Oh My Goddess!

ああっ女神さまっ

21

STORY AND ART BY
Kosuke Fujishima

TRANSLATION BY
Dana Lewis AND Lea Hernandez

LETTERING AND TOUCH-UP BY
Susie Lee AND Betty Dong
WITH Tom2K

DARK HORSE MANGA

CHAPTER 130

The Devil Inside

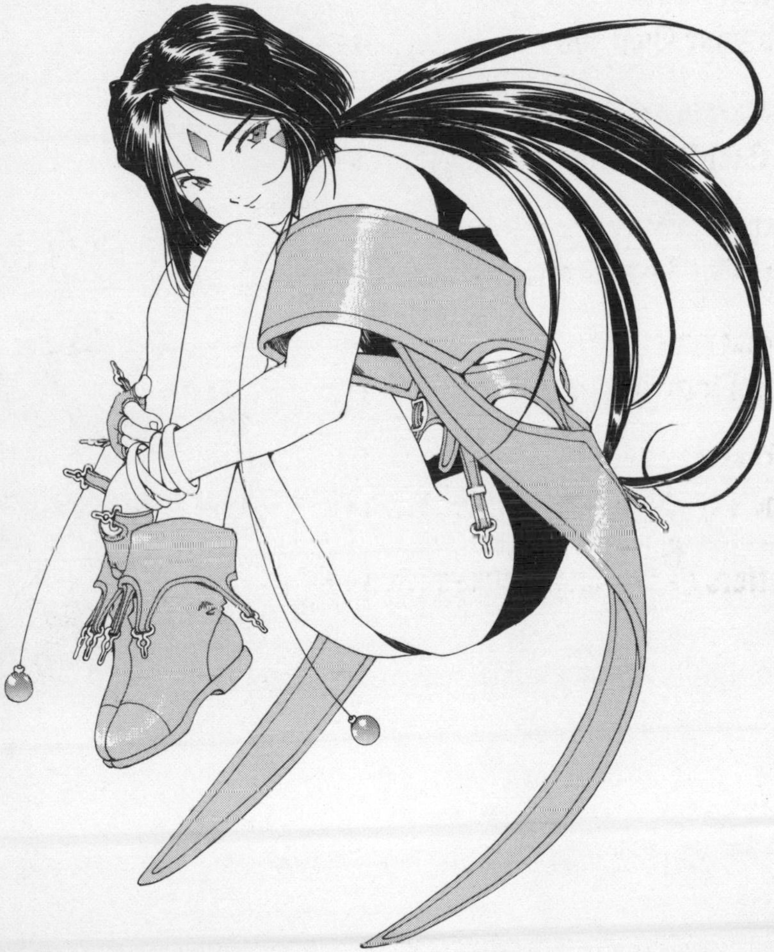

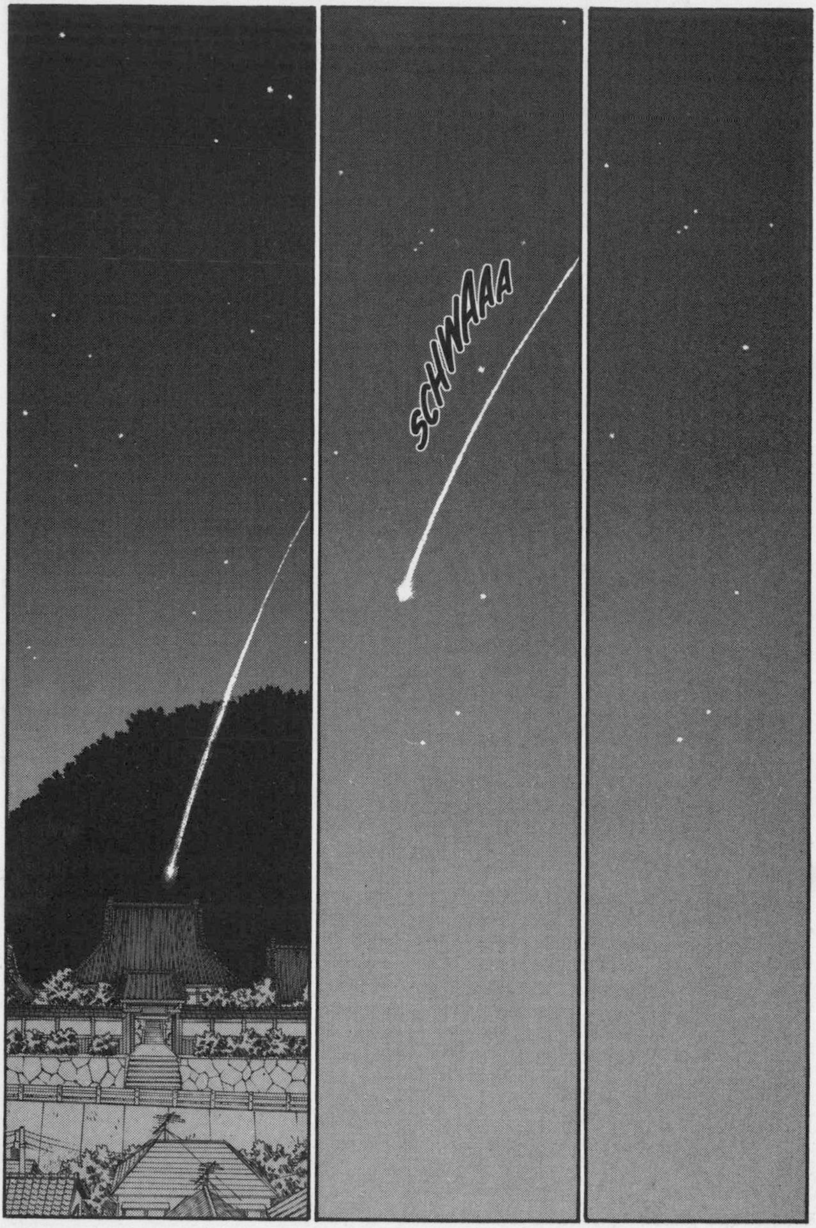
SCHWAAA

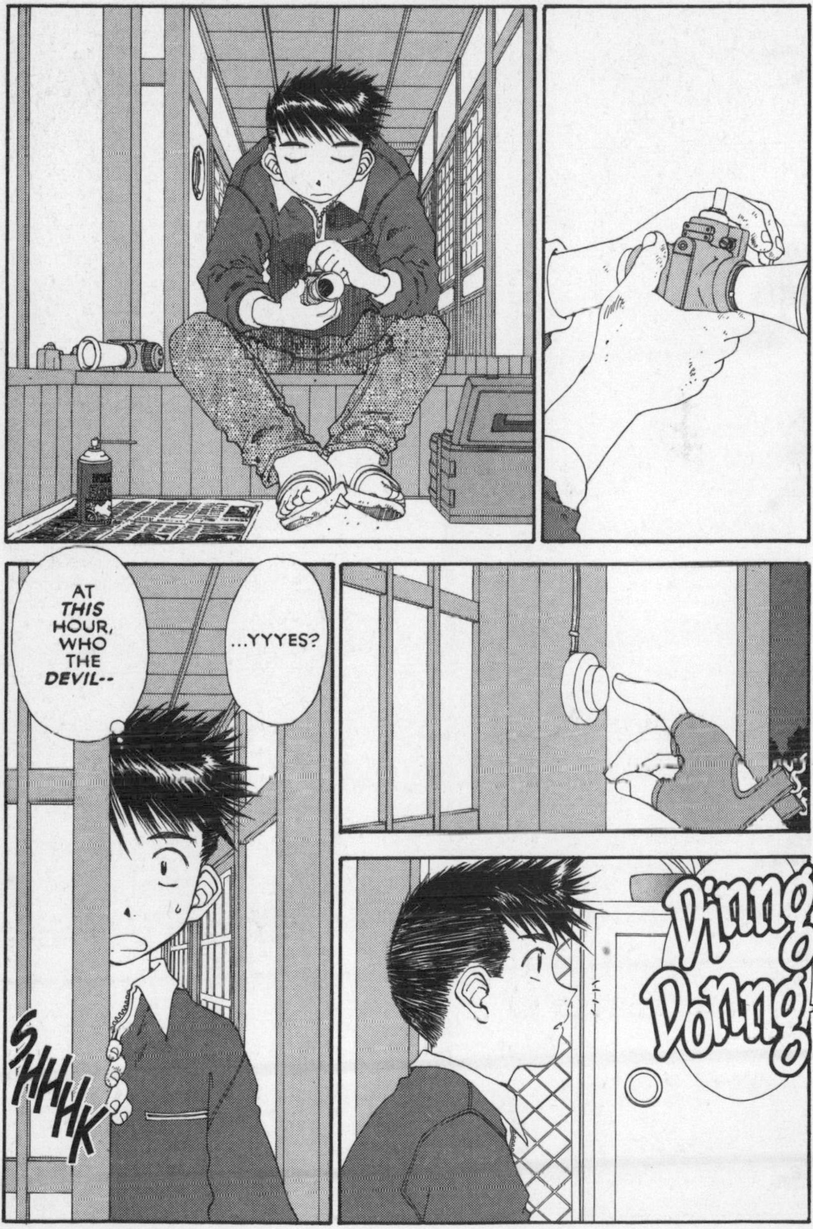
Dinng Donng
...YYYES?
AT THIS HOUR, WHO THE DEVIL--
SHHHK

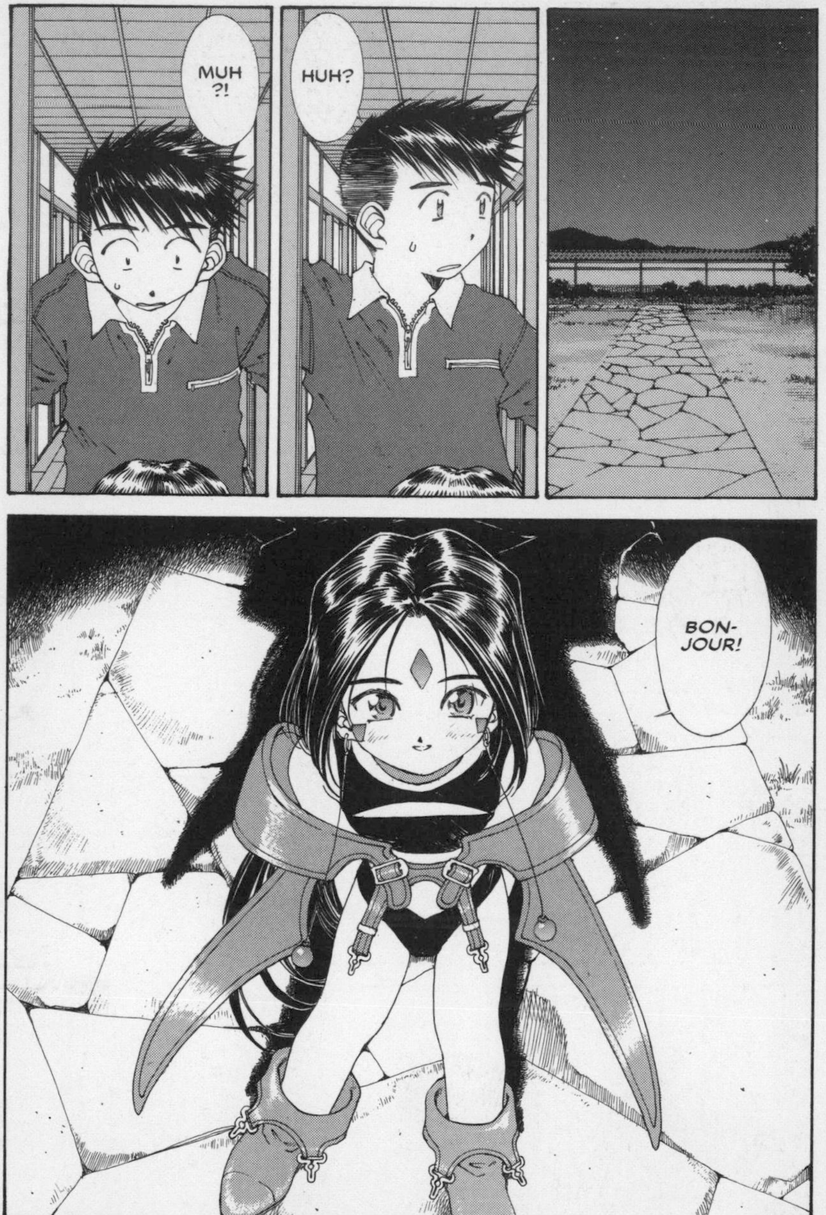
HUH?
MUH ?!
BON-
JOUR!

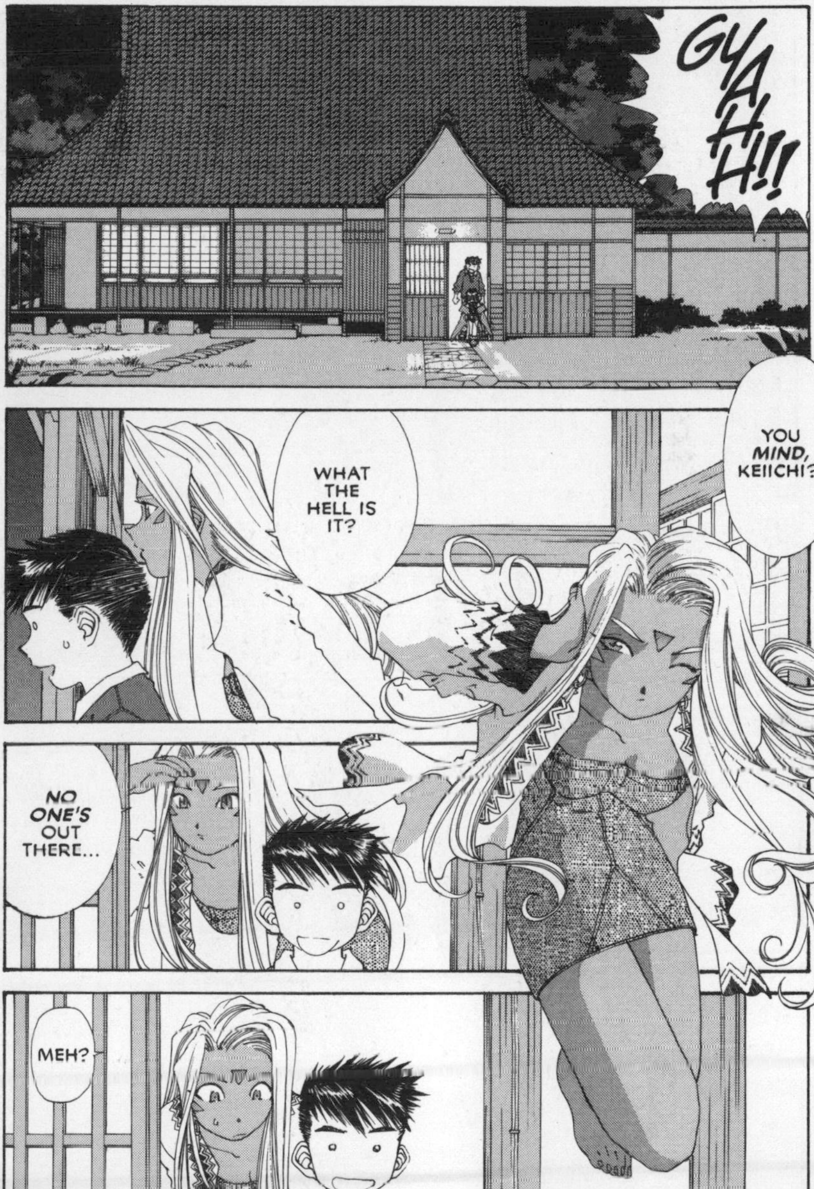
GYAHH!!
YOU MIND, KEIICHI?!
WHAT THE HELL IS IT?
NO ONE'S OUT THERE...
MEH?

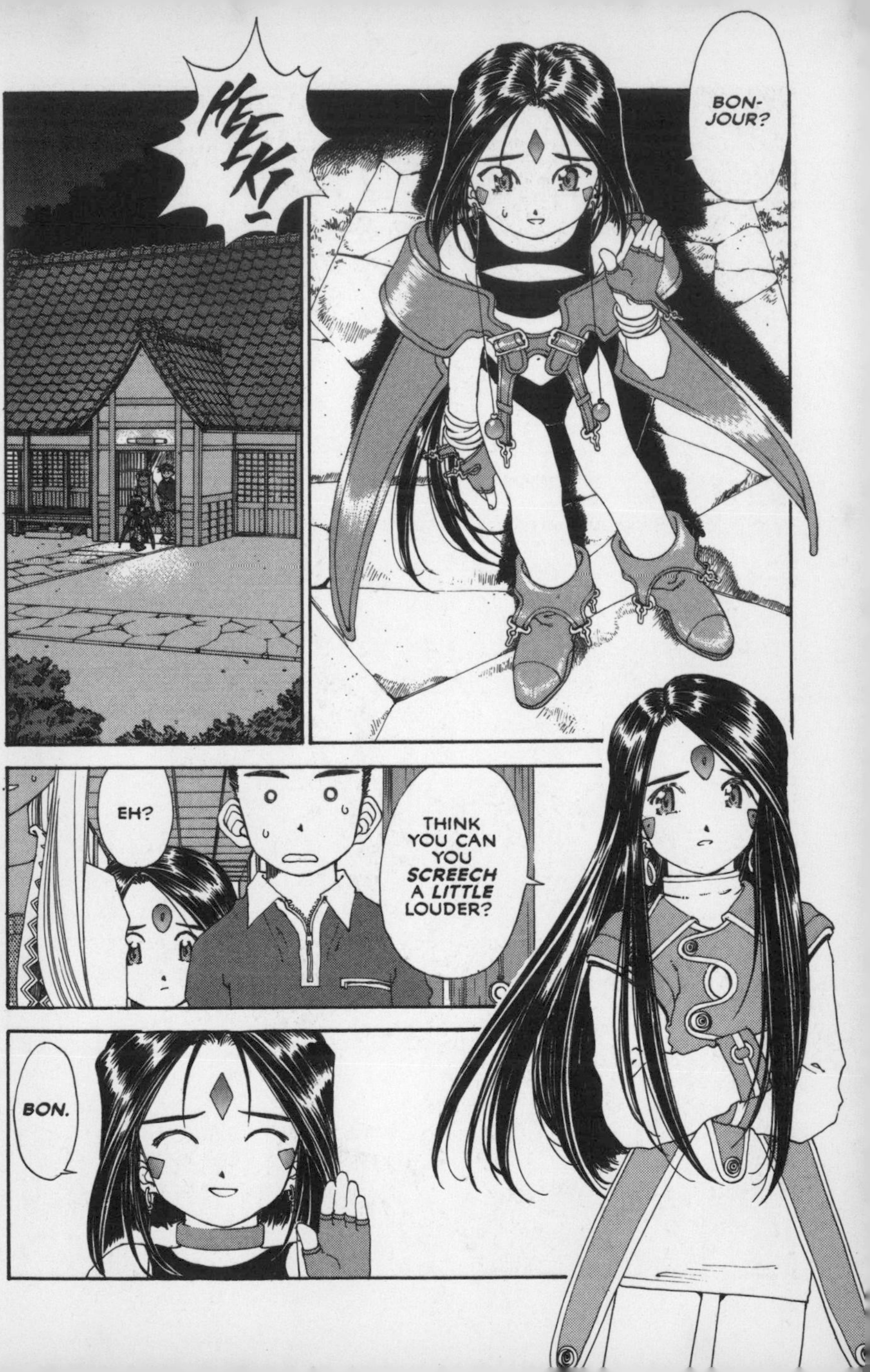
BON-JOUR?
HEEK!
THINK YOU CAN YOU *SCREECH* A *LITTLE* LOUDER?
EH?
BON.

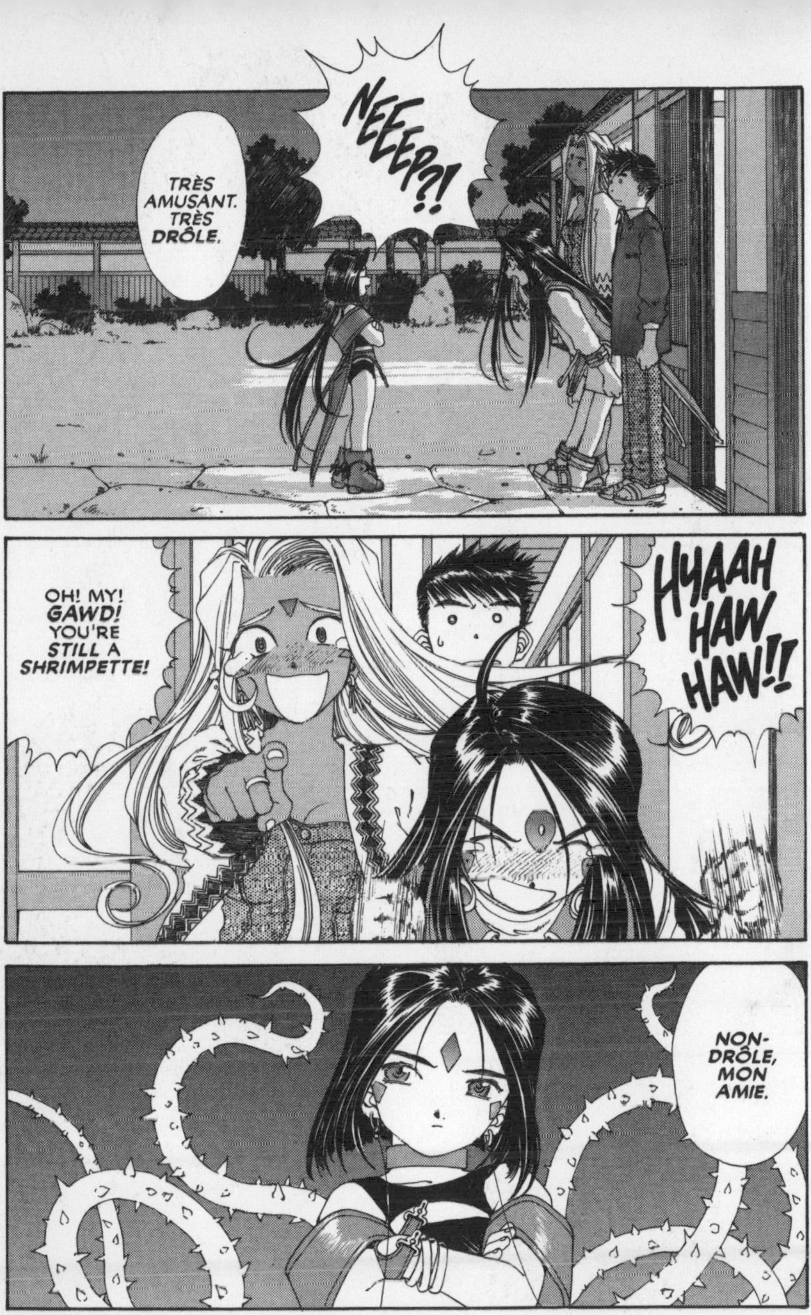
NEEEP?!
TRÈS AMUSANT. TRÈS DRÔLE.
HYAAH HAW HAW!!
OH! MY! GAWD! YOU'RE STILL A SHRIMPETTE!
NON-DRÔLE, MON AMIE.

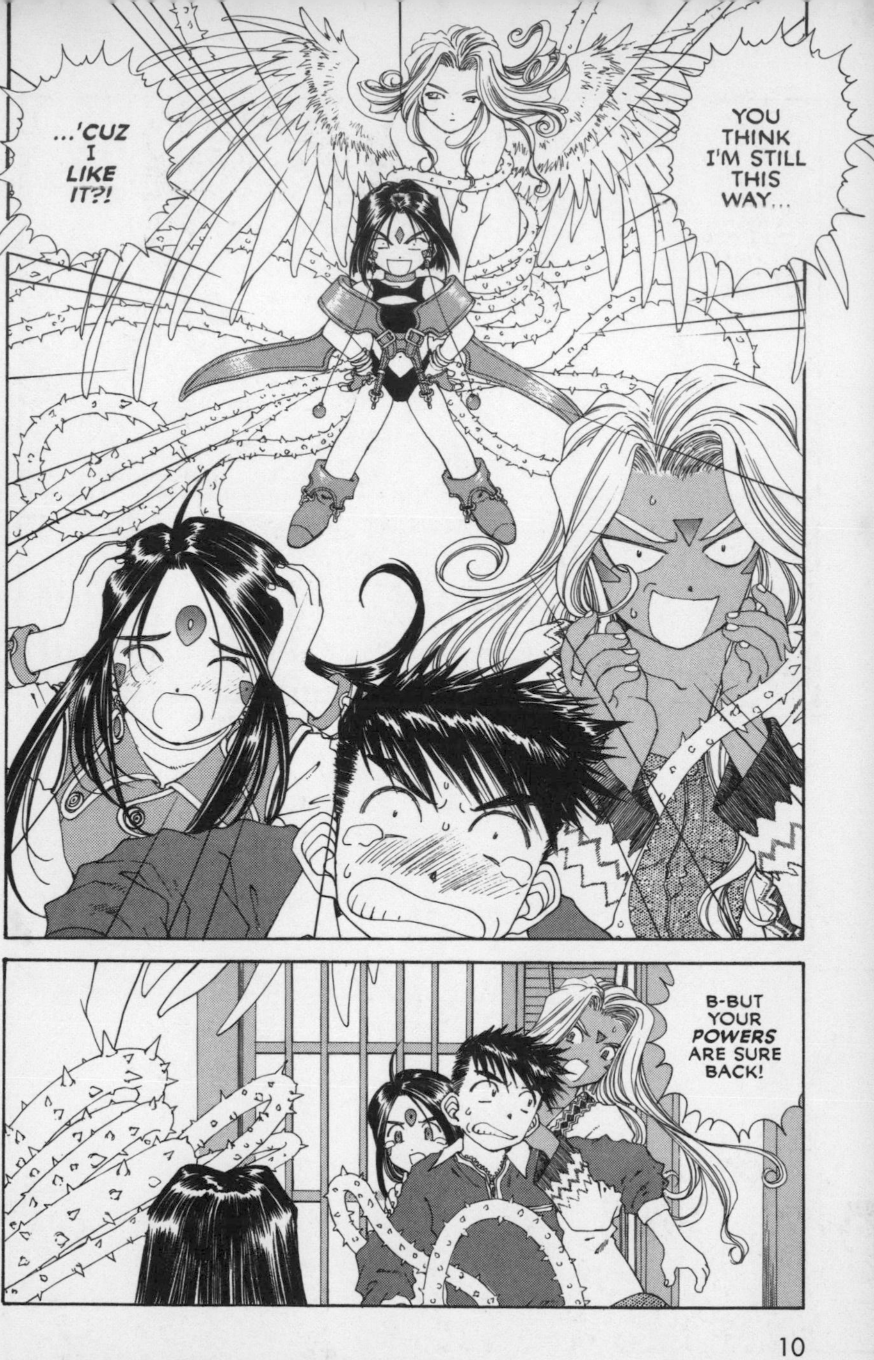
YOU THINK I'M STILL THIS WAY...
...'CUZ I *LIKE* IT?!
B-BUT YOUR *POWERS* ARE SURE BACK!

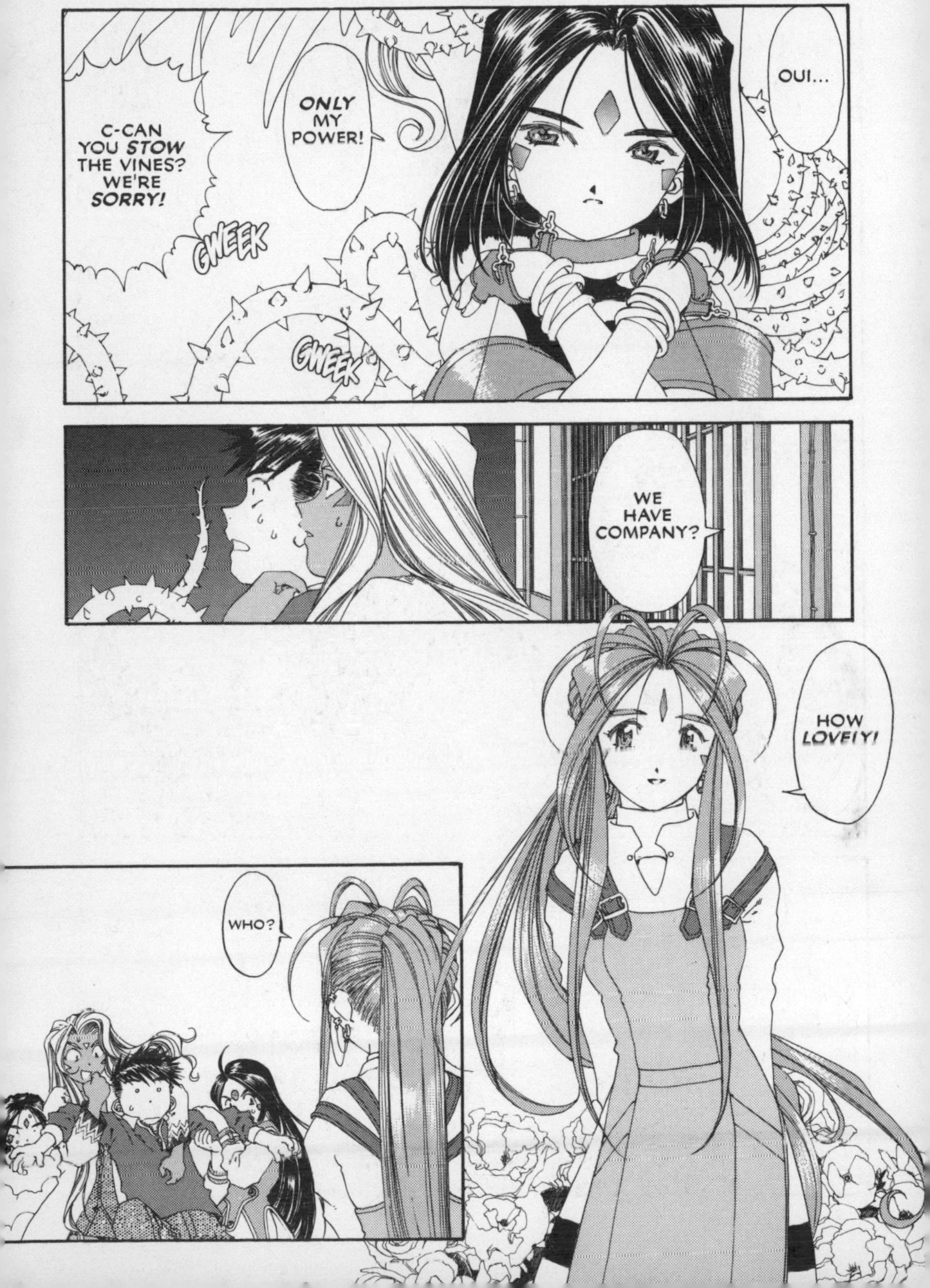
OUI...
ONLY MY POWER!
C-CAN YOU STOW THE VINES? WE'RE SORRY!
GWEEK
GWEEK
WE HAVE COMPANY?
HOW LOVELY!
WHO?

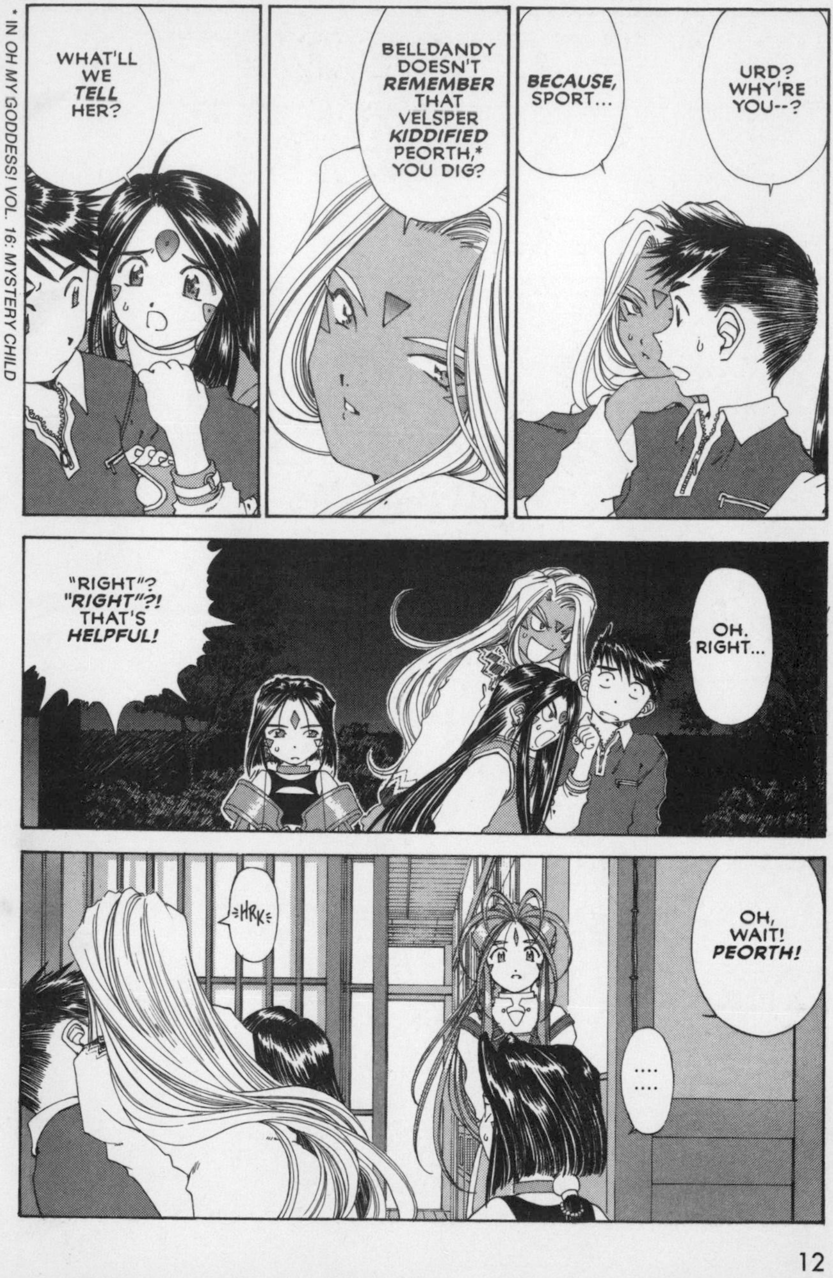
URD? WHY'RE YOU--?
BECAUSE, SPORT...
BELLDANDY DOESN'T REMEMBER THAT VELSPER KIDDIFIED PEORTH,* YOU DIG?
WHAT'LL WE TELL HER?
OH. RIGHT...
"RIGHT"? "RIGHT"?! THAT'S HELPFUL!
OH, WAIT! PEORTH!
HRK
....
....

* IN OH MY GODDESS! VOL. 16: MYSTERY CHILD

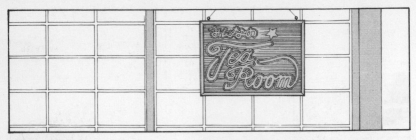

...WHY DO YOU LOOK LIKE A LITTLE GIRL?

PEORTH...

13

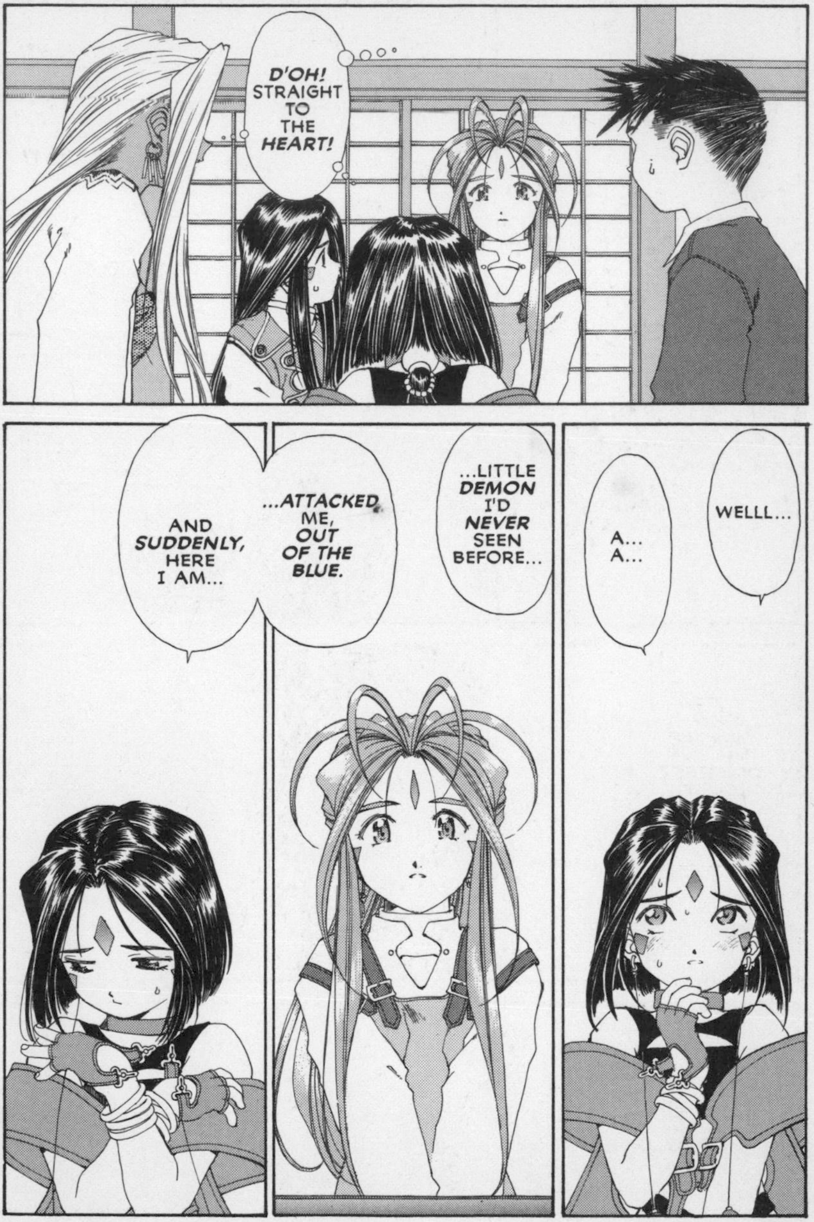
D'OH! STRAIGHT TO THE HEART!
WELLL...
A... A...
...LITTLE DEMON I'D NEVER SEEN BEFORE...
...ATTACKED ME, OUT OF THE BLUE.
AND SUDDENLY, HERE I AM...

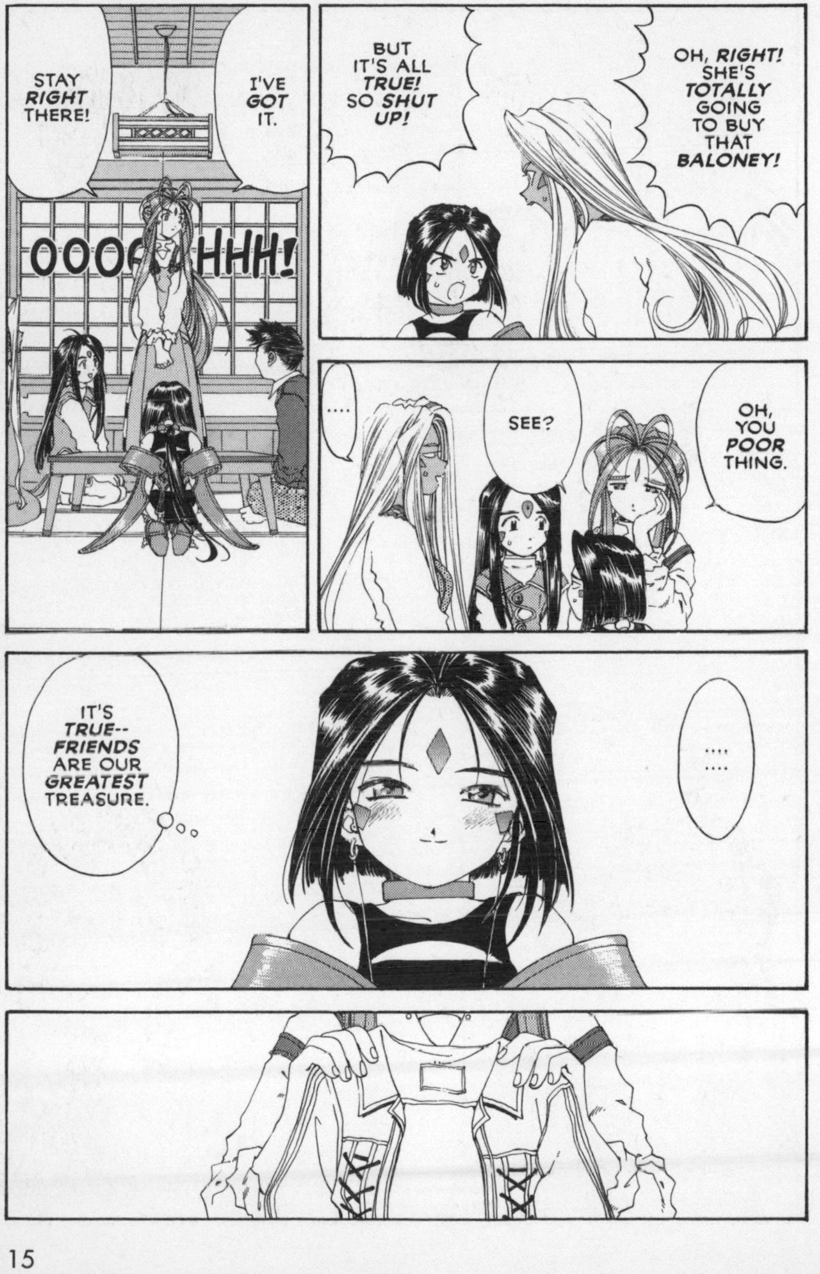
OH, RIGHT! SHE'S TOTALLY GOING TO BUY THAT BALONEY!
BUT IT'S ALL TRUE! SO SHUT UP!
OH, YOU POOR THING.
SEE?
....
I'VE GOT IT.
STAY RIGHT THERE!
OOOO HHH!
....
IT'S TRUE-- FRIENDS ARE OUR GREATEST TREASURE.

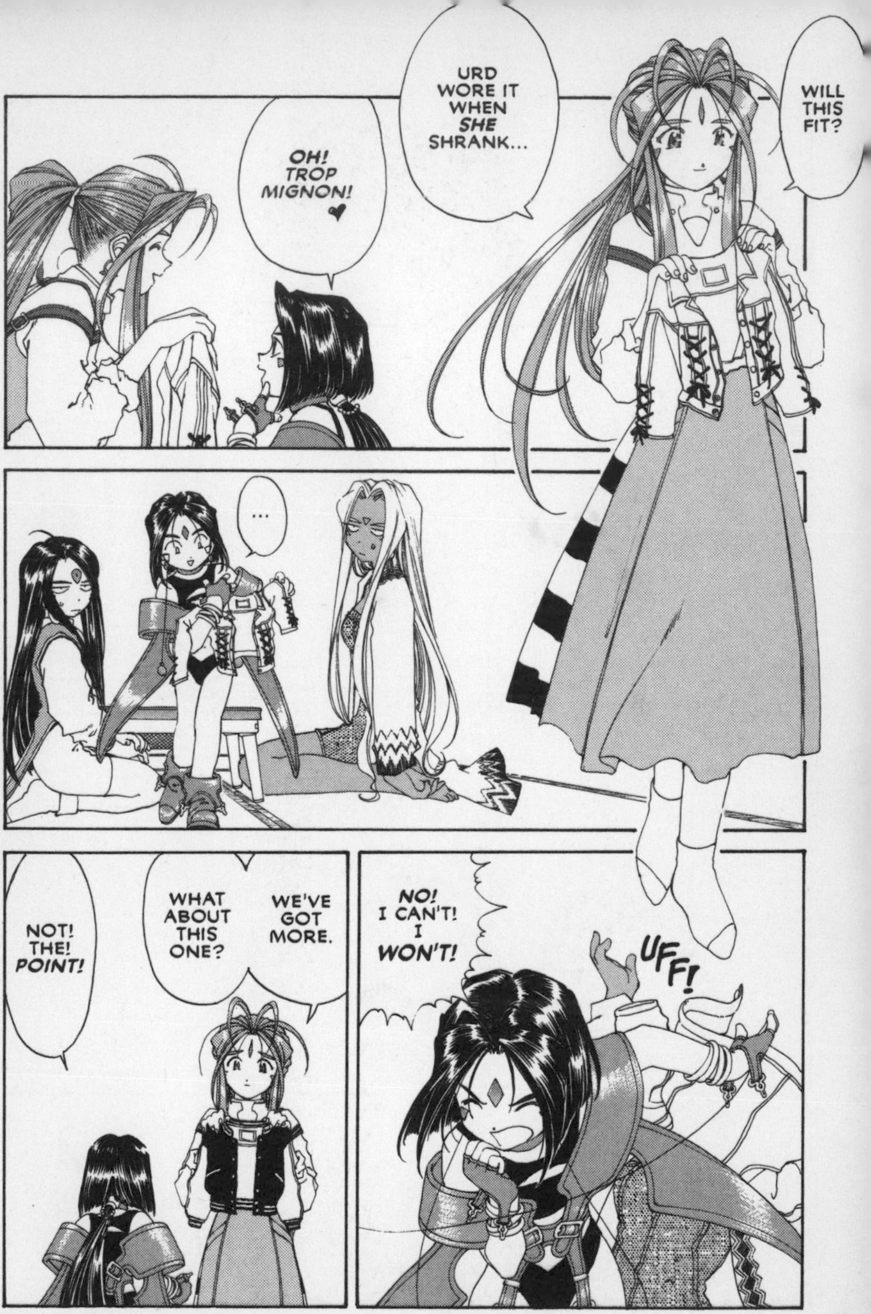
WILL THIS FIT?
URD WORE IT WHEN *SHE* SHRANK...
OH! TROP MIGNON! ♥
...
NO! I CAN'T! I *WON'T!*
UFF!
WE'VE GOT MORE.
WHAT ABOUT THIS ONE?
NOT! THE! *POINT!*

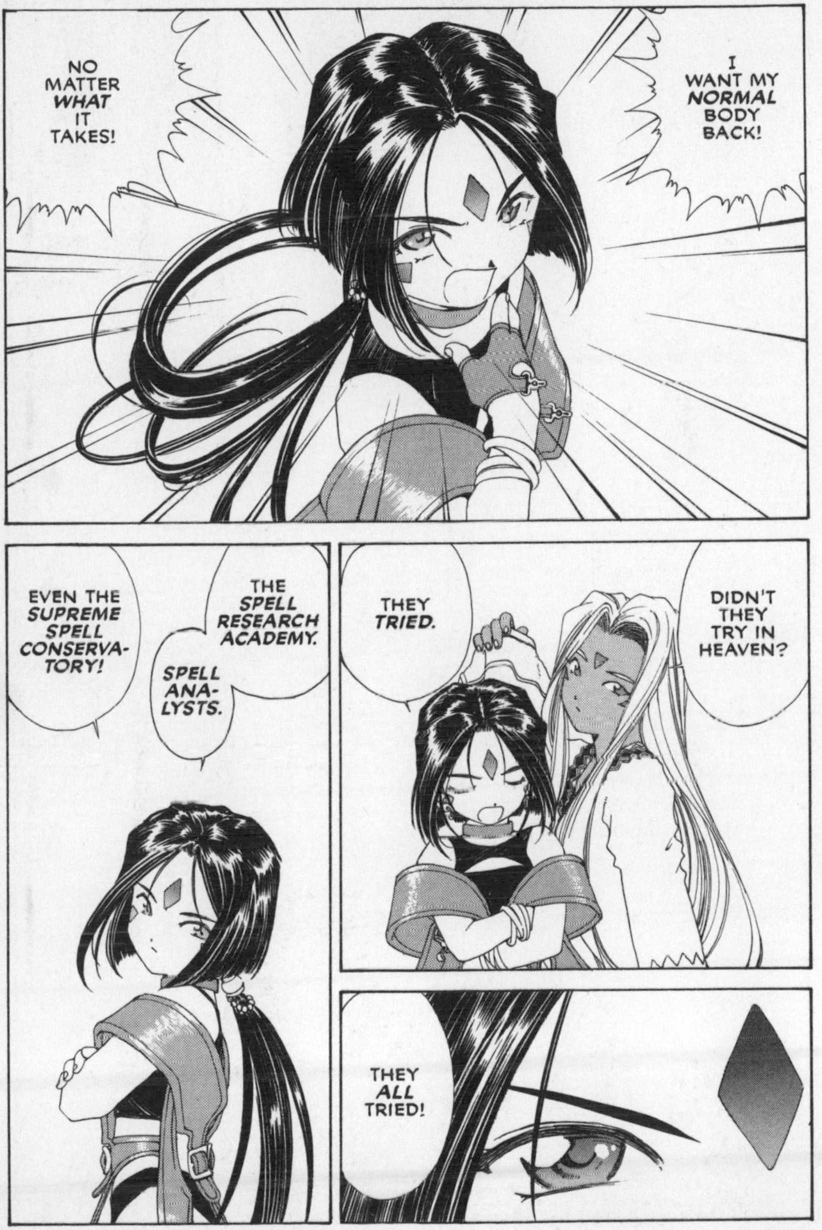
I WANT MY *NORMAL* BODY BACK!
NO MATTER *WHAT* IT TAKES!
DIDN'T THEY TRY IN HEAVEN?
THEY *TRIED.*
THEY *ALL* TRIED!
THE *SPELL RESEARCH ACADEMY.*
SPELL ANALYSTS.
EVEN THE *SUPREME SPELL CONSERVATORY!*

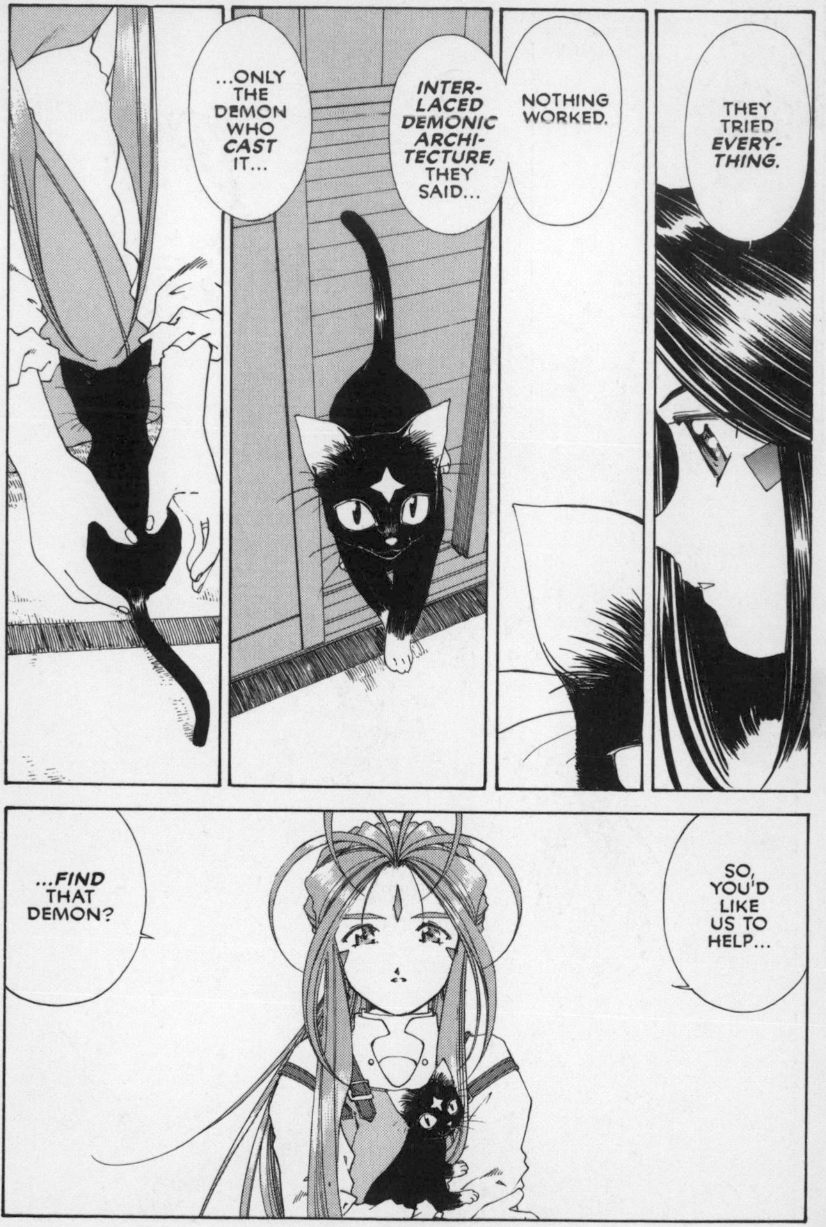
THEY TRIED EVERY-THING.
NOTHING WORKED.
INTER-LACED DEMONIC ARCHI-TECTURE, THEY SAID...
...ONLY THE DEMON WHO CAST IT...
SO, YOU'D LIKE US TO HELP...
...FIND THAT DEMON?

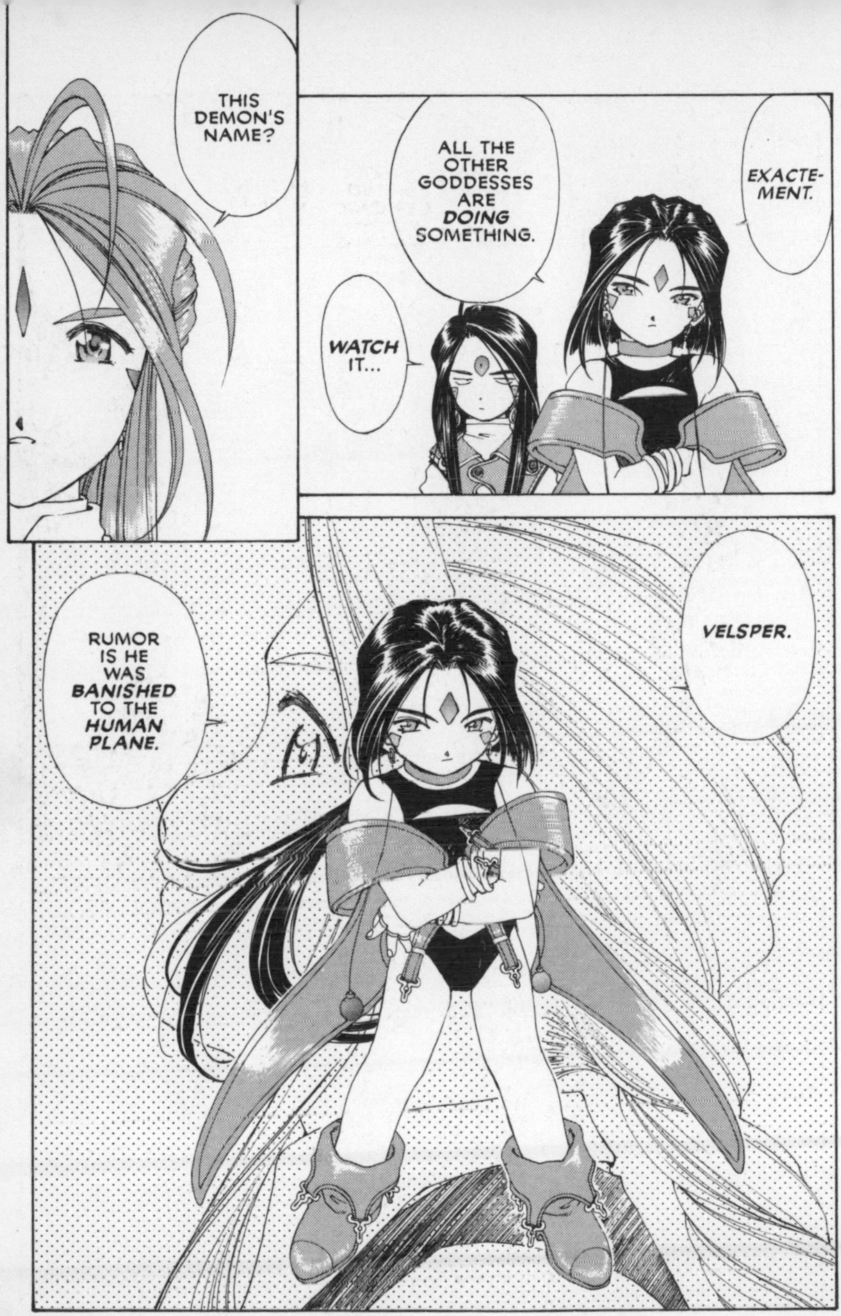
EXACTE-MENT.
ALL THE OTHER GODDESSES ARE *DOING* SOMETHING.
WATCH IT...
THIS DEMON'S NAME?
VELSPER.
RUMOR IS HE WAS *BANISHED* TO THE *HUMAN PLANE.*

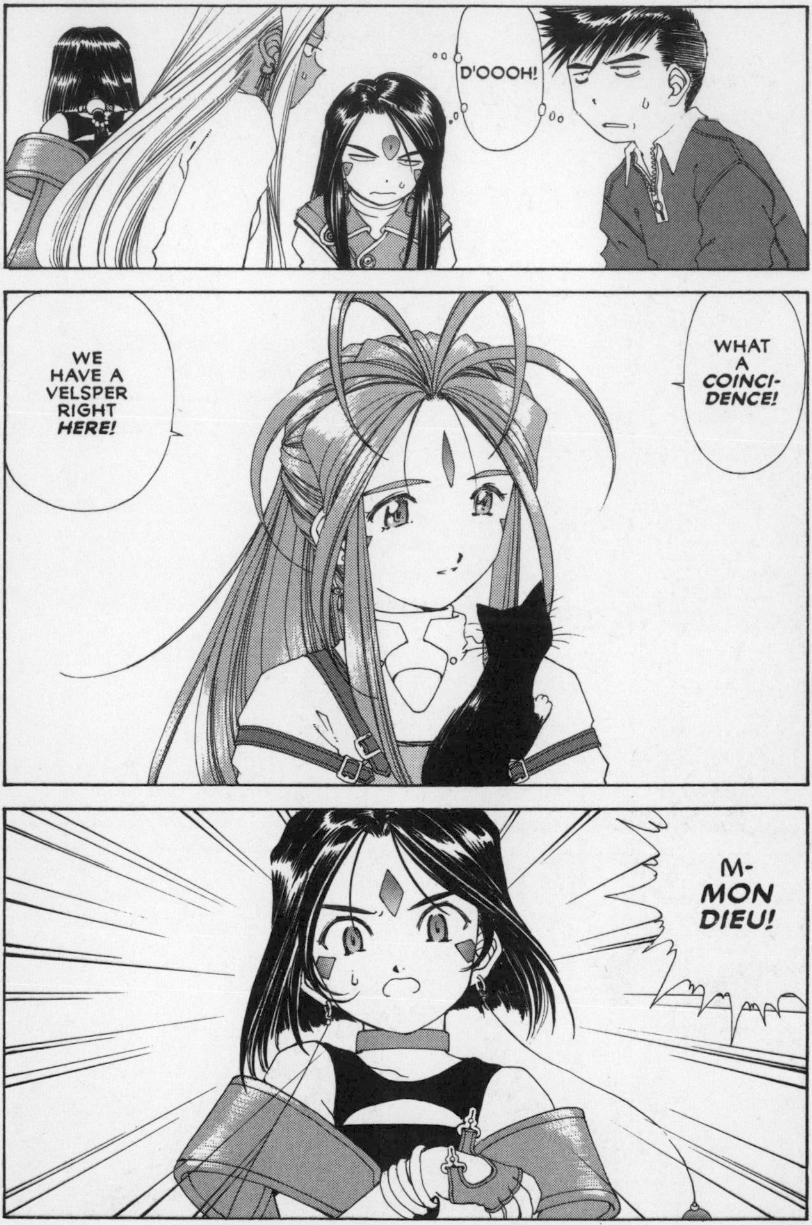
D'OOOH!
WHAT A COINCIDENCE!
WE HAVE A VELSPER RIGHT HERE!
M-MON DIEU!

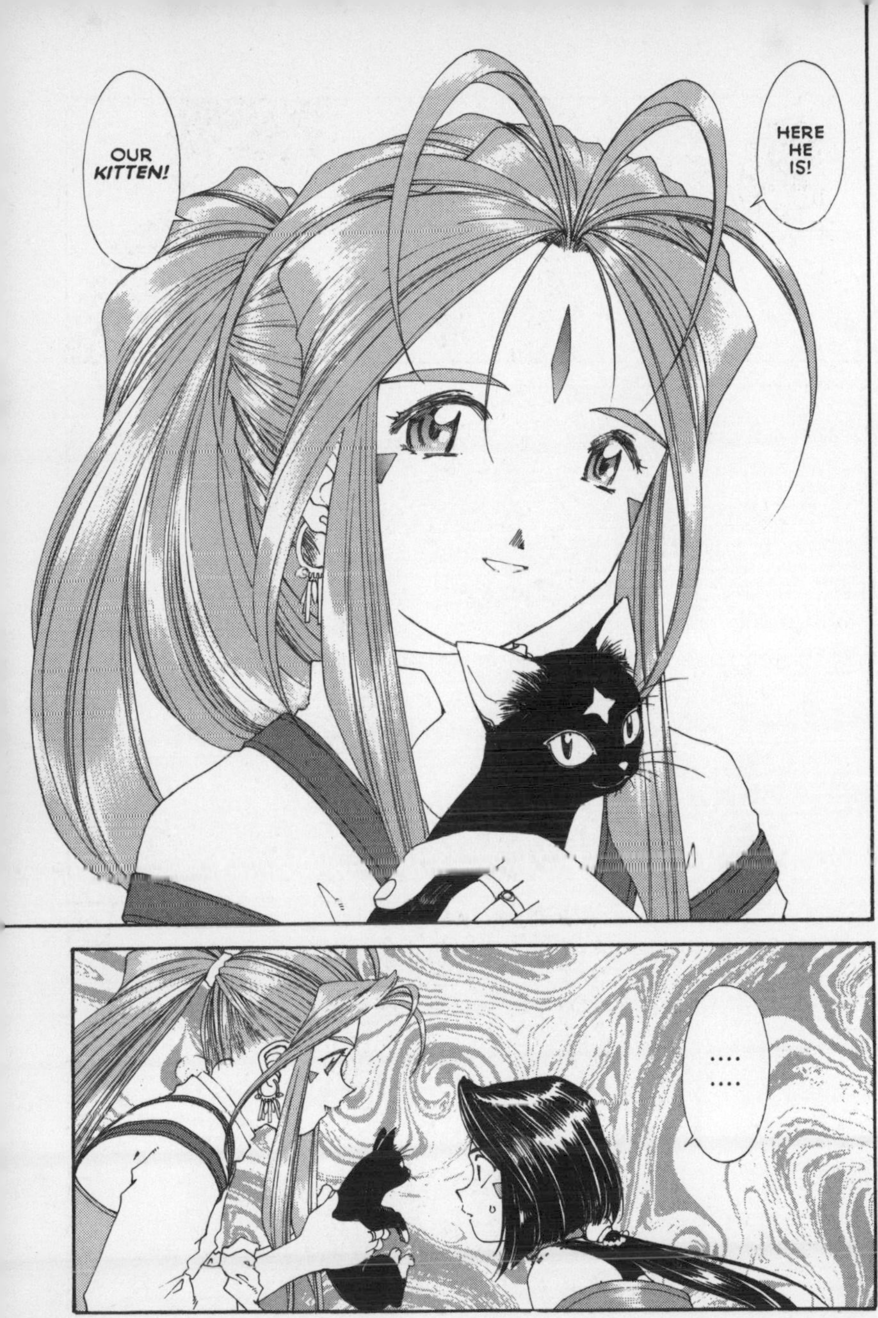
HERE HE IS!
OUR *KITTEN!*
....
....

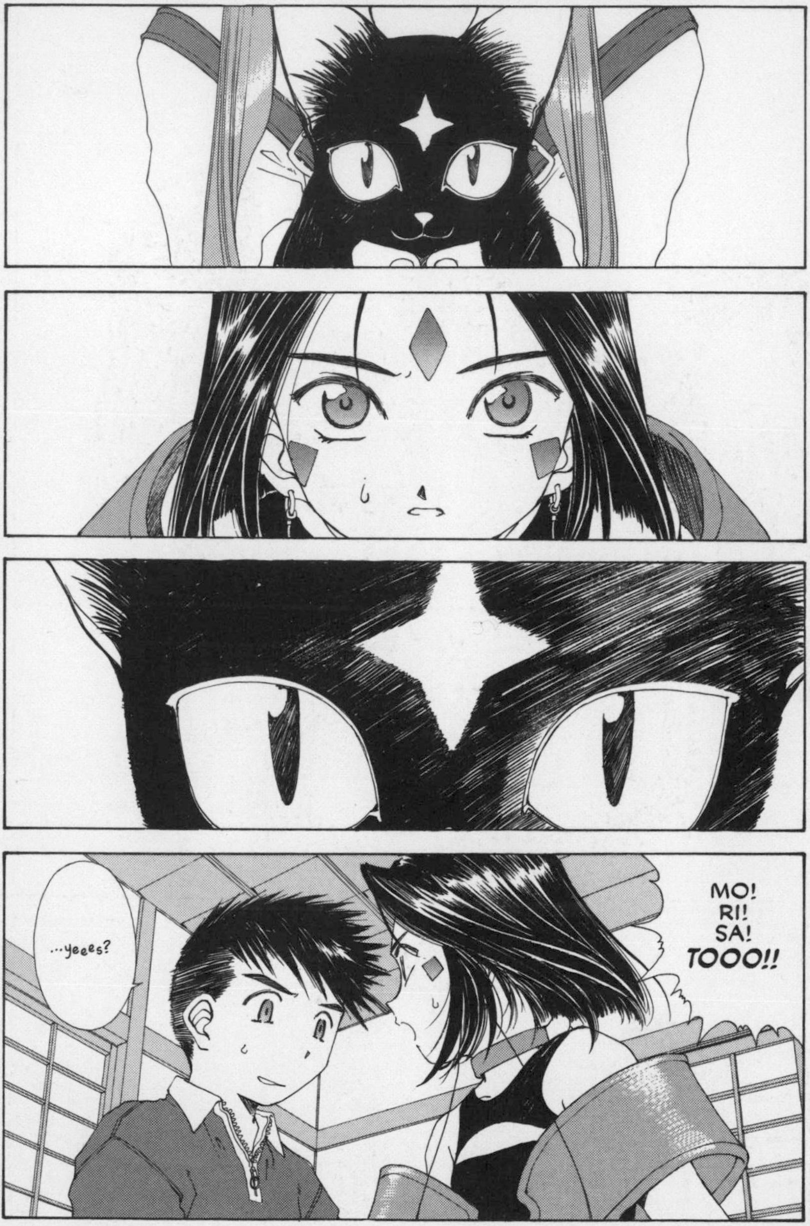
MO!
RI!
SA!
TOOO!!
...yeees?

CE CHAT...
UN MOMENT...
MUST... BRACE... SELF....
hahh
TH--
THAT FELINE IS--?
YES.

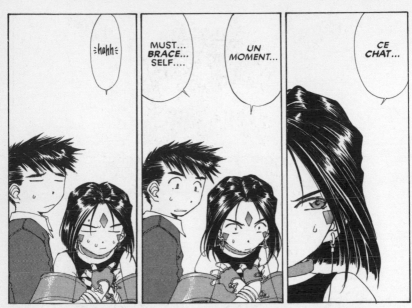

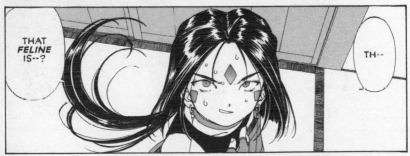

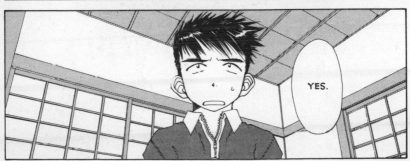

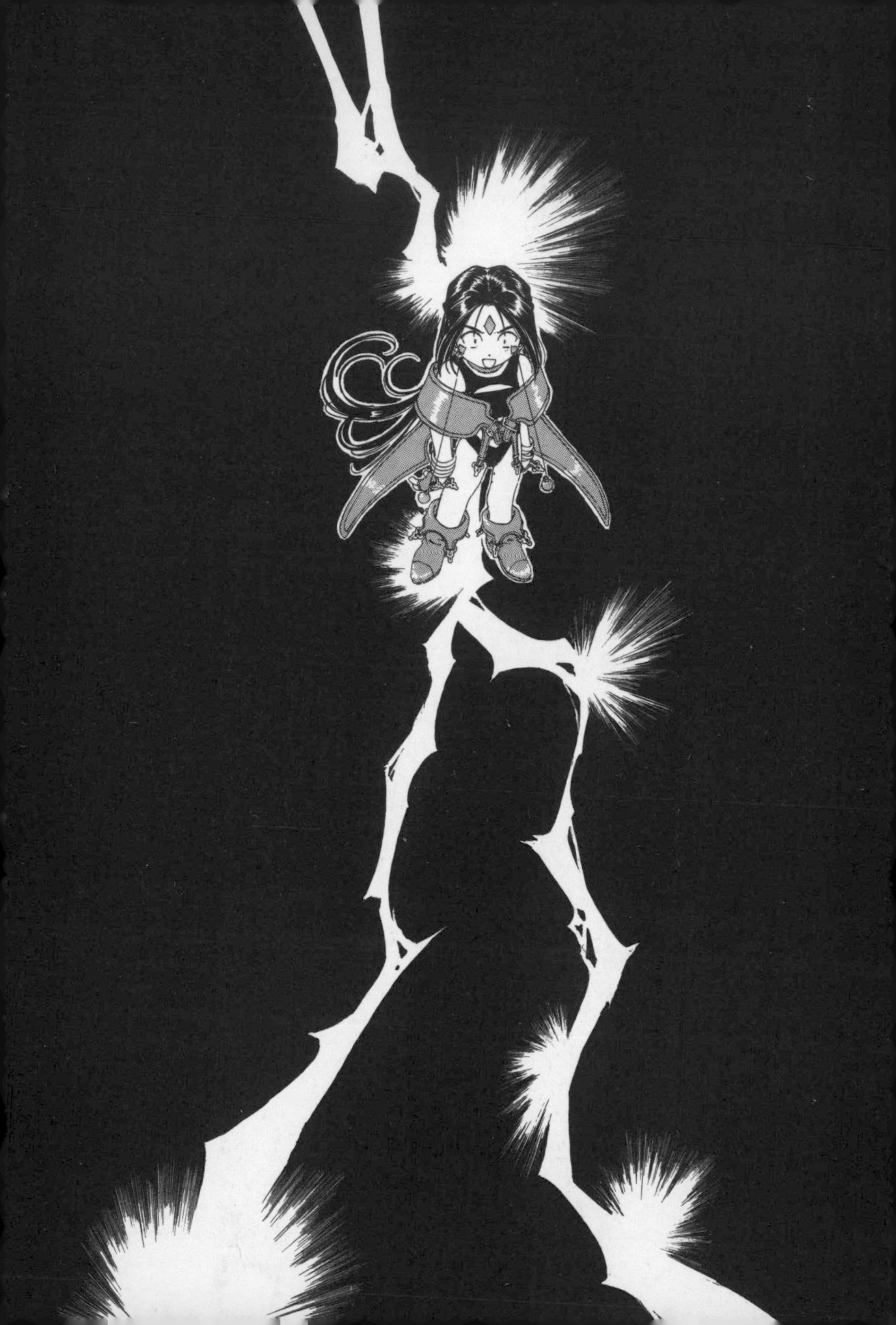

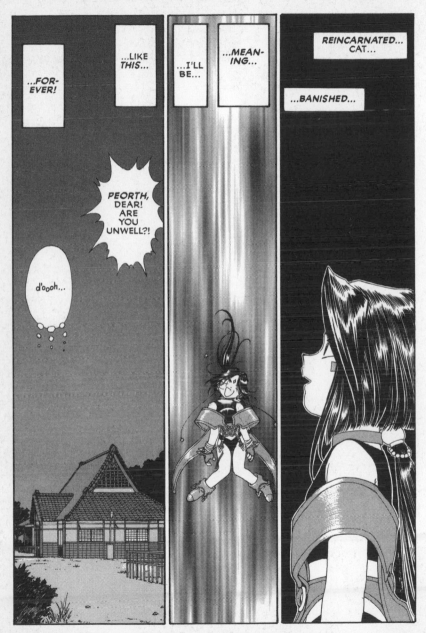

...FOR-
EVER!

...LIKE
THIS...

...I'LL
BE...

...MEAN-
ING...

REINCARNATED...
CAT...

...BANISHED...

PEORTH,
DEAR!
ARE
YOU
UNWELL?!

d'oooh...

END CHAPTER 130

OH MY GODDESS!
BELLDANDY

CHAPTER 131

Go Your Own Way

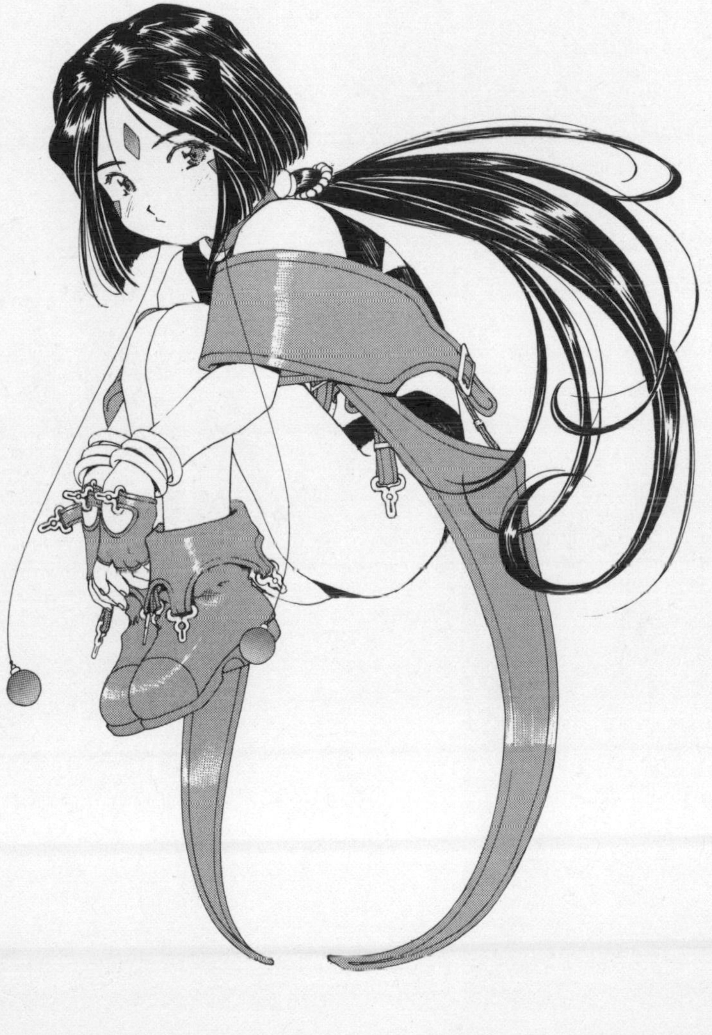

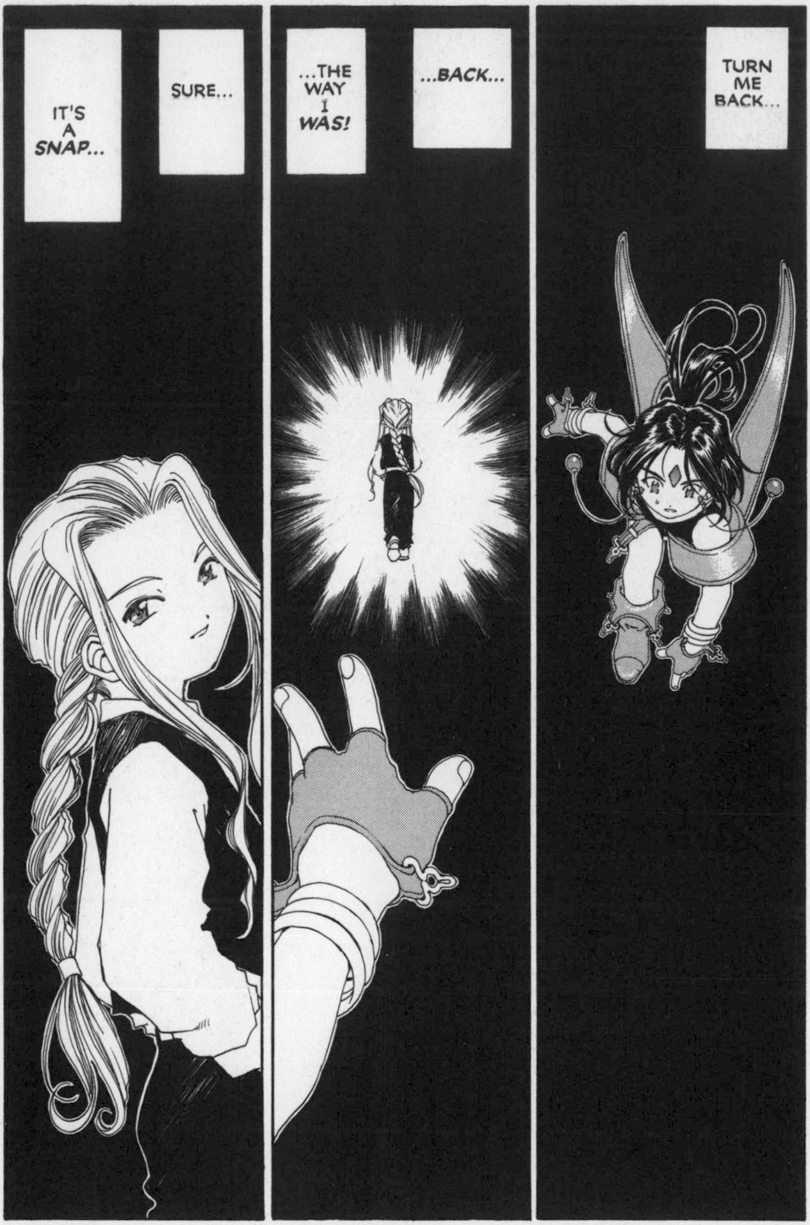
TURN ME BACK...
...BACK...
...THE WAY I WAS!
SURE...
IT'S A SNAP...

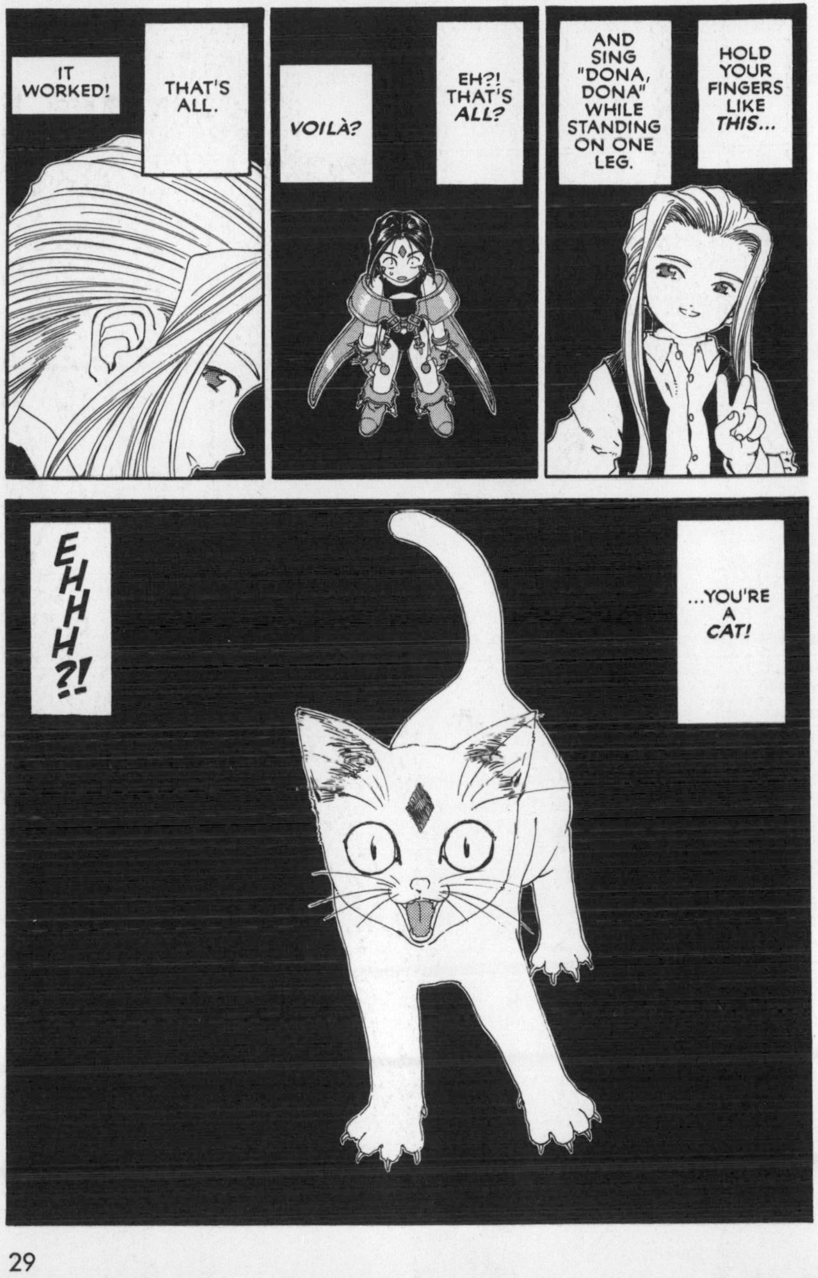
HOLD YOUR FINGERS LIKE *THIS*...
AND SING "DONA, DONA" WHILE STANDING ON ONE LEG.
EH?! THAT'S *ALL?*
VOILÀ?
THAT'S ALL.
IT WORKED!
...YOU'RE A *CAT!*
EHHHH?!

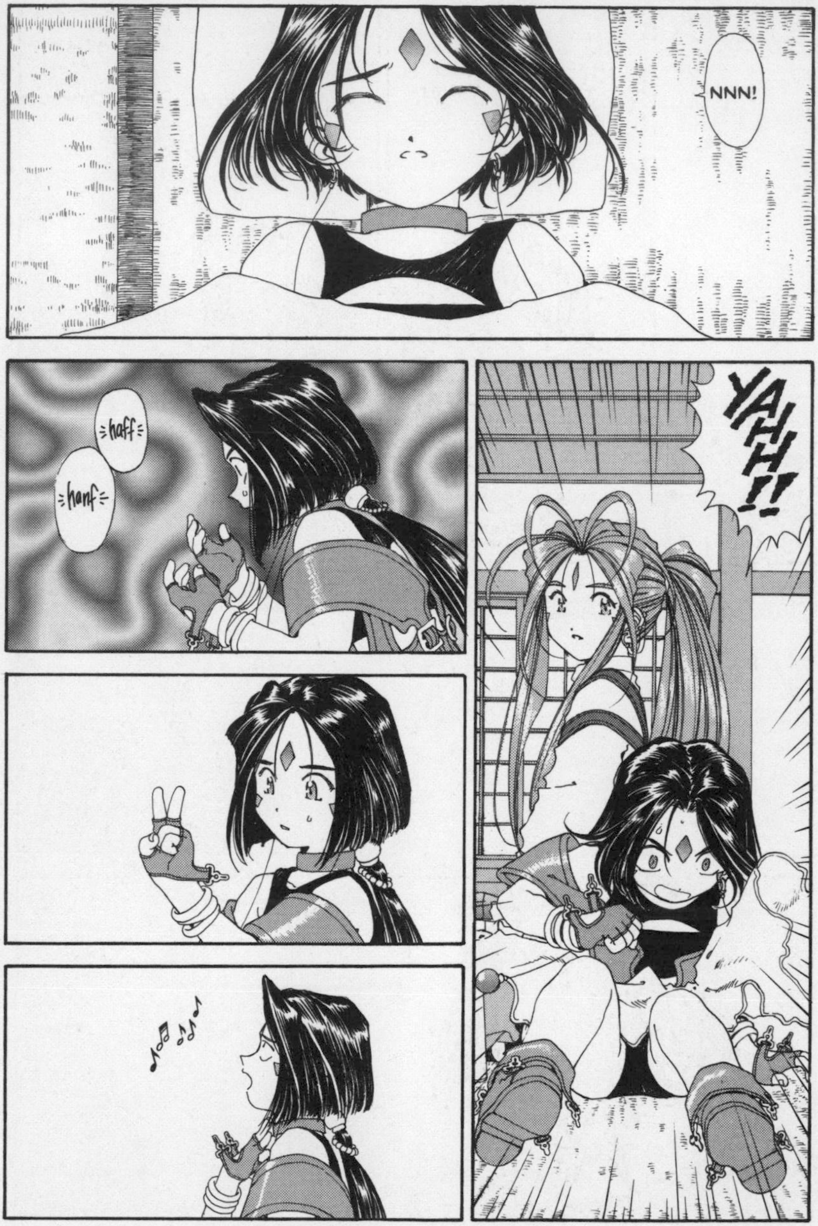
NNN!
YAHH!!
haff
hanf

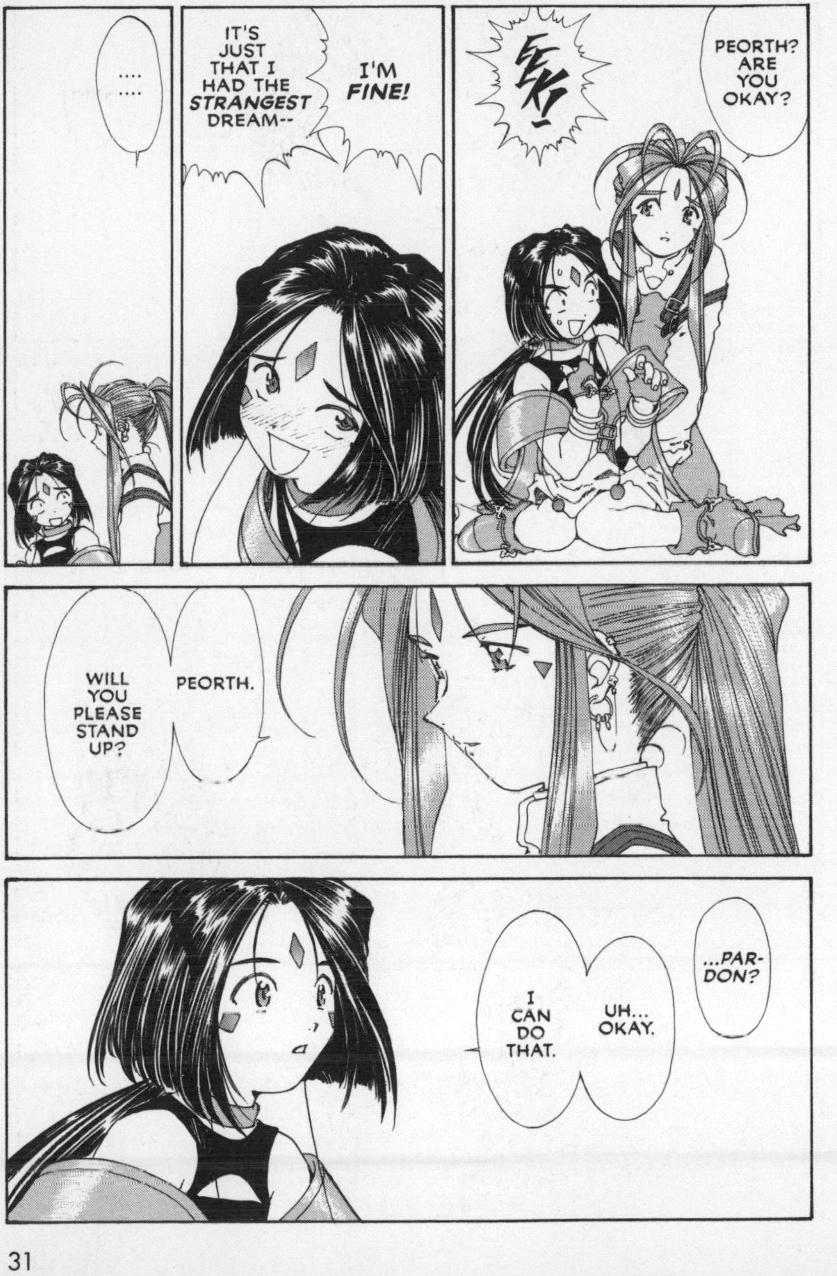
PEORTH? ARE YOU OKAY?
EEK!
I'M FINE!
IT'S JUST THAT I HAD THE STRANGEST DREAM--
....
PEORTH.
WILL YOU PLEASE STAND UP?
...PAR-DON?
UH... OKAY.
I CAN DO THAT.

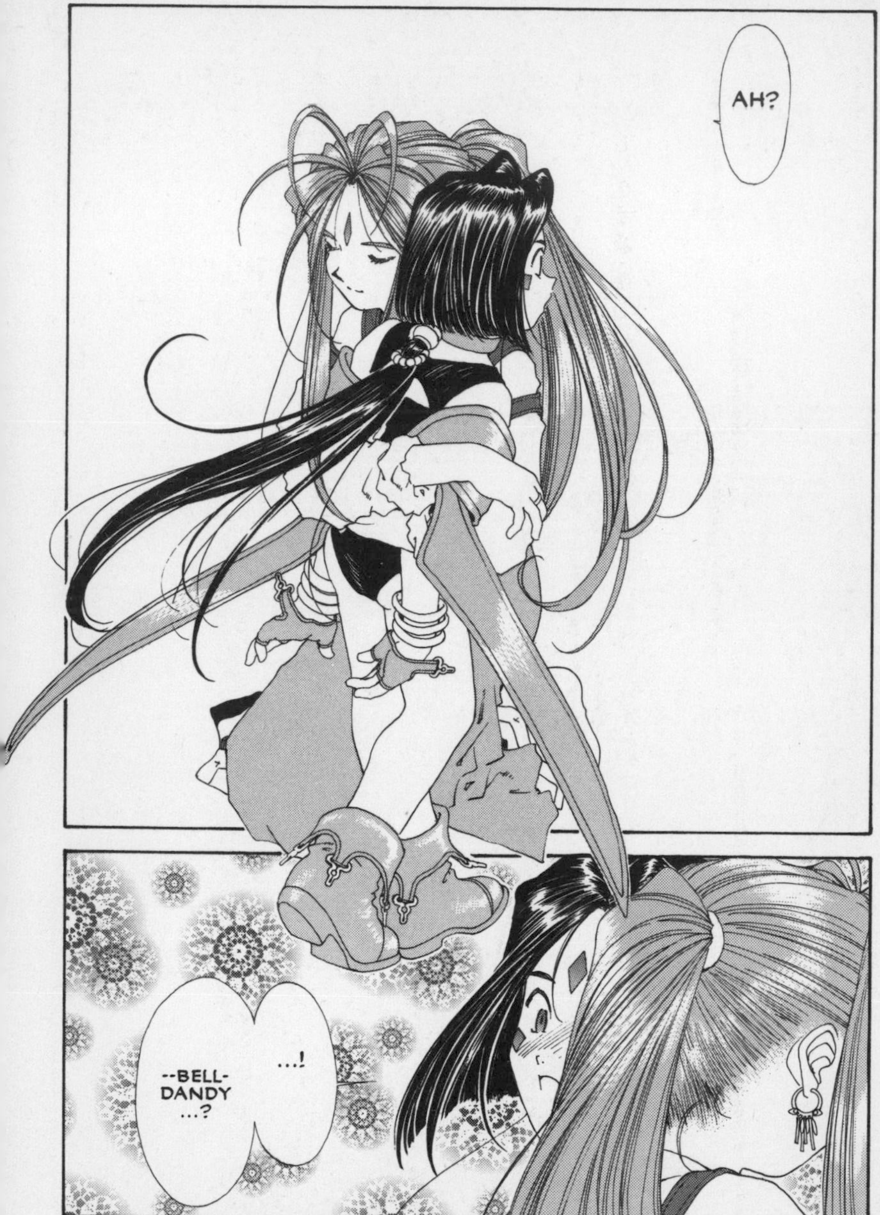
AH?
...!
--BELL-DANDY ...?

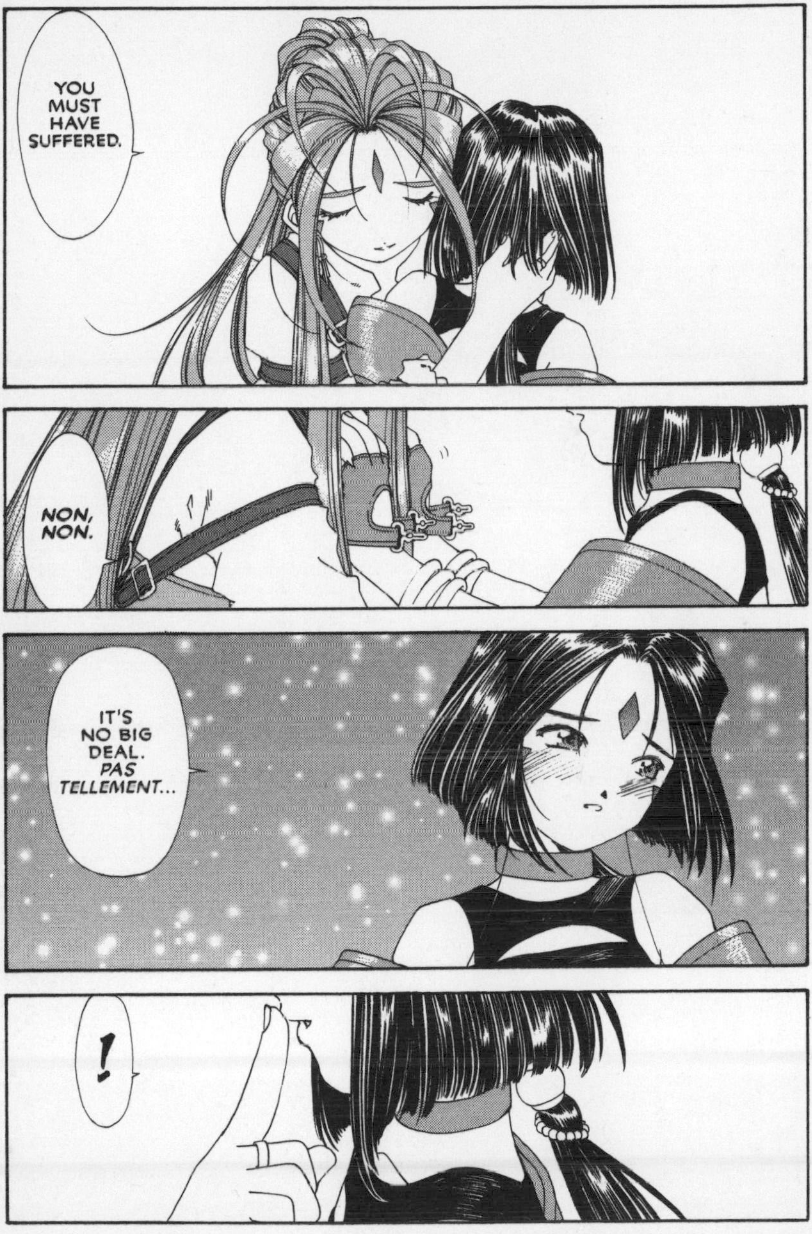
YOU MUST HAVE SUFFERED.
NON, NON.
IT'S NO BIG DEAL. *PAS TELLEMENT...*
!

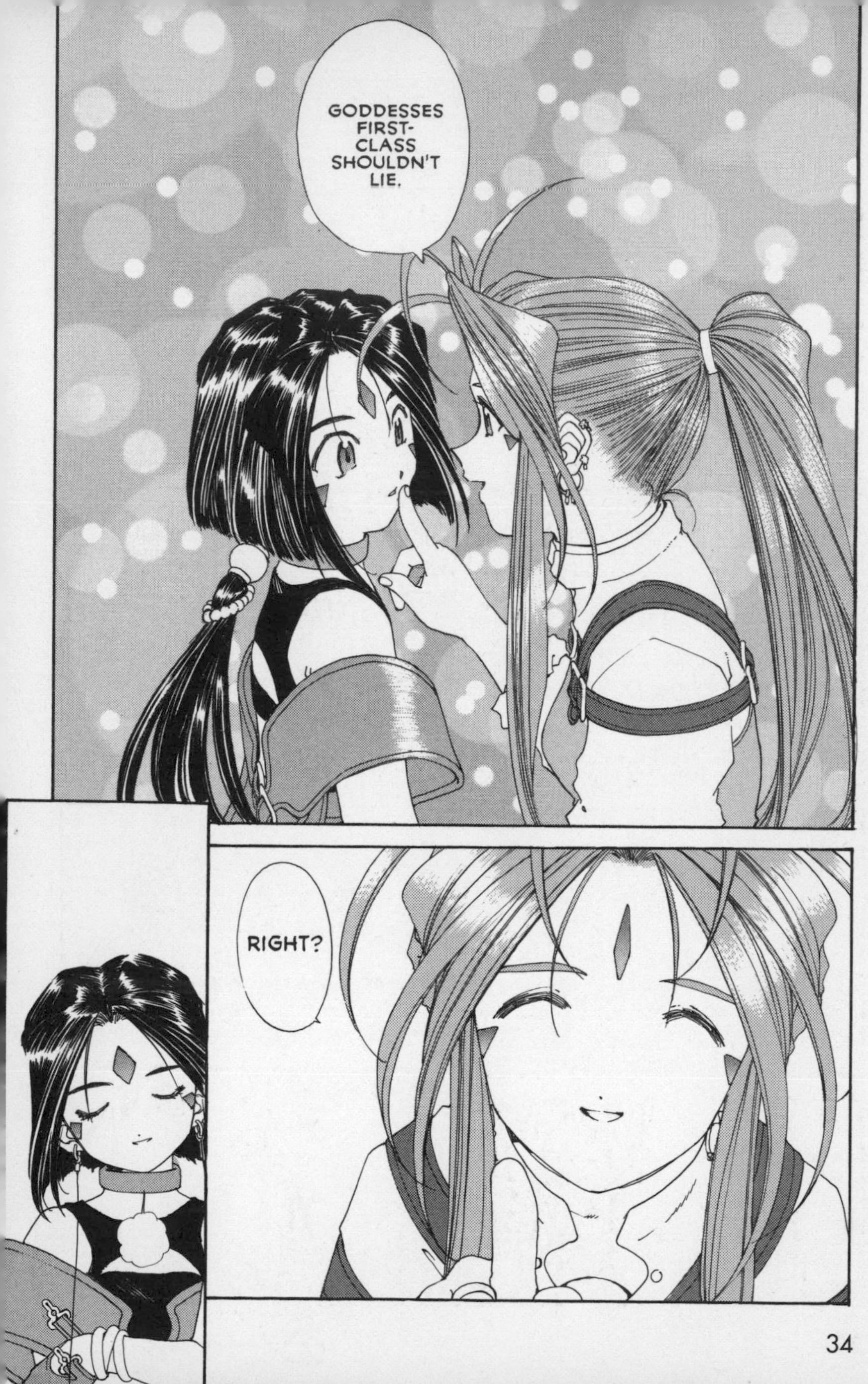
GODDESSES FIRST-CLASS SHOULDN'T LIE.
RIGHT?

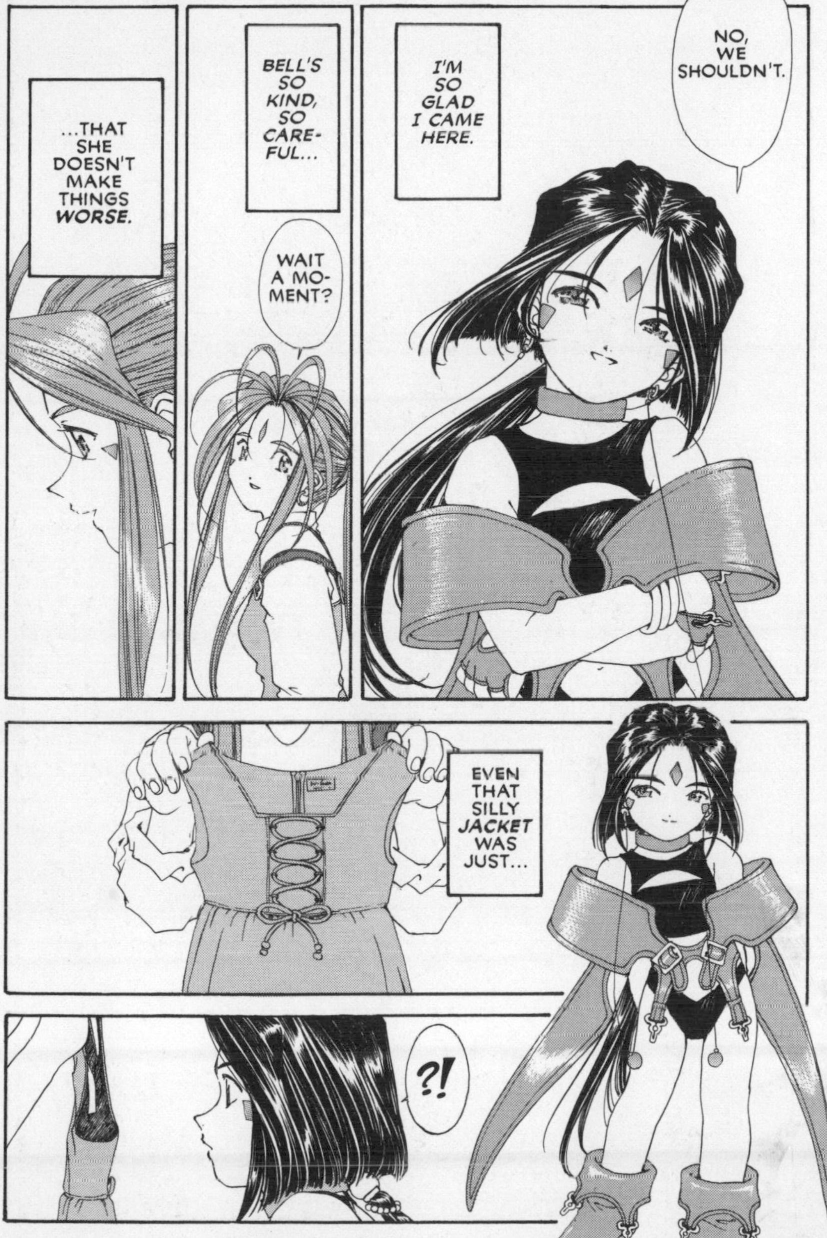
NO, WE SHOULDN'T.
I'M SO GLAD I CAME HERE.
BELL'S SO KIND, SO CAREFUL...
WAIT A MOMENT?
...THAT SHE DOESN'T MAKE THINGS *WORSE.*
EVEN THAT SILLY *JACKET* WAS JUST...
?!

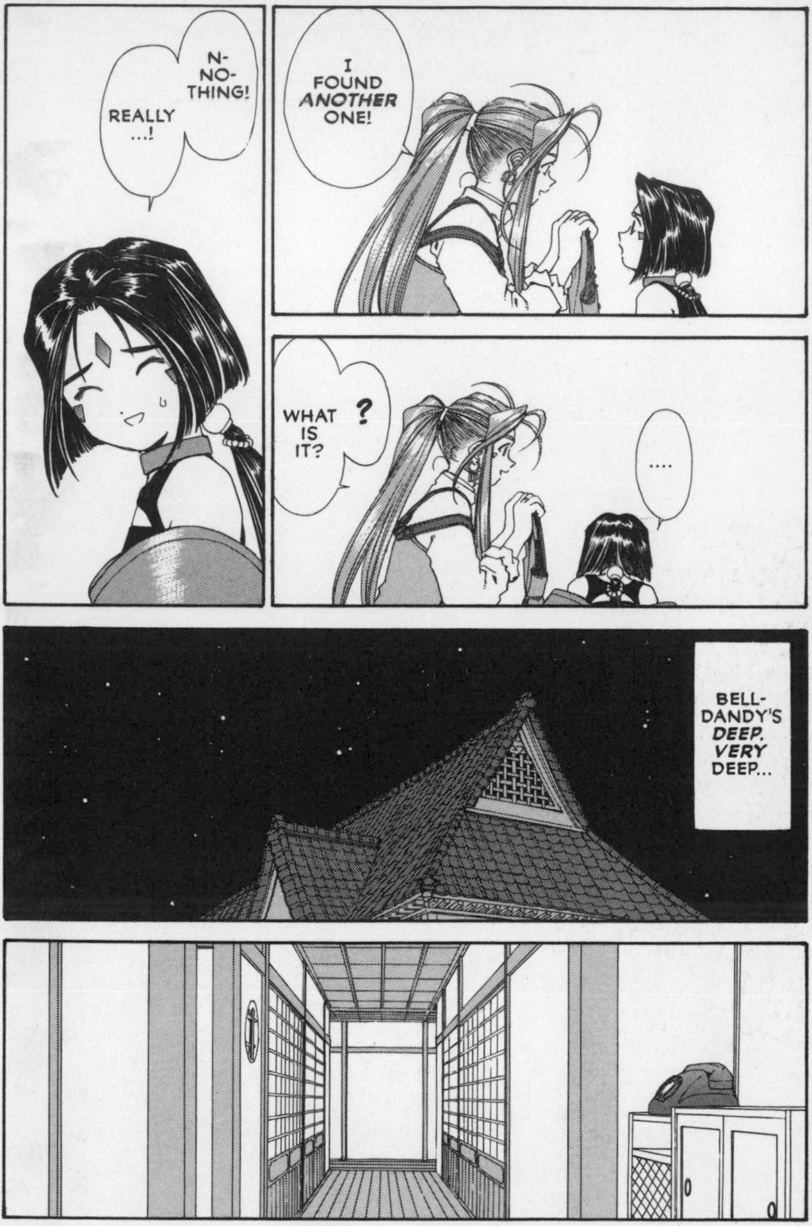
I FOUND ANOTHER ONE!
....
WHAT IS IT? ?
N-NO-THING! REALLY...!
BELL-DANDY'S DEEP. VERY DEEP...

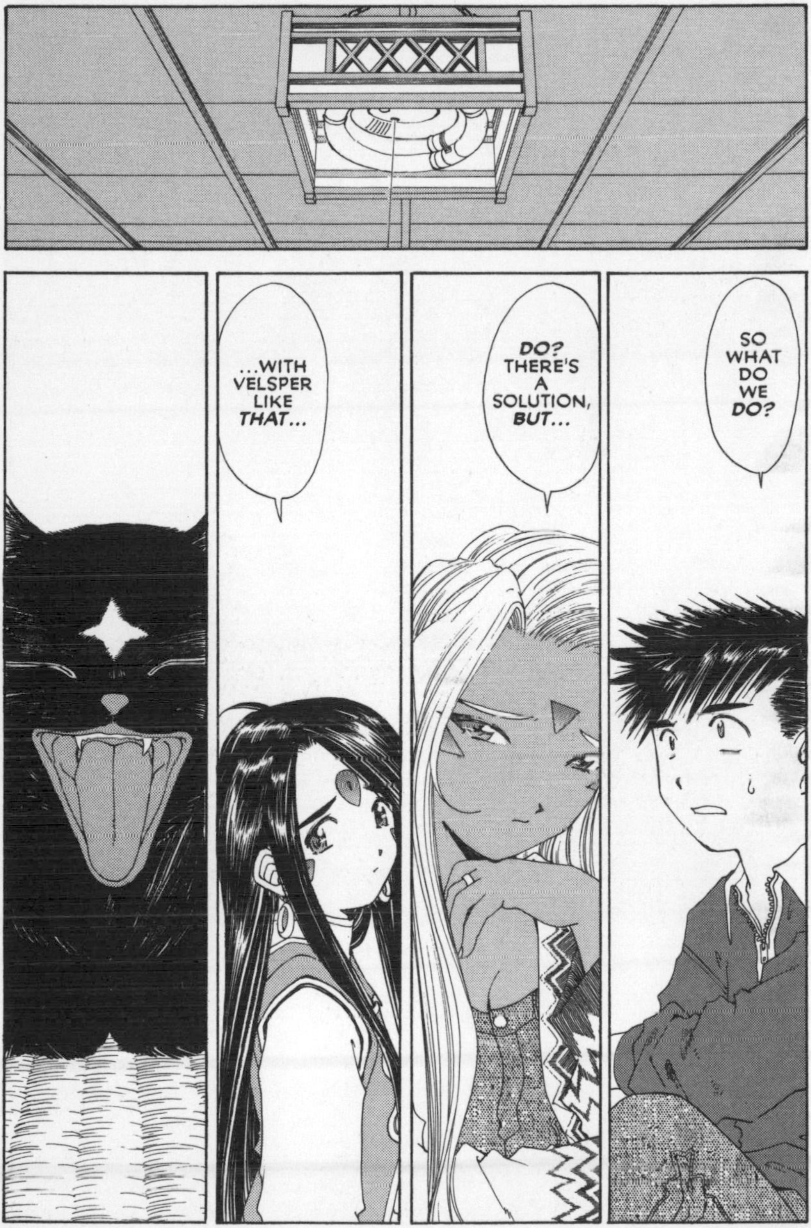
SO WHAT DO WE *DO?*
DO? THERE'S A SOLUTION, *BUT...*
...WITH VELSPER LIKE *THAT...*

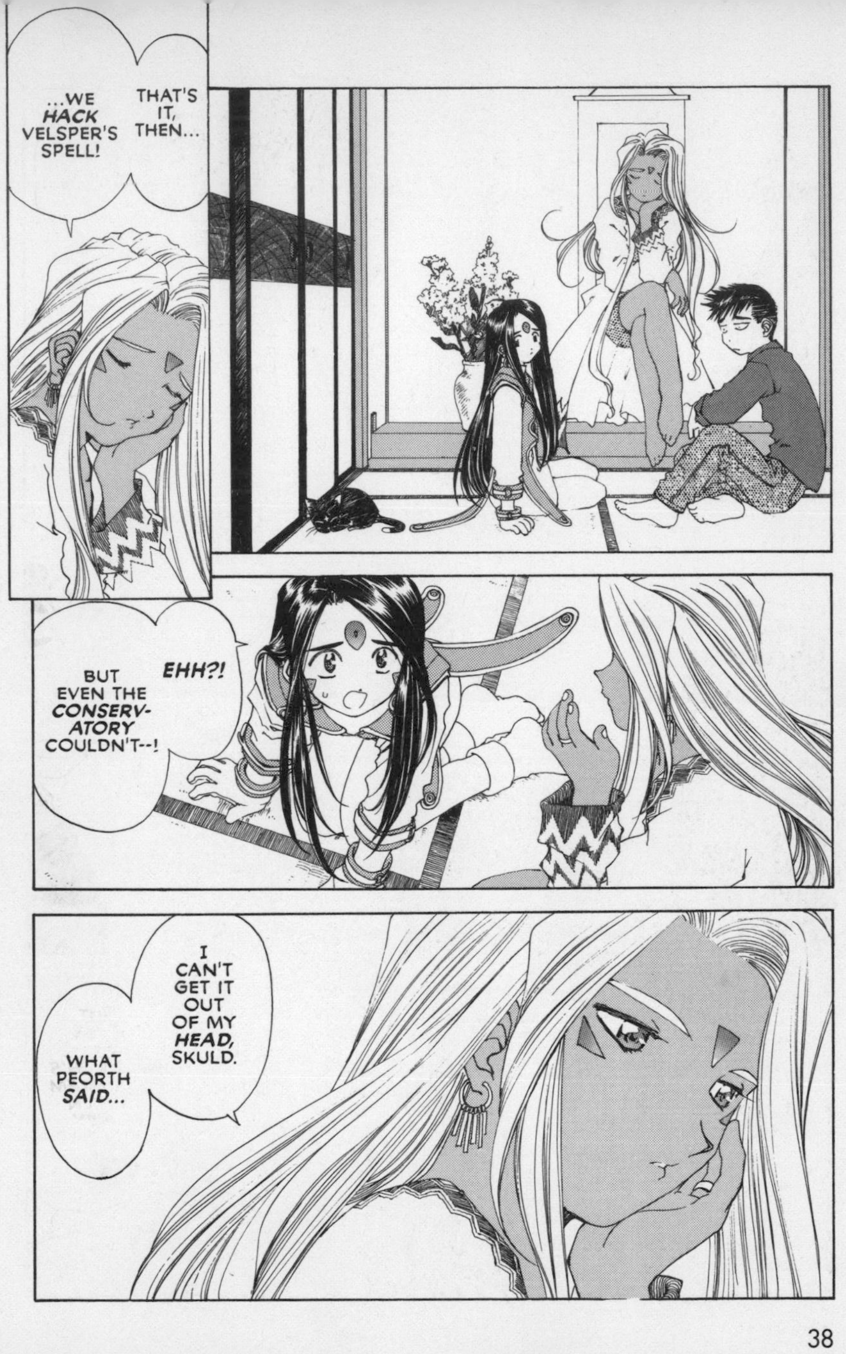
THAT'S IT, THEN... ...WE HACK VELSPER'S SPELL!
EHH?!
BUT EVEN THE CONSERVATORY COULDN'T--!
I CAN'T GET IT OUT OF MY HEAD, SKULD.
WHAT PEORTH SAID...

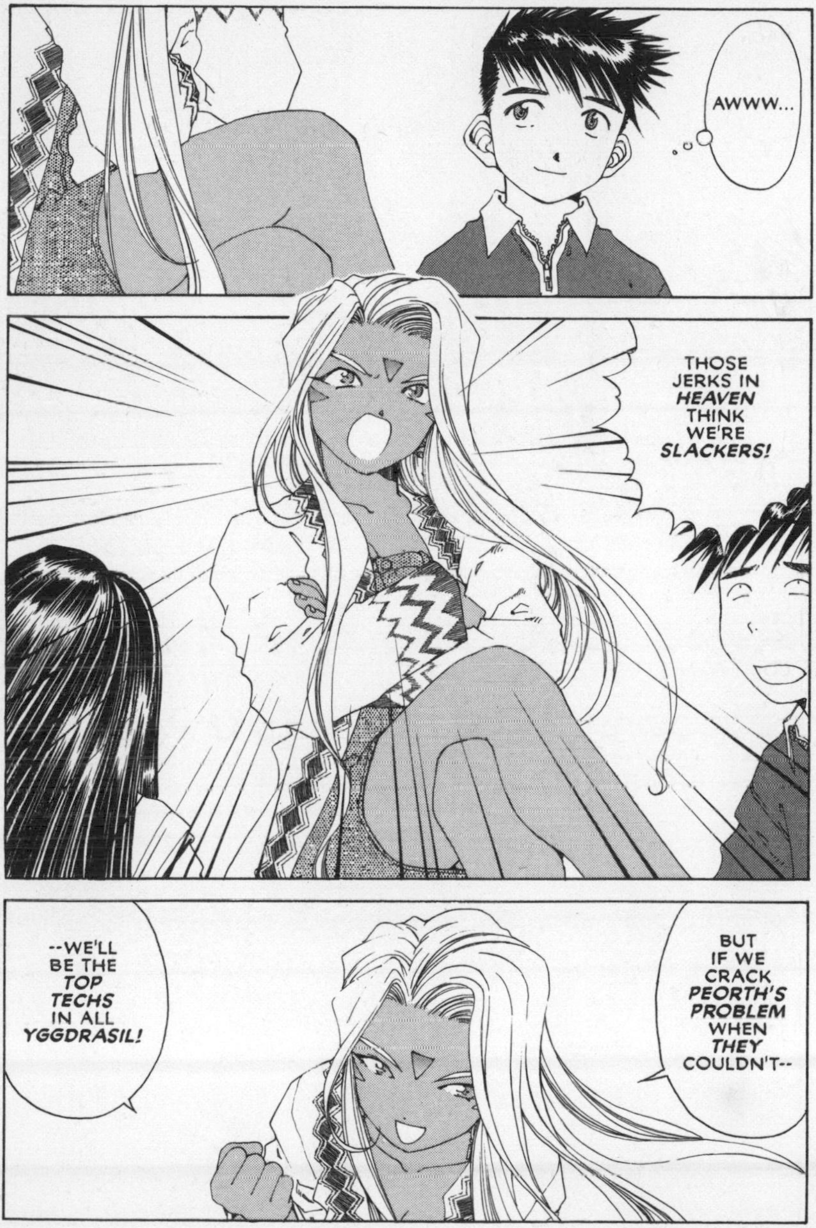
AWWW...
THOSE JERKS IN HEAVEN THINK WE'RE SLACKERS!
BUT IF WE CRACK PEORTH'S PROBLEM WHEN THEY COULDN'T--
--WE'LL BE THE TOP TECHS IN ALL YGGDRASIL!

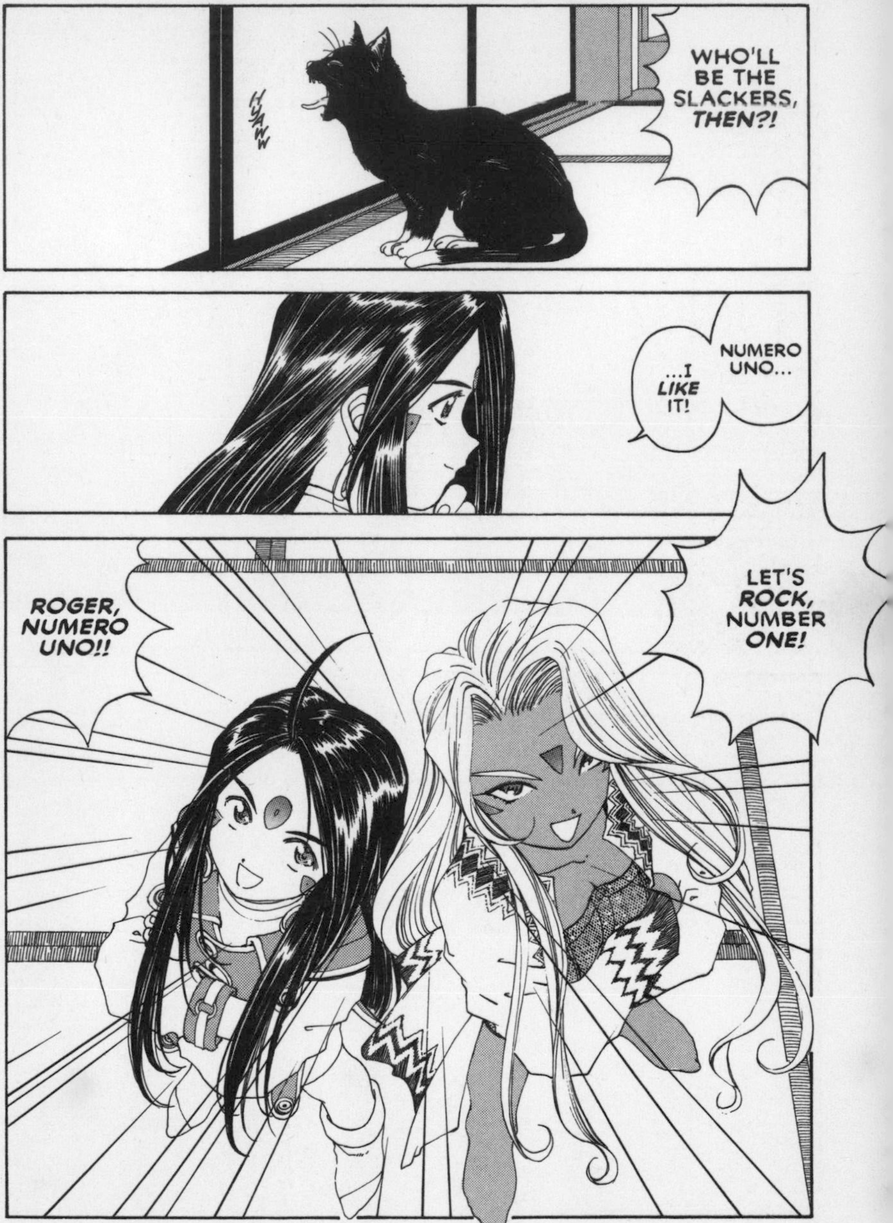
WHO'LL BE THE SLACKERS, *THEN?!*
HYAWW
NUMERO UNO...
...I *LIKE* IT!
LET'S *ROCK,* NUMBER *ONE!*
ROGER, NUMERO UNO!!

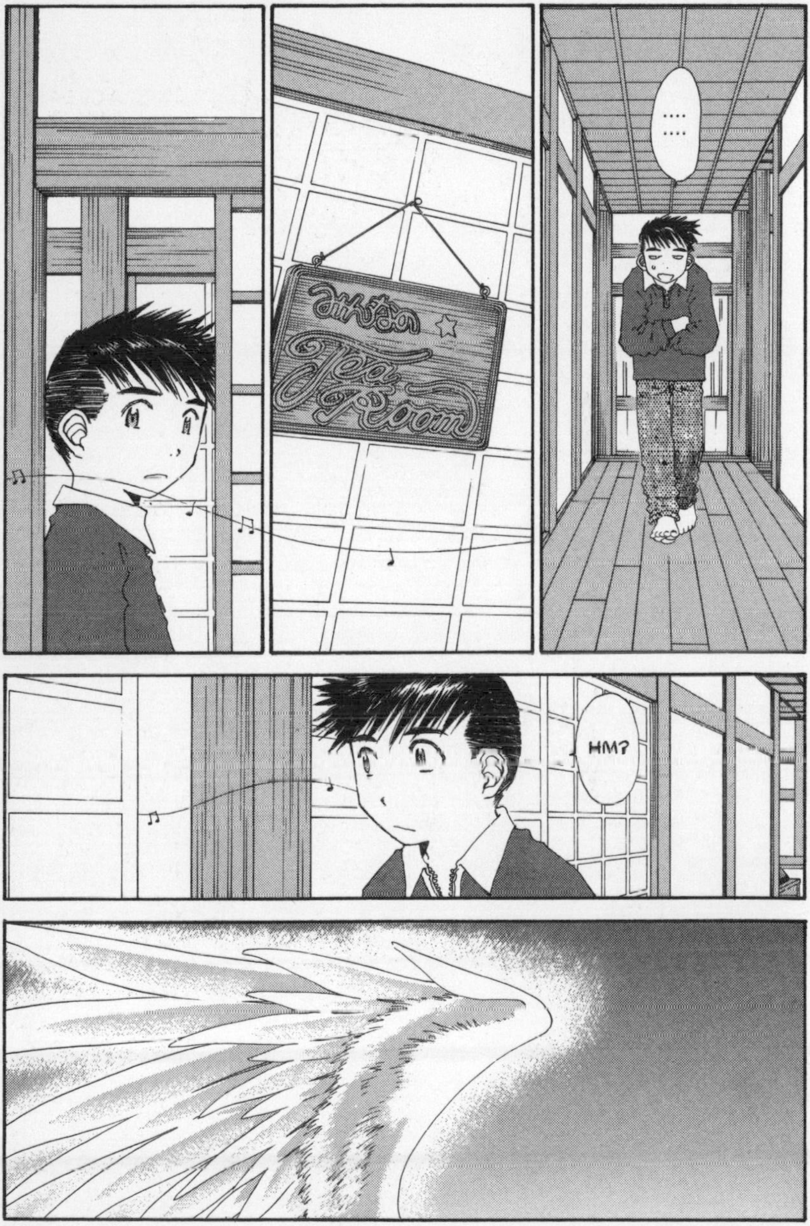
....
....
みんなの
Tea Room
HM?

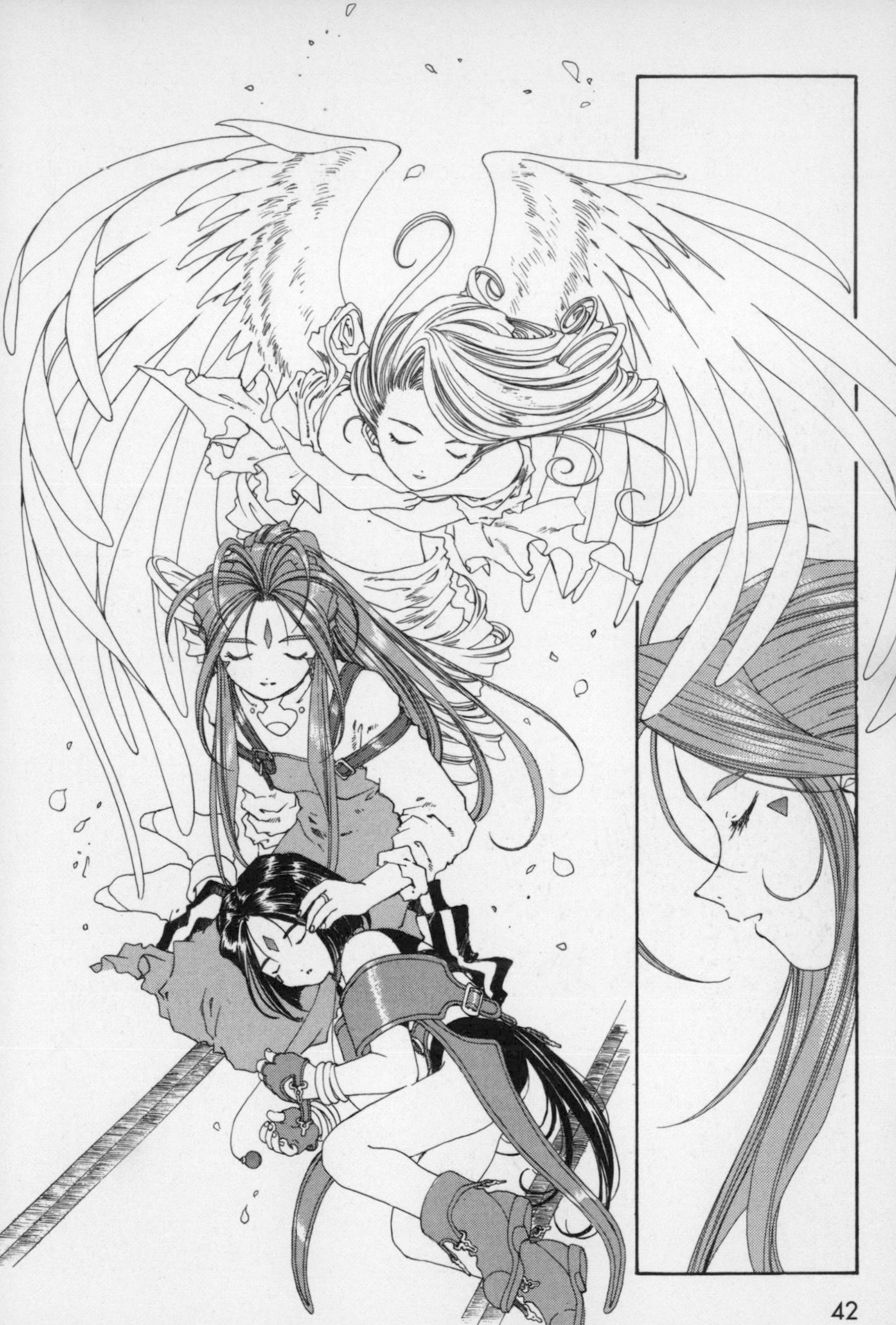

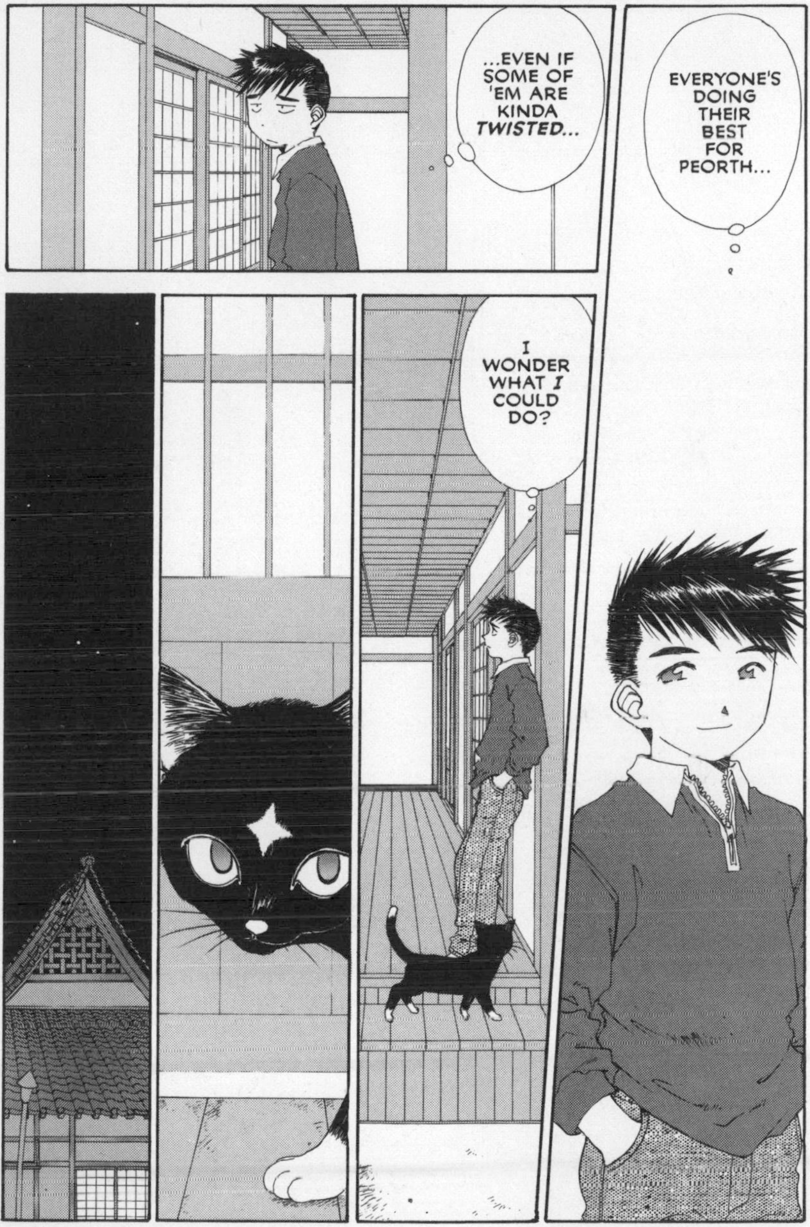
EVERYONE'S DOING THEIR BEST FOR PEORTH...
...EVEN IF SOME OF 'EM ARE KINDA *TWISTED...*
I WONDER WHAT *I* COULD DO?

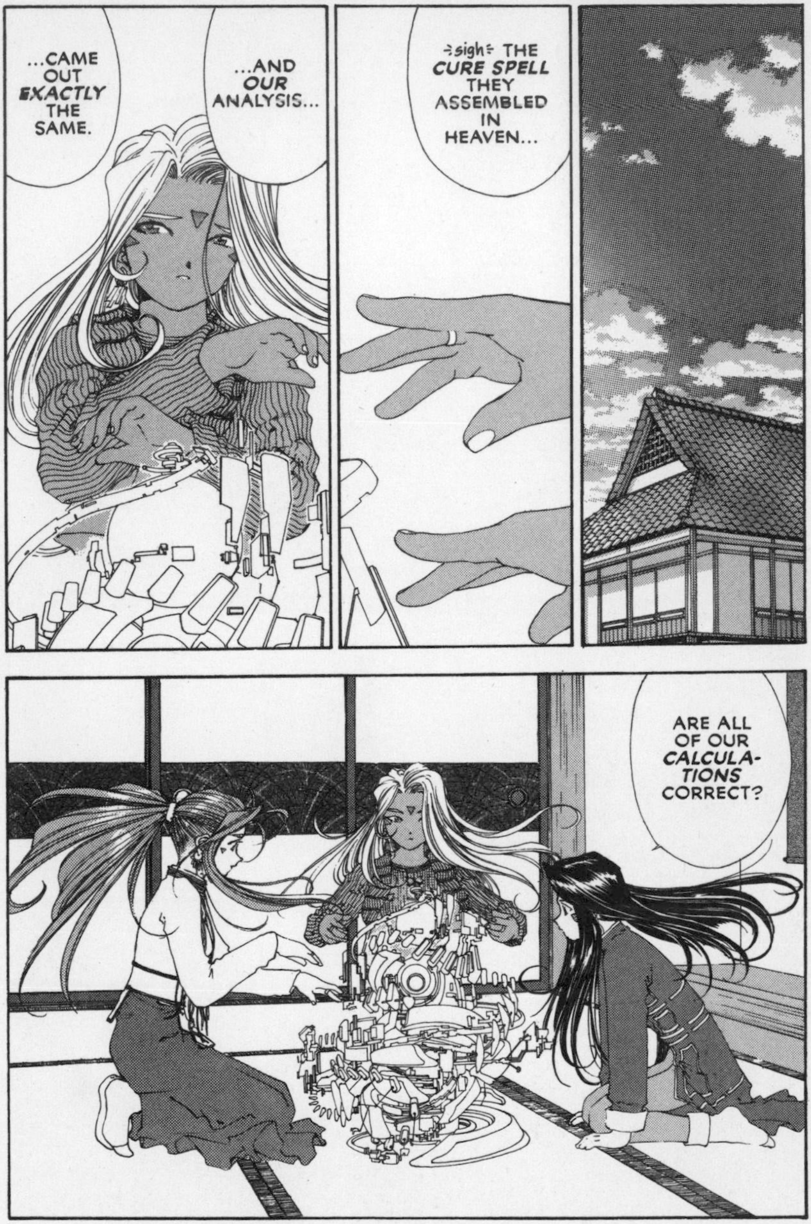
=sigh= THE CURE SPELL THEY ASSEMBLED IN HEAVEN...
...AND OUR ANALYSIS...
...CAME OUT EXACTLY THE SAME.
ARE ALL OF OUR CALCULATIONS CORRECT?

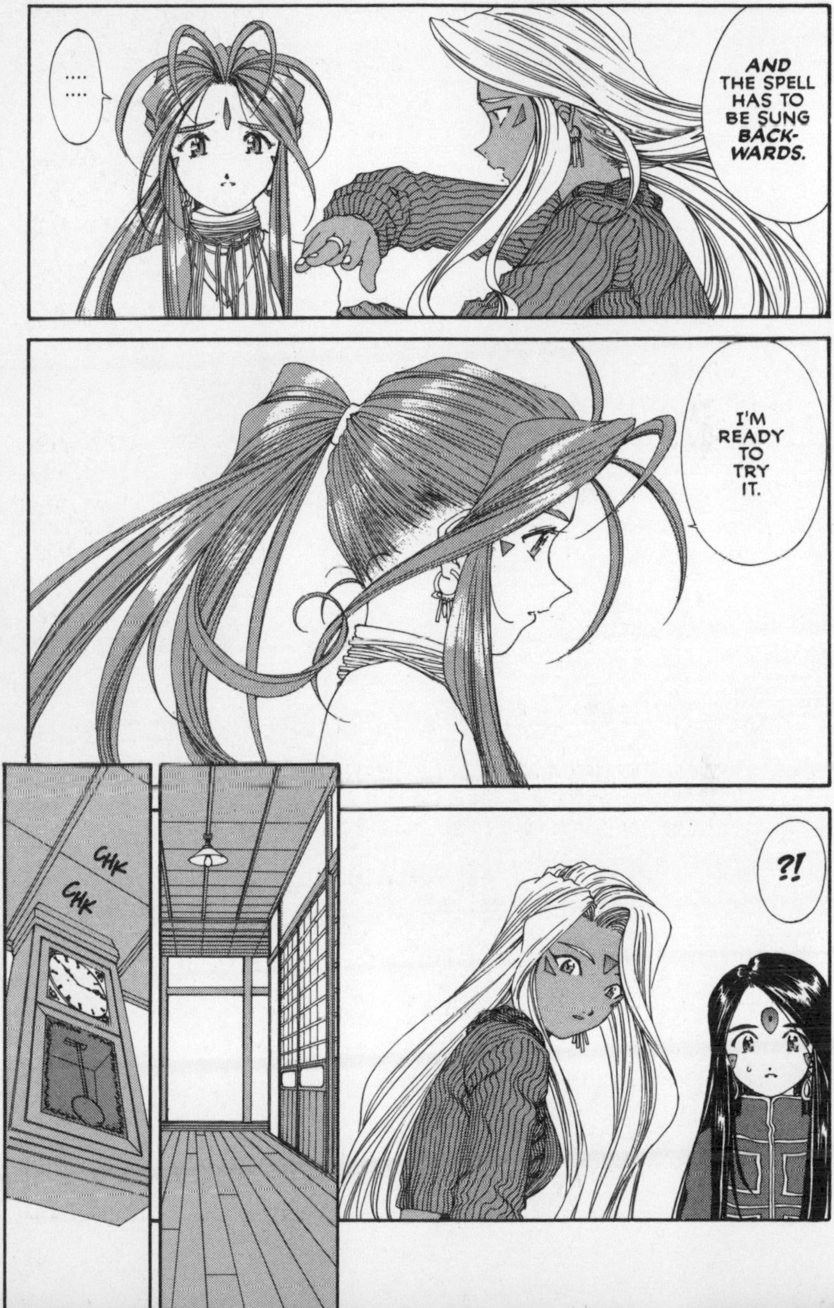
AND THE SPELL HAS TO BE SUNG BACKWARDS.
....
....
I'M READY TO TRY IT.
?!
CHK
CHK

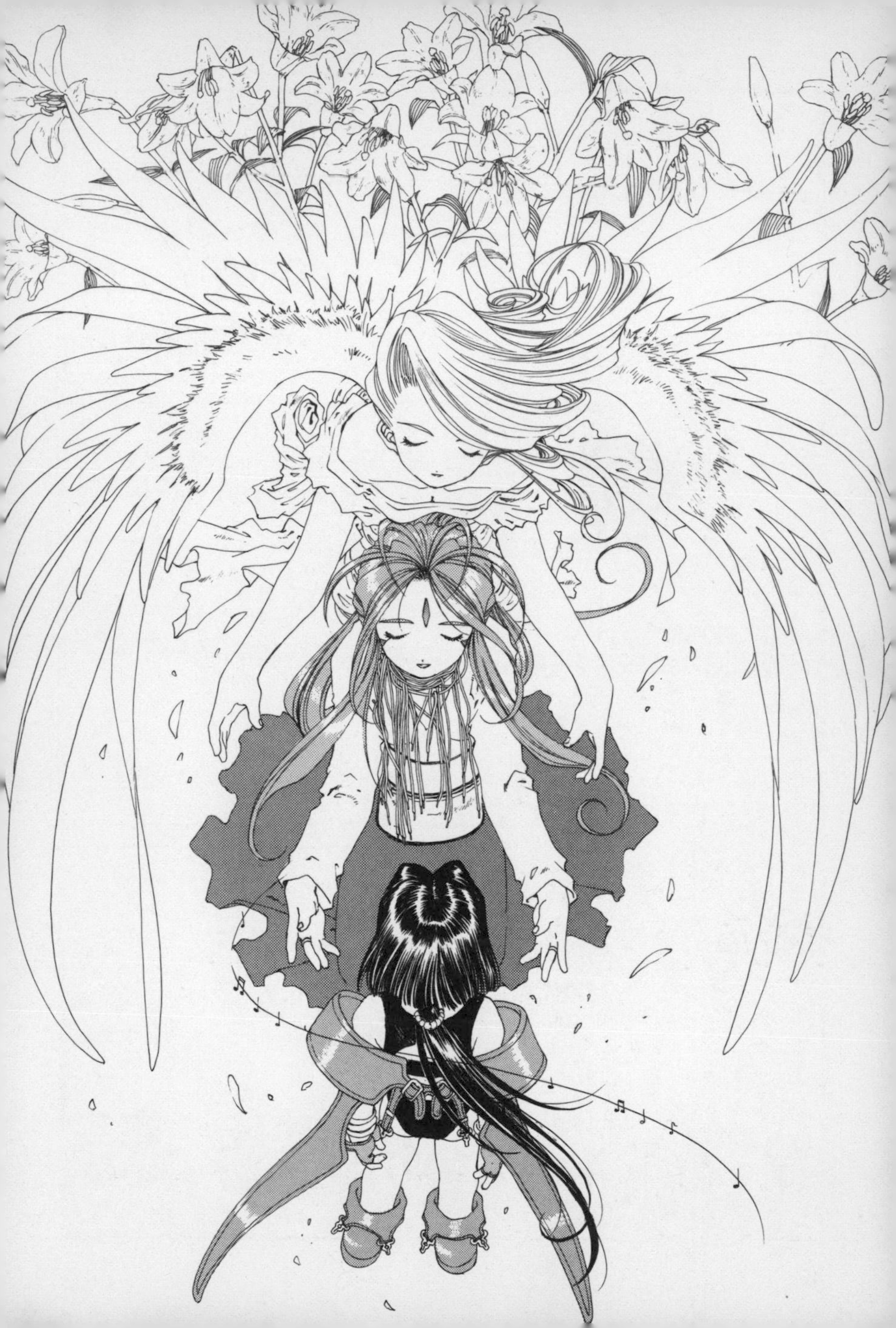

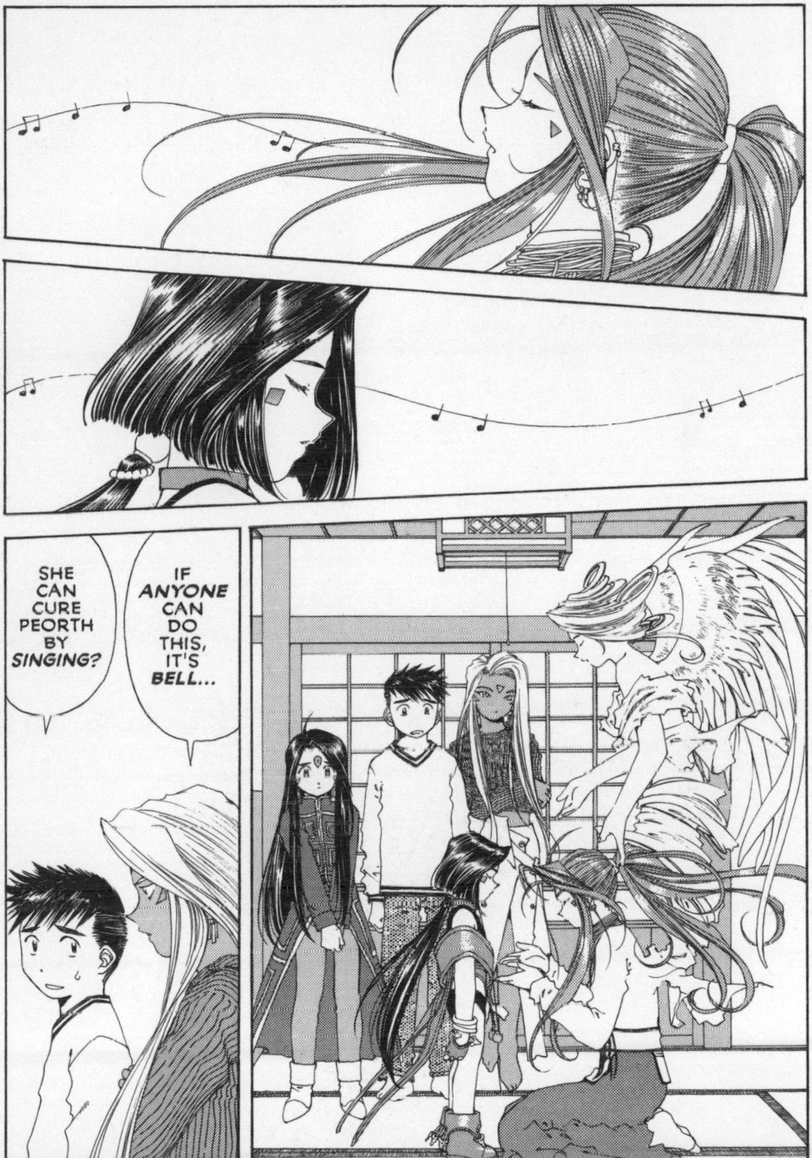
IF ANYONE CAN DO THIS, IT'S BELL...
SHE CAN CURE PEORTH BY SINGING?

WHAT *SOUNDS* LIKE SONGS TO YOU--

--ARE *COMPRESSED SPELL COMMANDS.*

FREQUENCY SHIFTS FROM NOTE TO NOTE...

...*EXECUTE* THE SPELL *SUB-ROUTINES.*

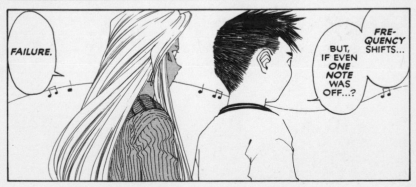

FRE-QUENCY SHIFTS...

BUT, IF EVEN *ONE NOTE* WAS OFF...?

FAILURE.

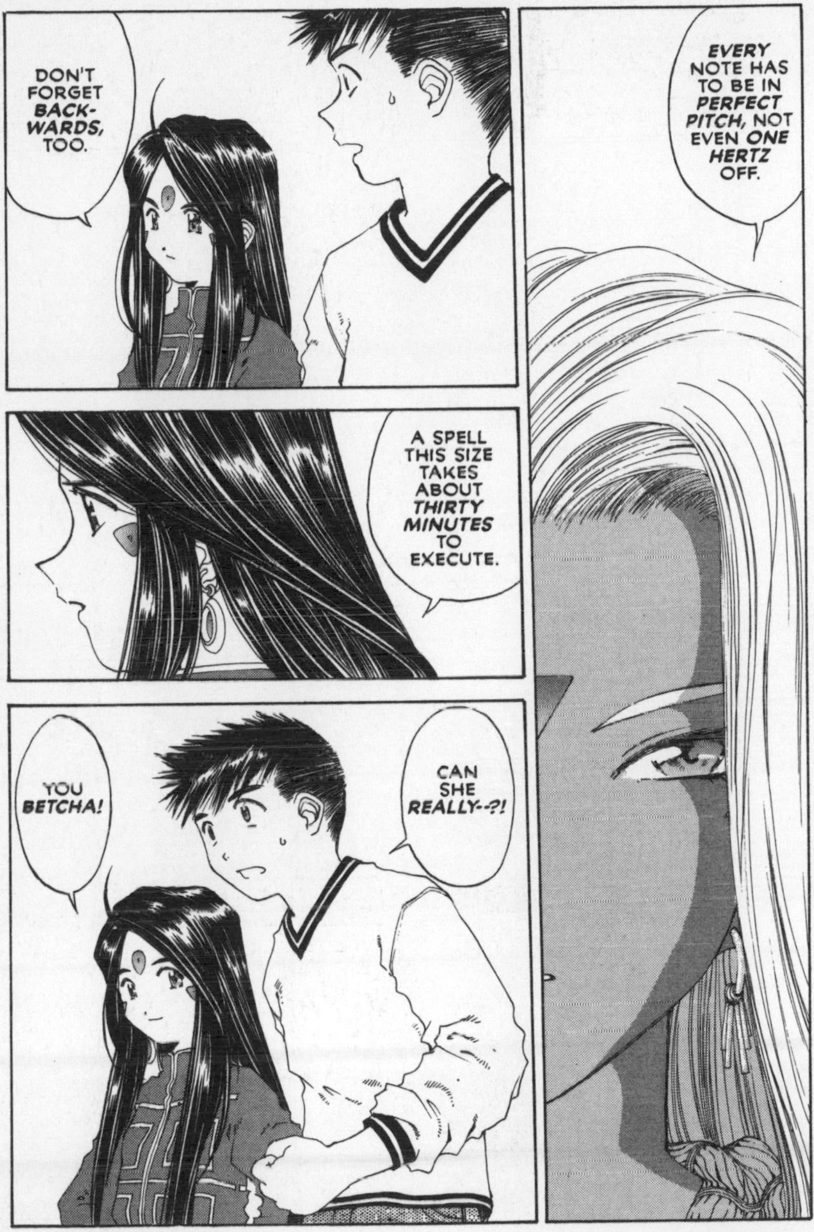
EVERY NOTE HAS TO BE IN PERFECT PITCH, NOT EVEN ONE HERTZ OFF.
DON'T FORGET BACKWARDS, TOO.
A SPELL THIS SIZE TAKES ABOUT THIRTY MINUTES TO EXECUTE.
CAN SHE REALLY--?!
YOU BETCHA!

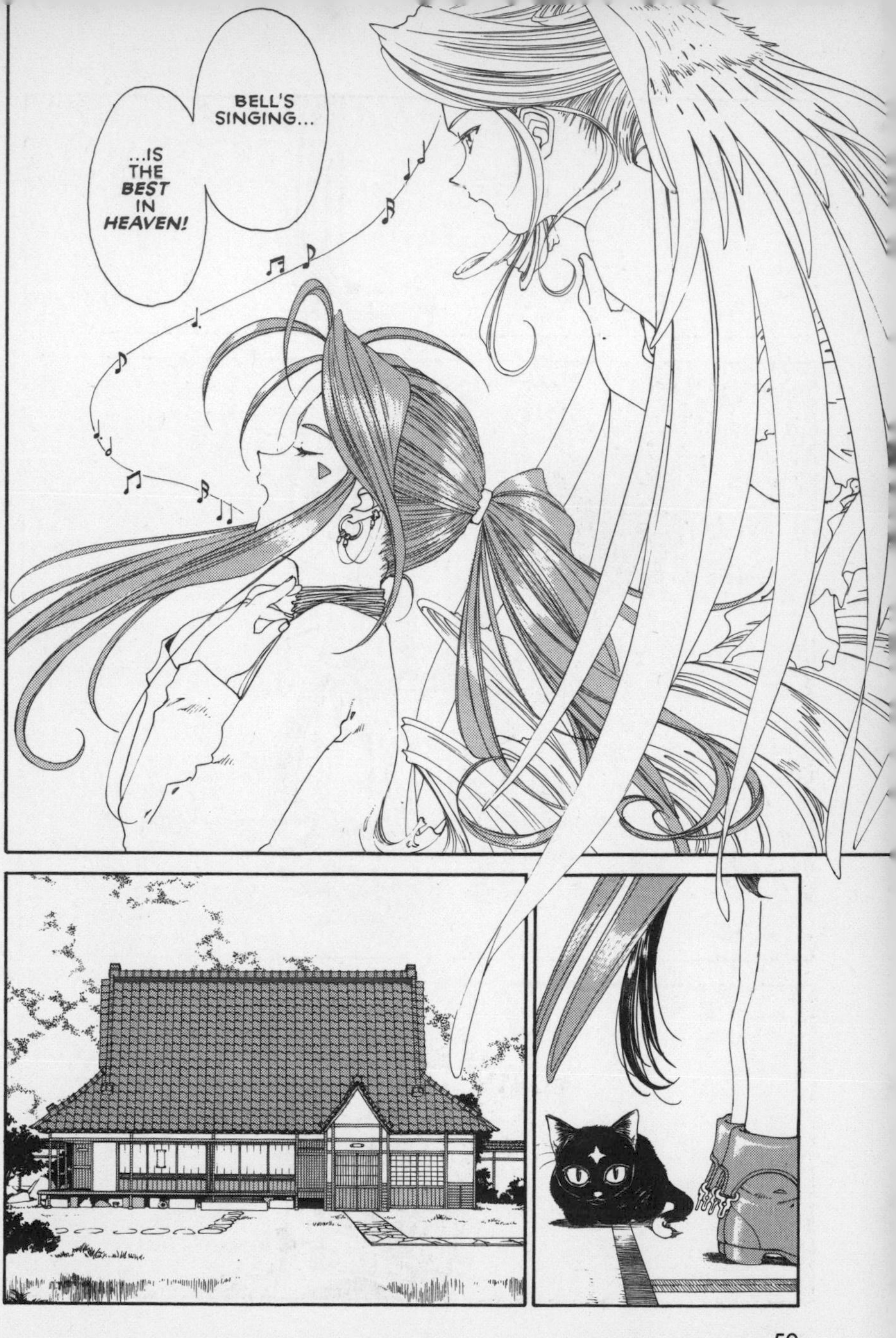
BELL'S SINGING...
...IS THE *BEST* IN *HEAVEN!*

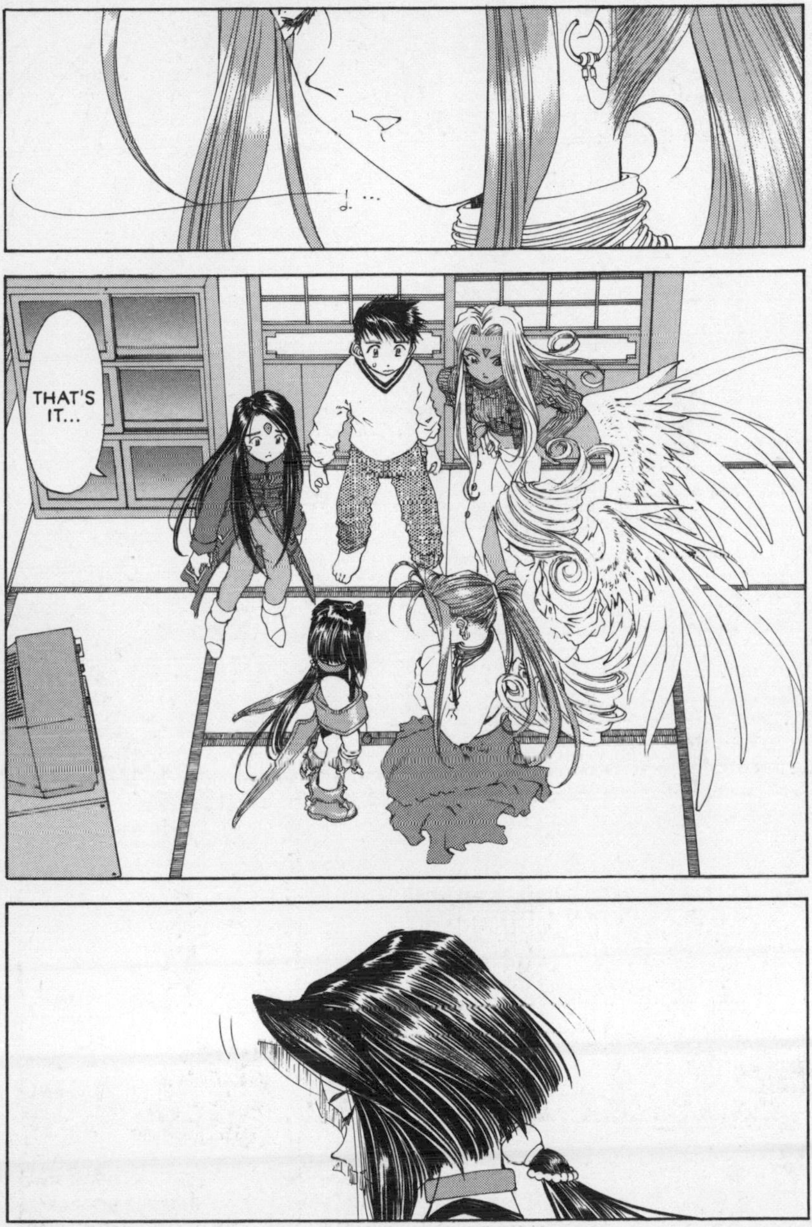
THAT'S IT...

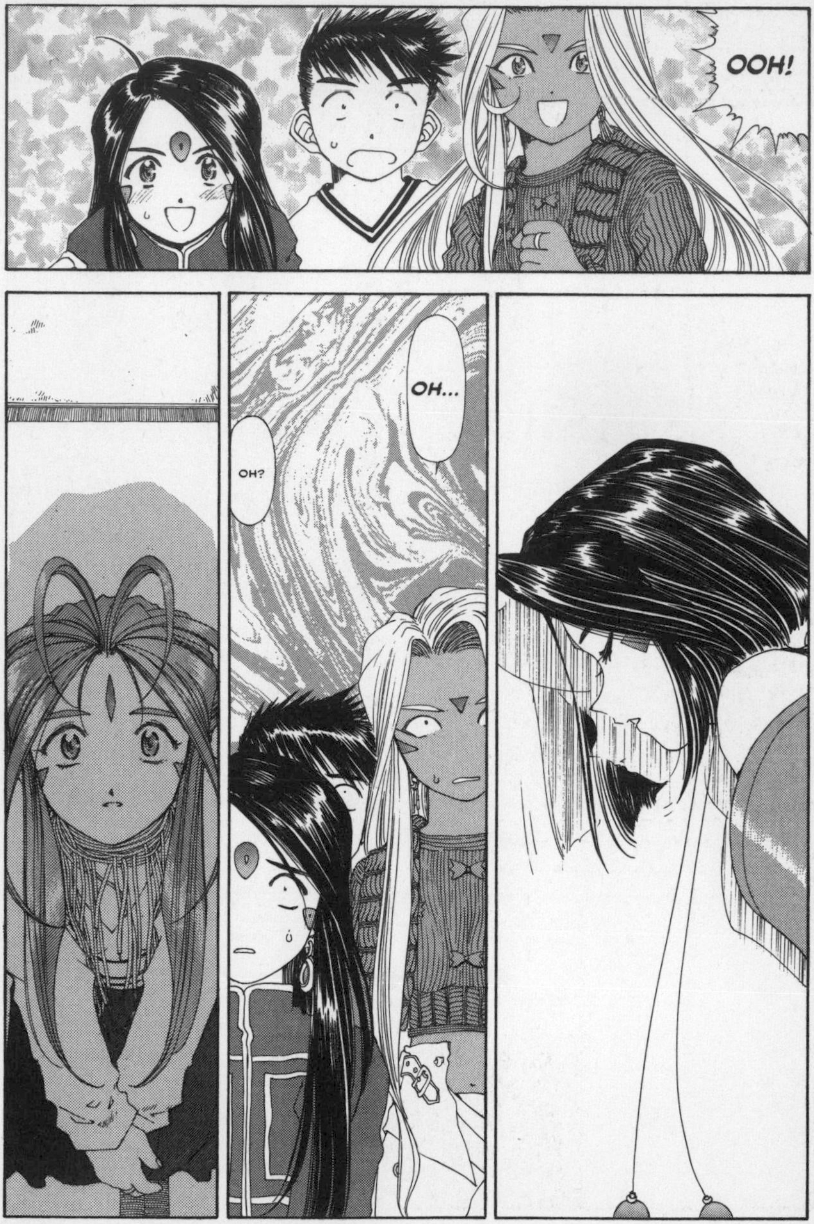
OOH!
OH...
OH?

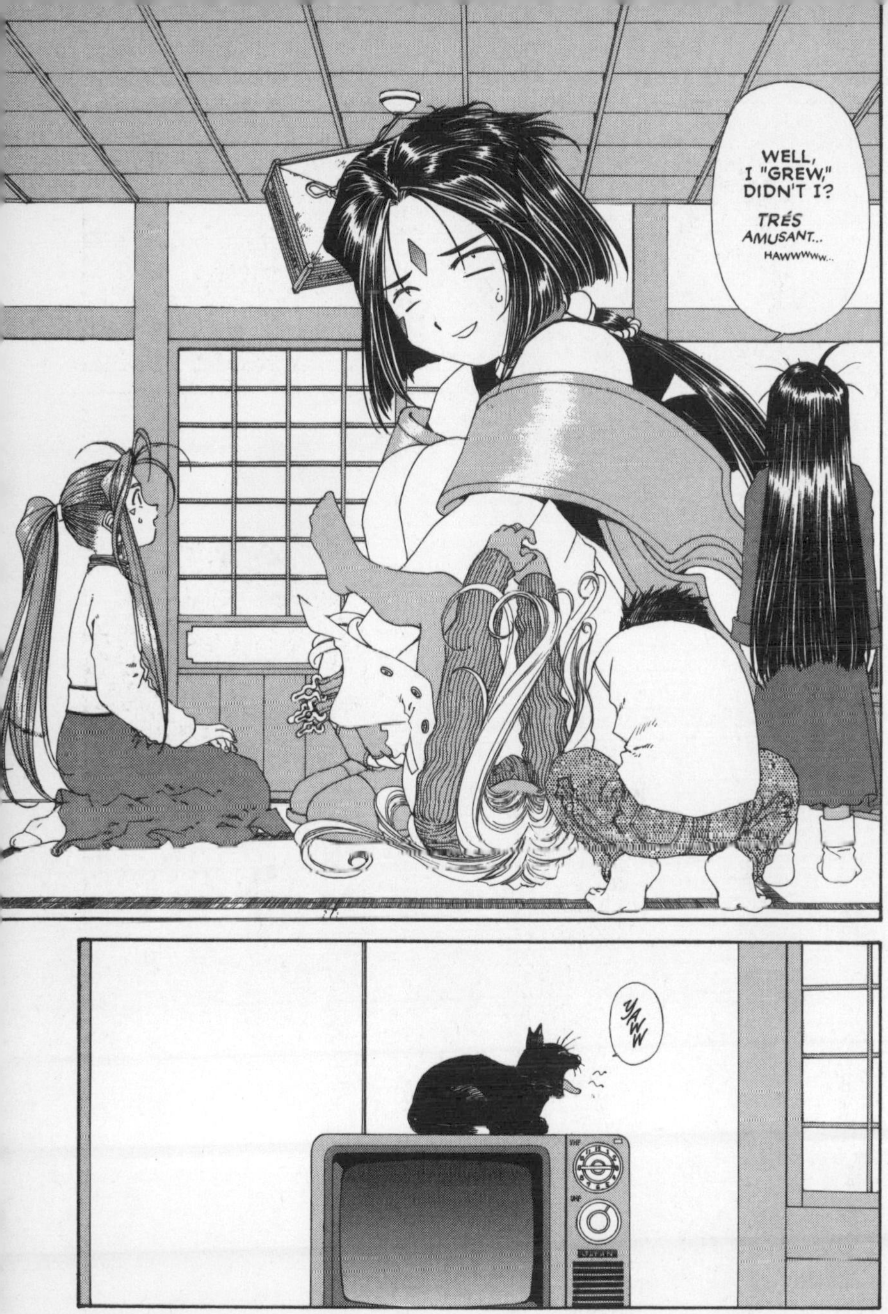
WELL, I "GREW," DIDN'T I?
TRÉS AMUSANT...
HAWWWWW...
YAWW

END CHAPTER 131

OH MY GODDESS!
P E O R T H

CHAPTER 132

A Goddess Never Forgets

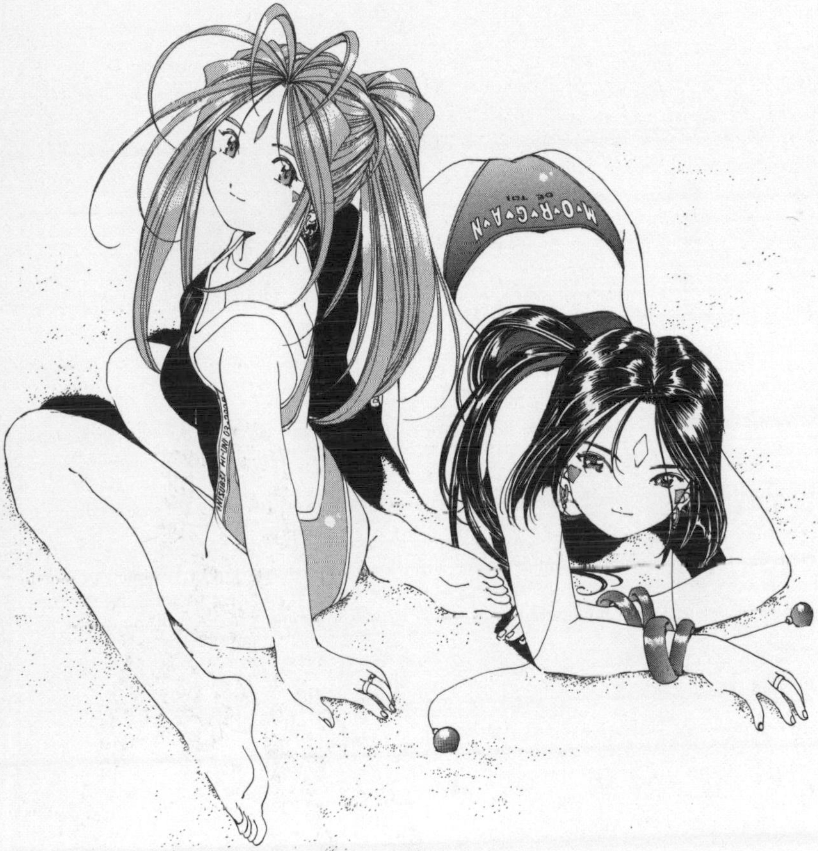

牧野○製
コンサバ号

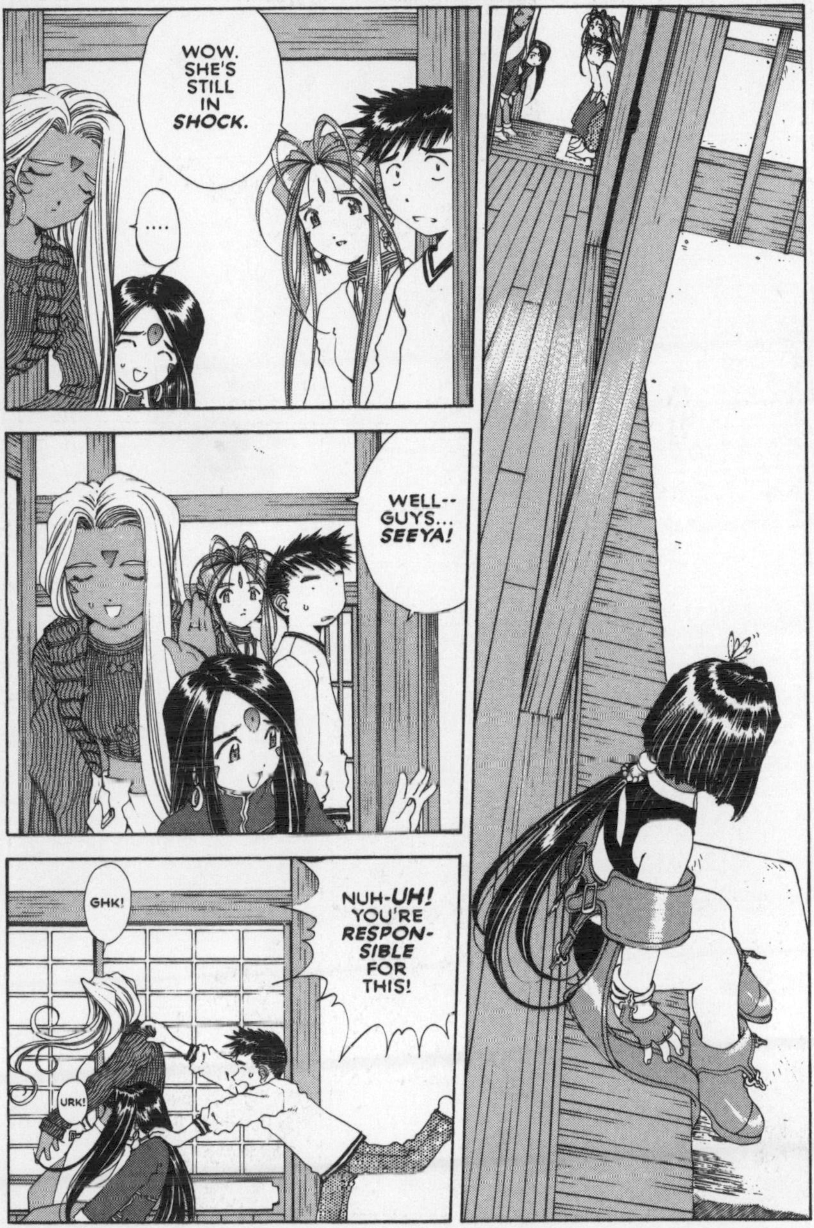

WOW. SHE'S STILL IN SHOCK.
....
WELL-- GUYS... SEEYA!
NUH-UH! YOU'RE RESPONSIBLE FOR THIS!
GHK!
URK!

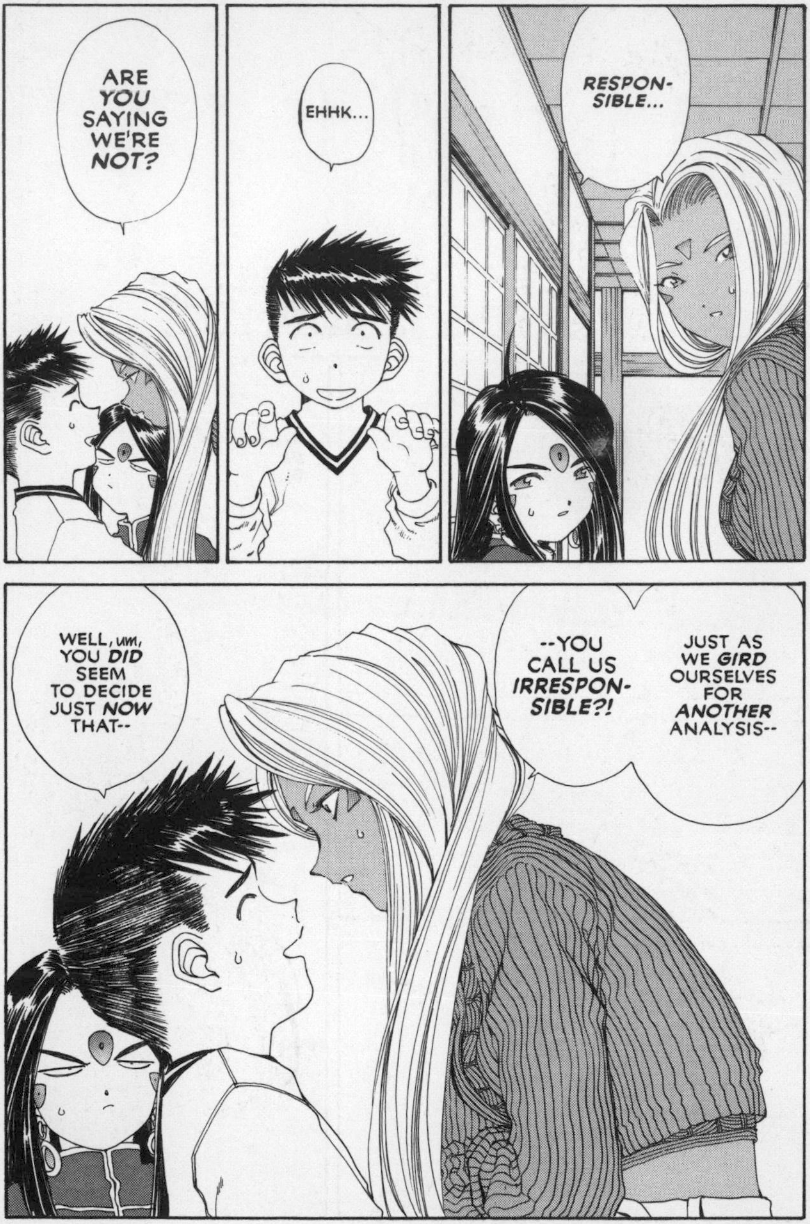
RESPONSIBLE...
EHHK...
ARE YOU SAYING WE'RE NOT?
JUST AS WE GIRD OURSELVES FOR ANOTHER ANALYSIS--
--YOU CALL US IRRESPONSIBLE?!
WELL, um, YOU DID SEEM TO DECIDE JUST NOW THAT--

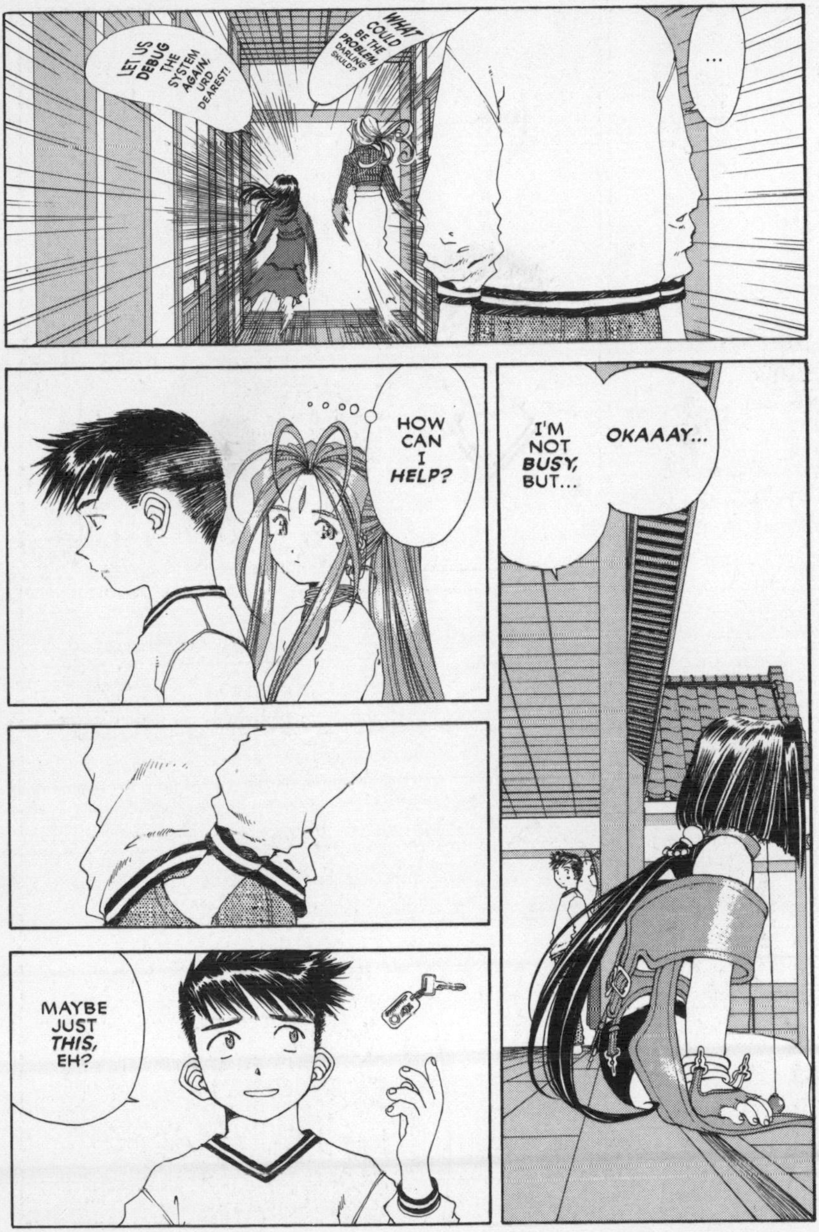
...
WHAT COULD BE THE PROBLEM, DARLING SKULD?
LET US DEBUG THE SYSTEM AGAIN, URD DEAREST!
OKAAAY...
I'M NOT BUSY, BUT...
HOW CAN I HELP?
MAYBE JUST THIS, EH?

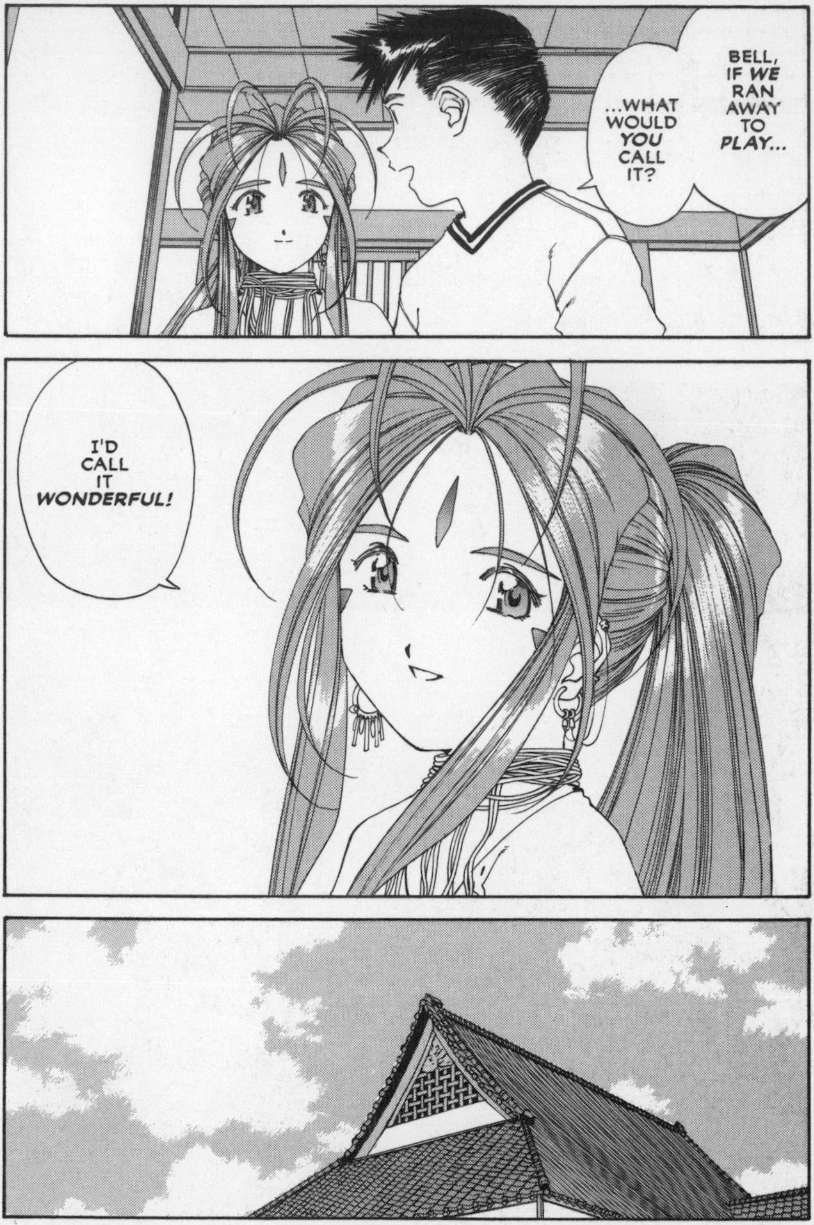
BELL, IF WE RAN AWAY TO PLAY...
...WHAT WOULD YOU CALL IT?
I'D CALL IT WONDERFUL!

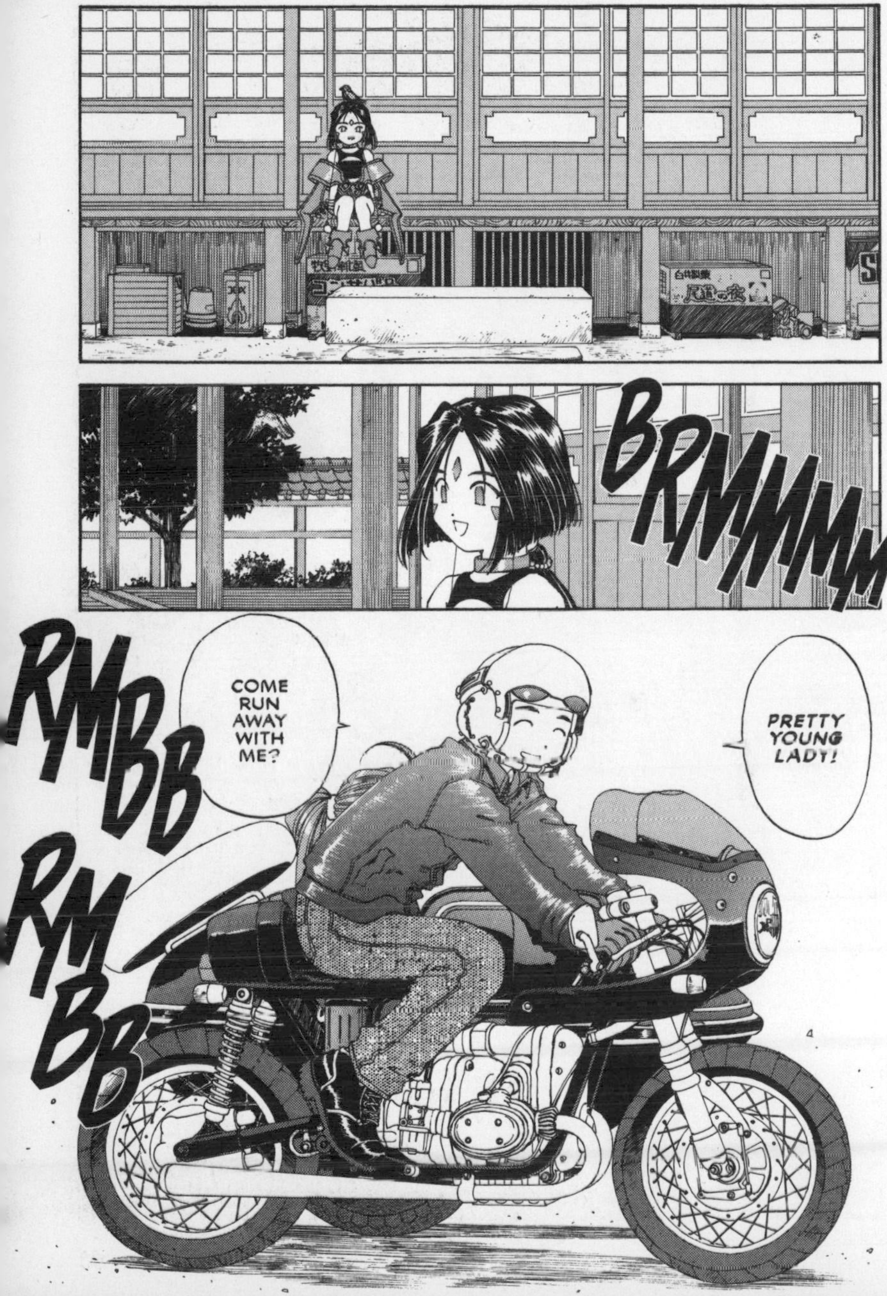
BRMMMMM
PRETTY YOUNG LADY!
COME RUN AWAY WITH ME?
RMBB RMBB

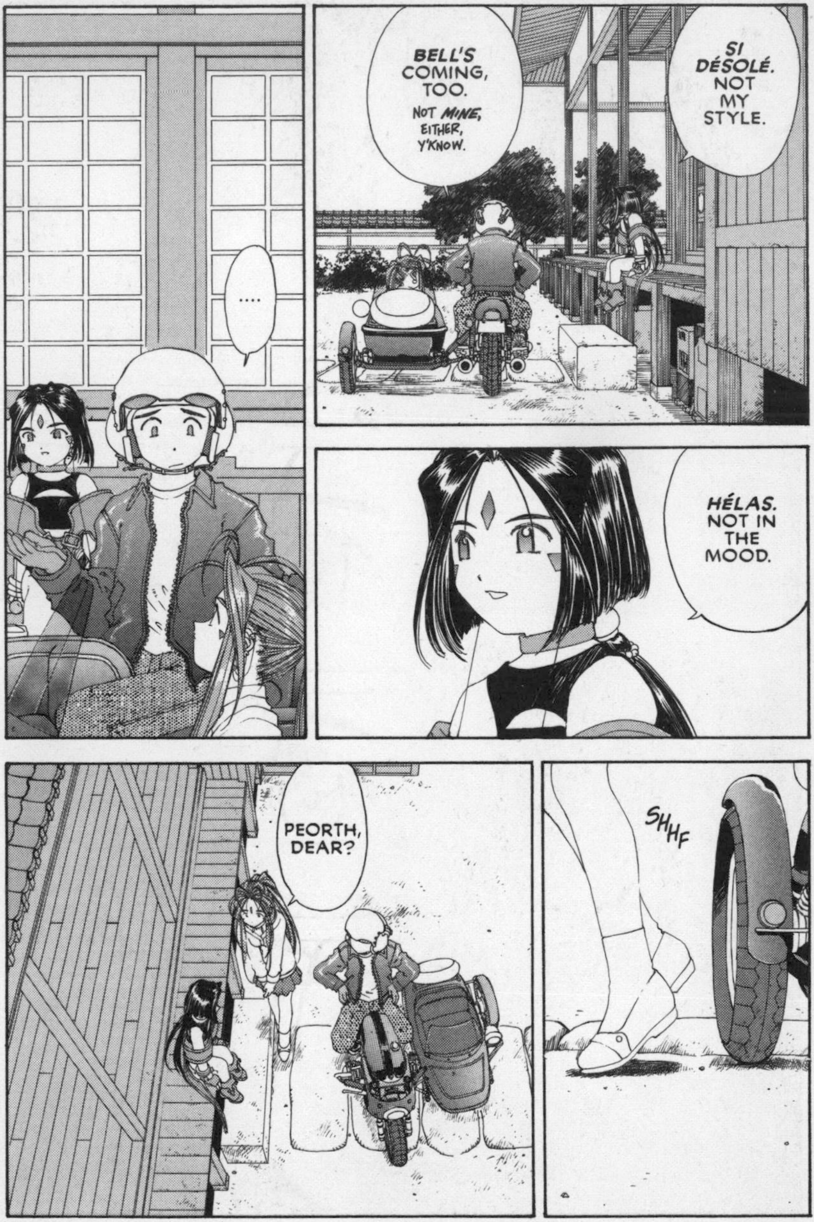
SI DÉSOLÉ. NOT MY STYLE.
BELL'S COMING, TOO.
NOT MINE, EITHER, Y'KNOW.
HÉLAS. NOT IN THE MOOD.
....
SHHF
PEORTH, DEAR?

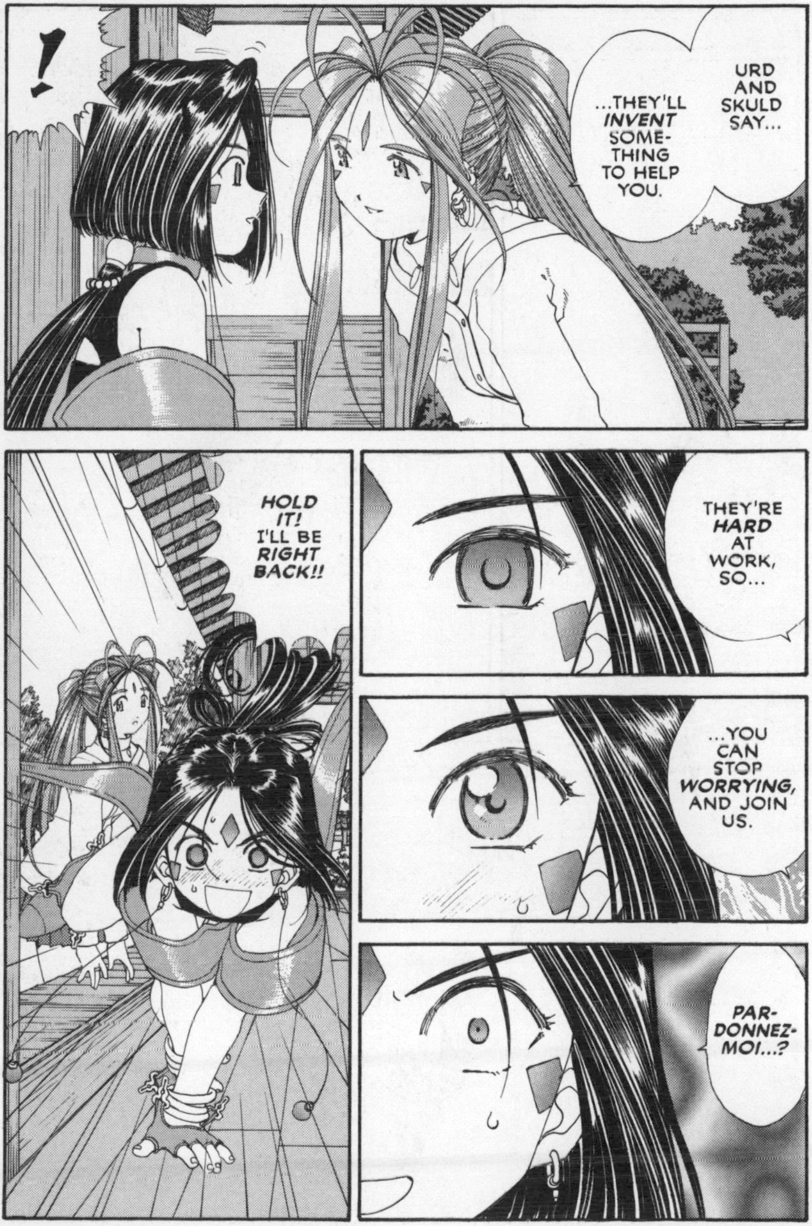
URD AND SKULD SAY...
...THEY'LL *INVENT* SOME-THING TO HELP YOU.
!
THEY'RE *HARD* AT WORK, SO...
...YOU CAN STOP *WORRYING*, AND JOIN US.
PAR-DONNEZ-MOI...?
HOLD IT! I'LL BE *RIGHT BACK!!*

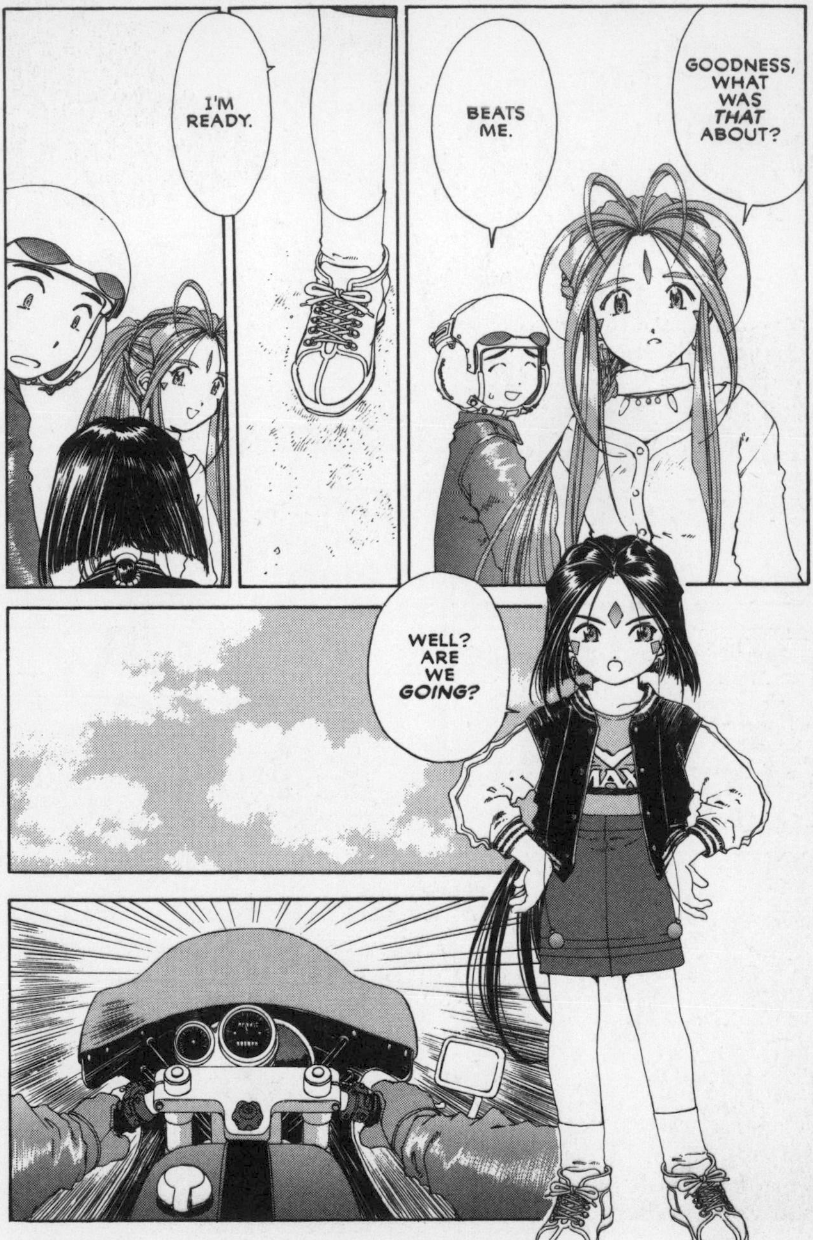
GOODNESS, WHAT WAS *THAT* ABOUT?
BEATS ME.
I'M READY.
WELL? ARE WE *GOING*?

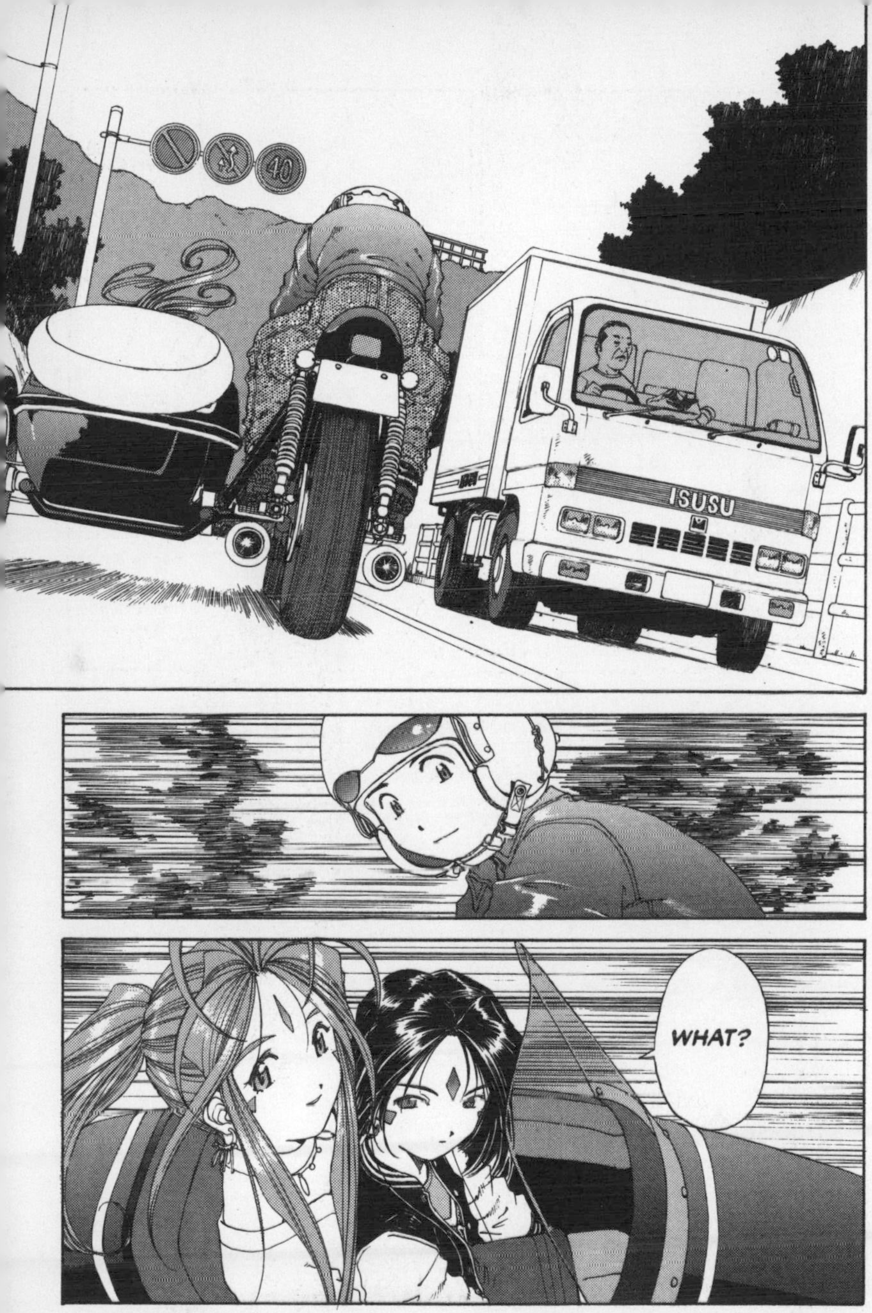
ISUSU
WHAT?

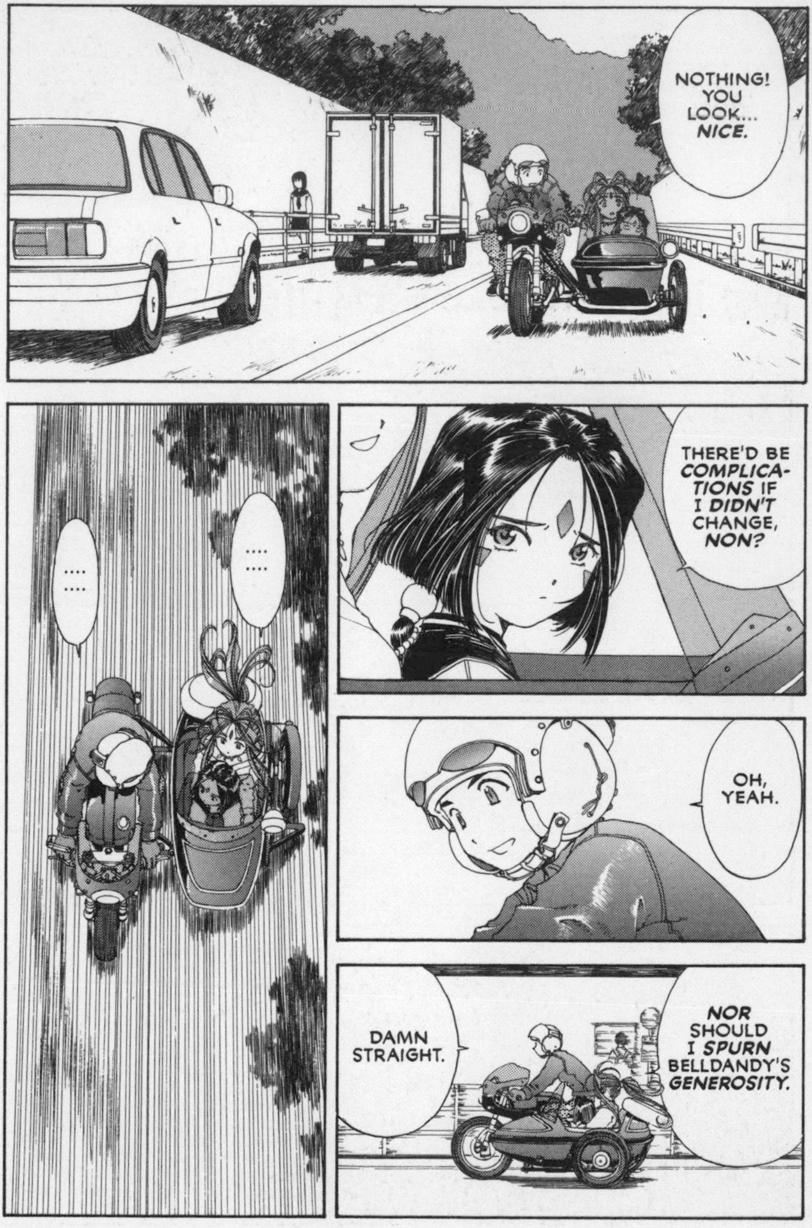
NOTHING! YOU LOOK... *NICE.*
THERE'D BE *COMPLICATIONS* IF I *DIDN'T* CHANGE, *NON?*
OH, YEAH.
NOR SHOULD I *SPURN* BELLDANDY'S *GENEROSITY.*
DAMN STRAIGHT.
....
....

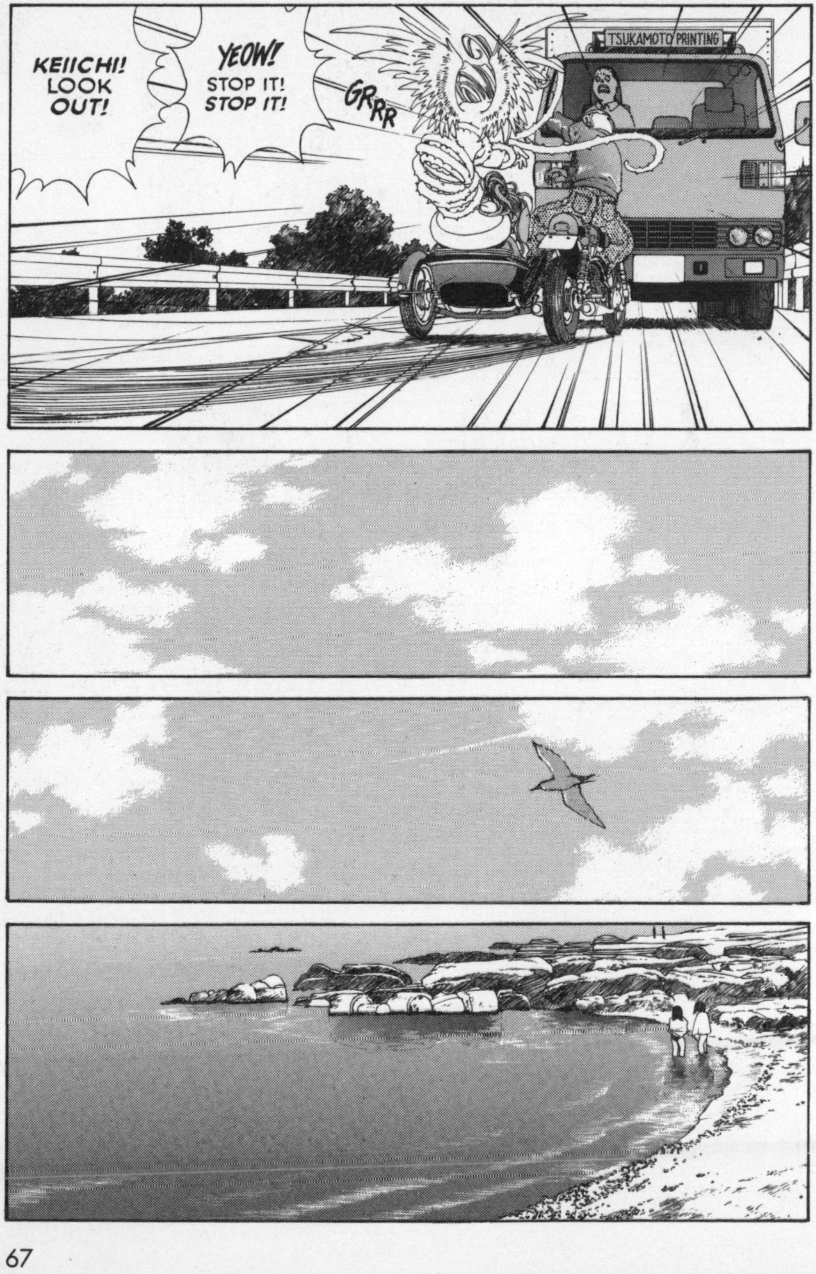
TSUKAMOTO PRINTING
GRRR
YEOW! STOP IT! STOP IT!
KEIICHI! LOOK OUT!

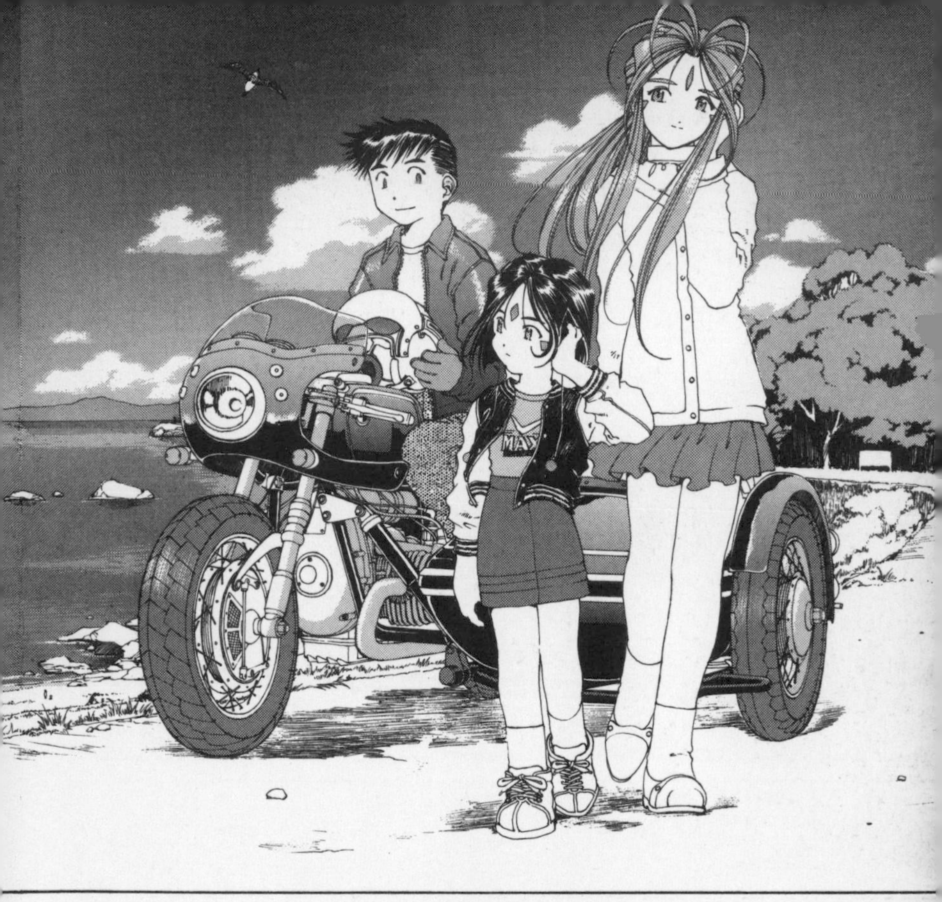

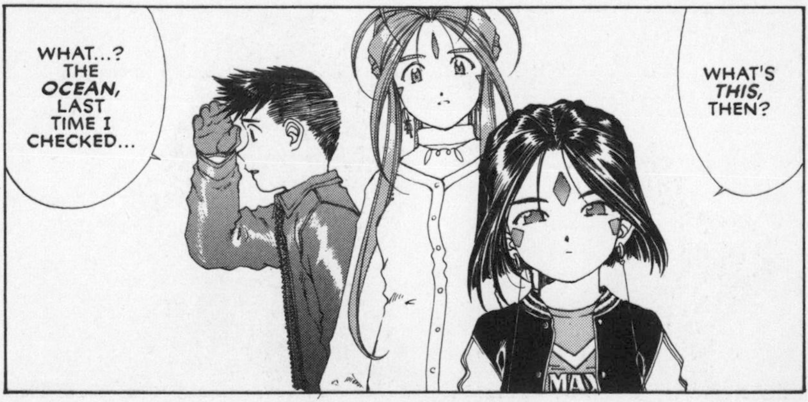
WHAT'S *THIS,* THEN?
WHAT...? THE *OCEAN,* LAST TIME I CHECKED...

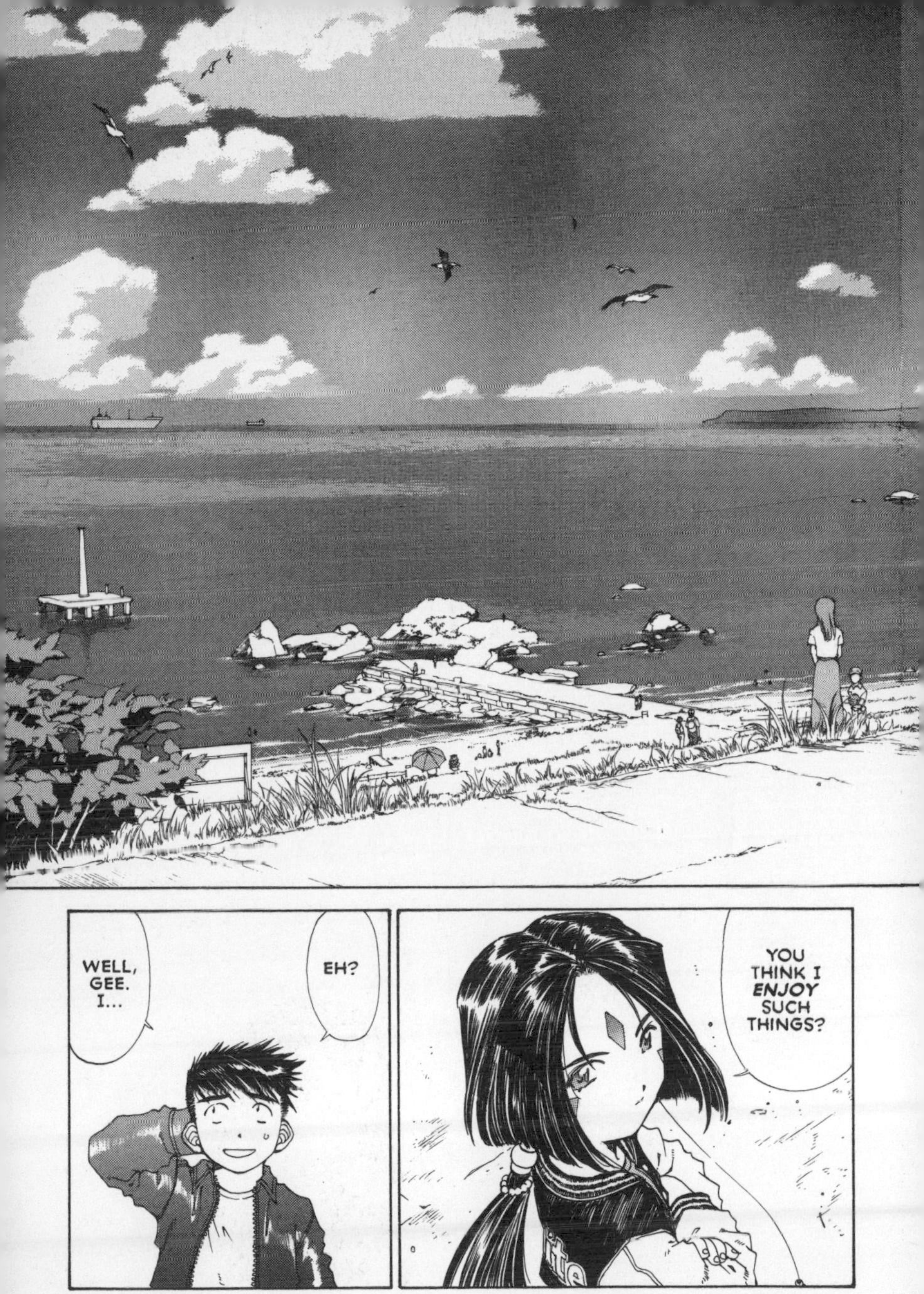
YOU THINK I *ENJOY* SUCH THINGS?
EH?
WELL, GEE. I...

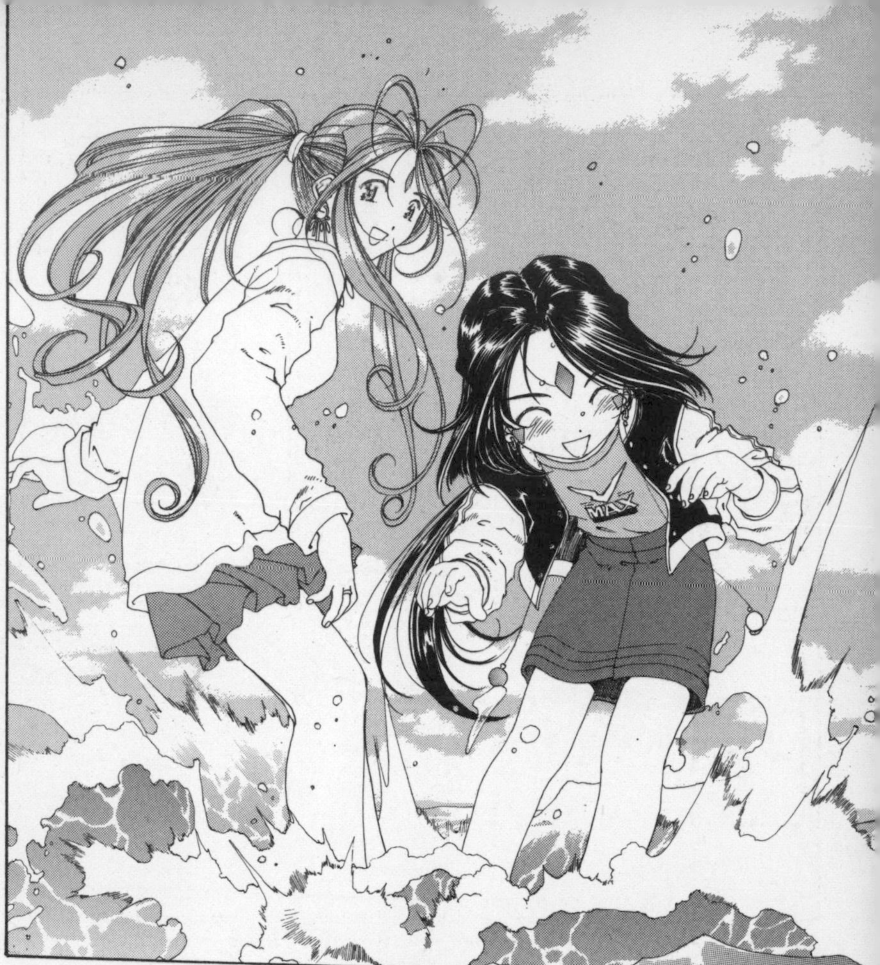
MAX

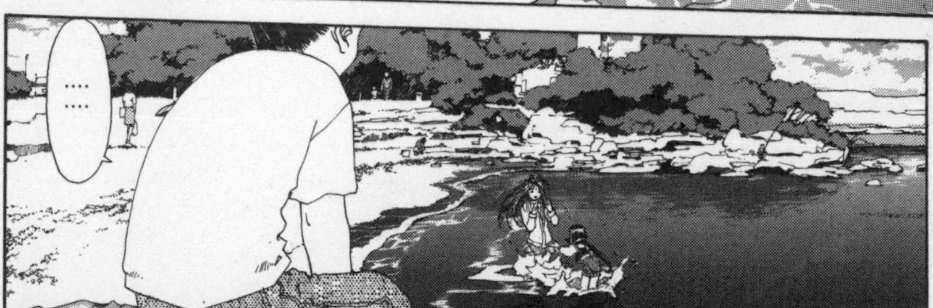
....
....

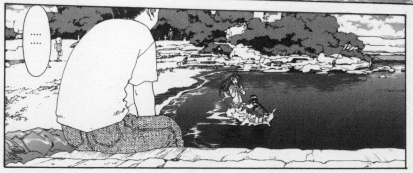

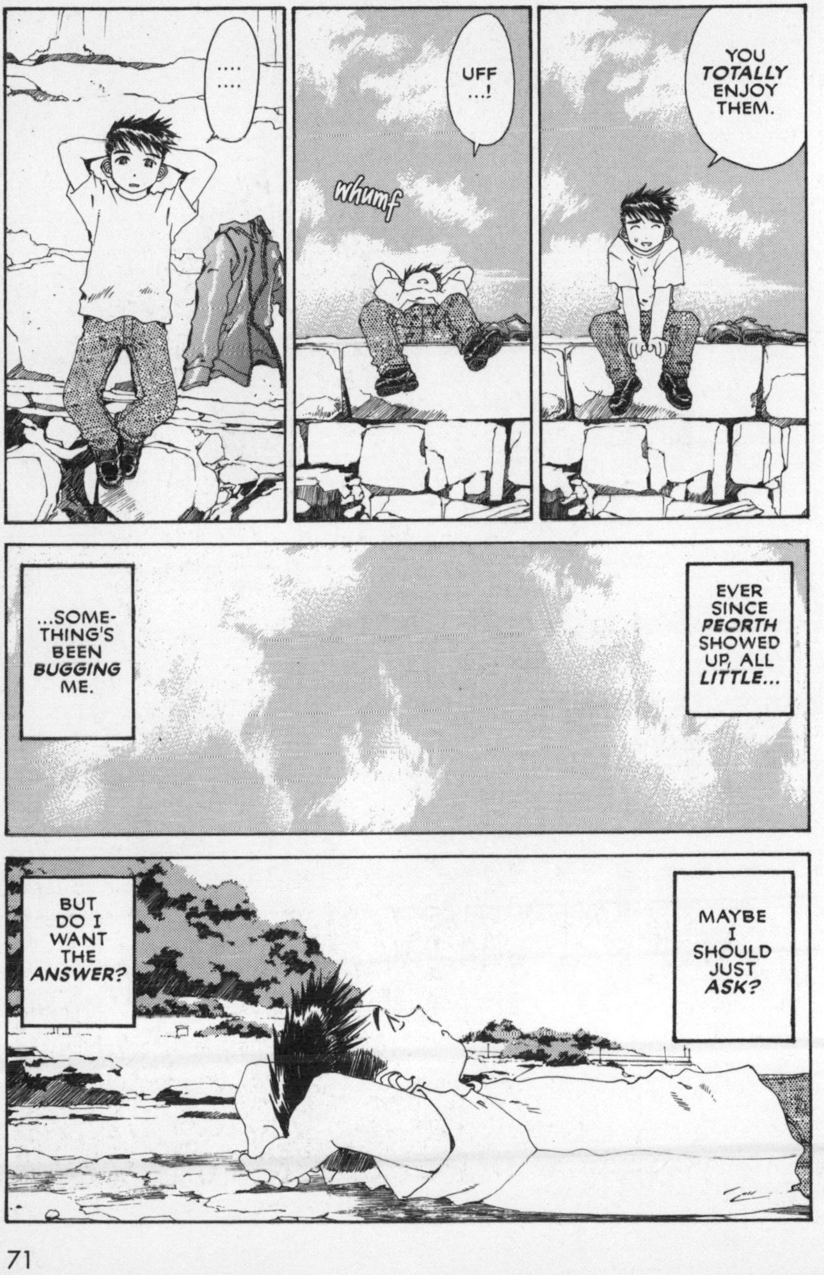
YOU *TOTALLY* ENJOY THEM.
UFF ...!
whumf
....
EVER SINCE *PEORTH* SHOWED UP, ALL *LITTLE...*
...SOME-THING'S BEEN *BUGGING* ME.
MAYBE I SHOULD JUST *ASK?*
BUT DO I WANT THE *ANSWER?*

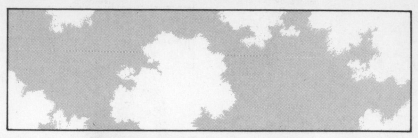

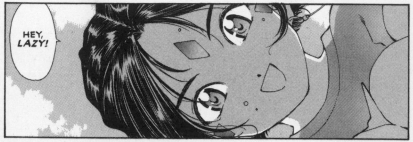

HEY, LAZY!
YEEK!
WHAT ARE YOU MOPING ABOUT?
DID WE NOT COME HERE TO CHEER ME UP?
YEAH... WE DID.
SURE.

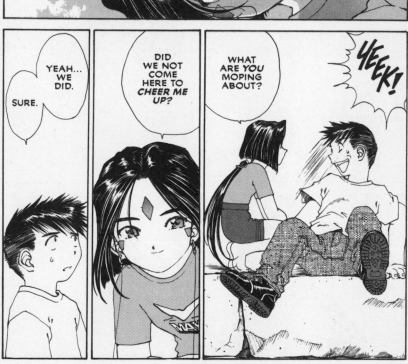

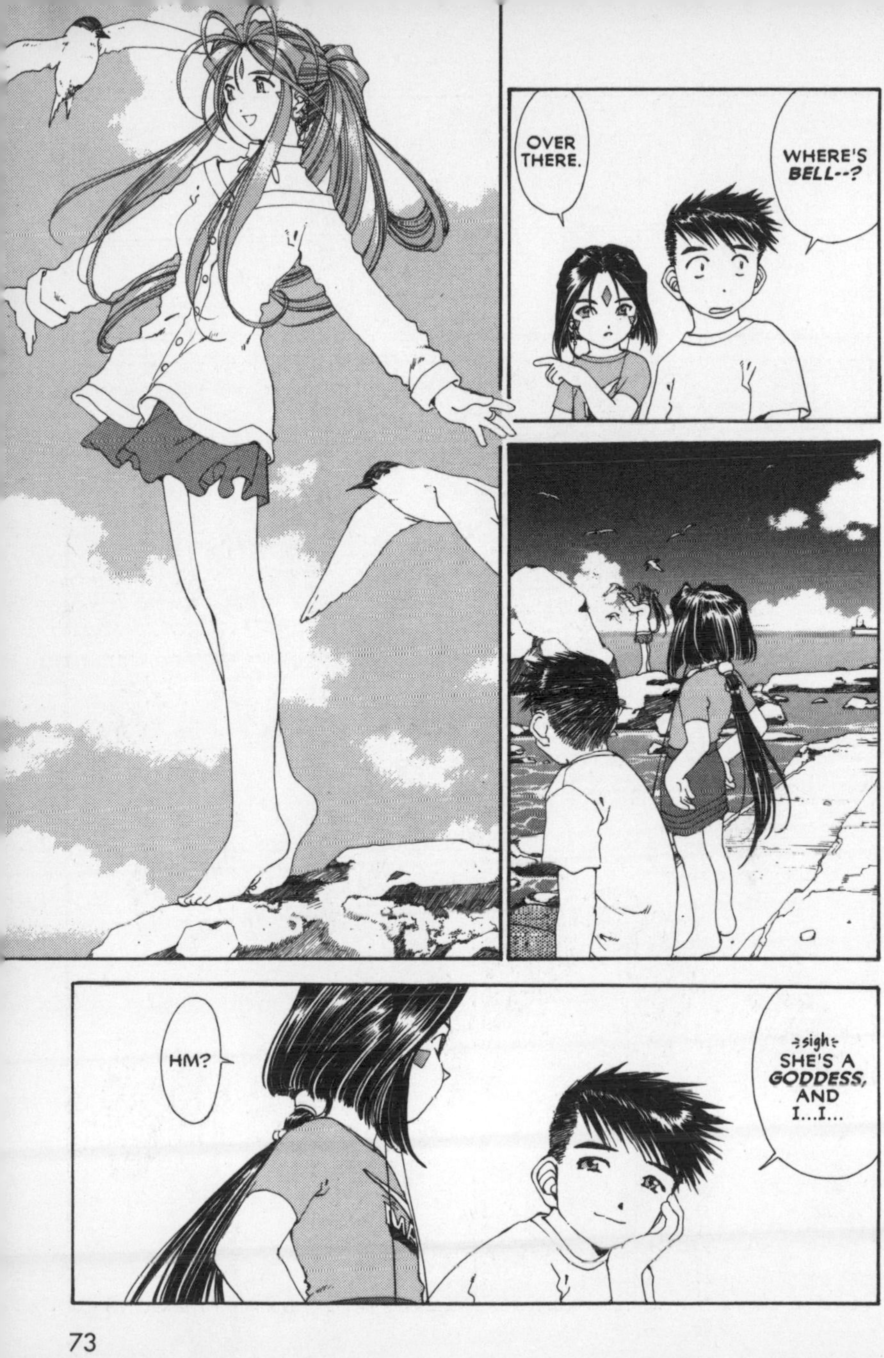
WHERE'S *BELL--?*
OVER THERE.
≈sigh≈ SHE'S A *GODDESS,* AND I...I...
HM?

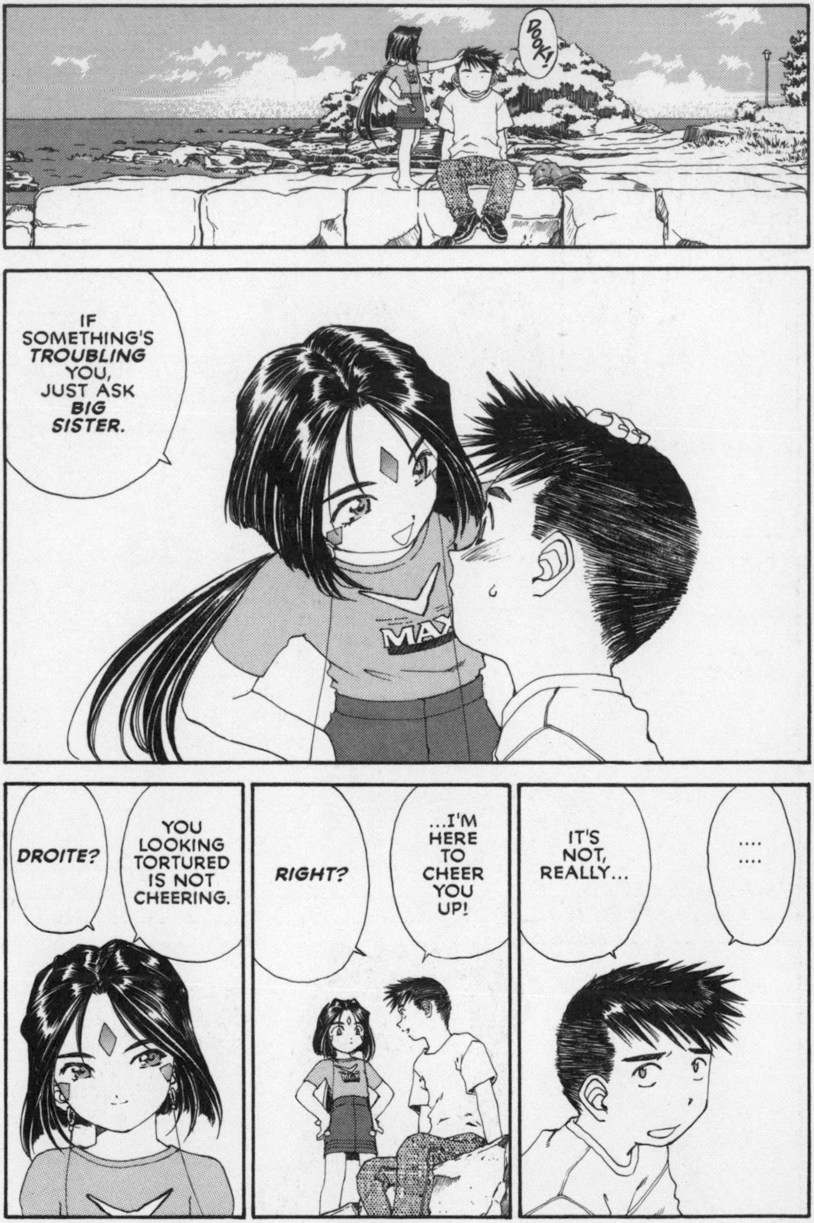
DOOK!
IF SOMETHING'S *TROUBLING* YOU, JUST ASK *BIG SISTER.*
....
....
IT'S NOT, REALLY...
...I'M HERE TO CHEER YOU UP!
RIGHT?
YOU LOOKING TORTURED IS NOT CHEERING.
DROITE?

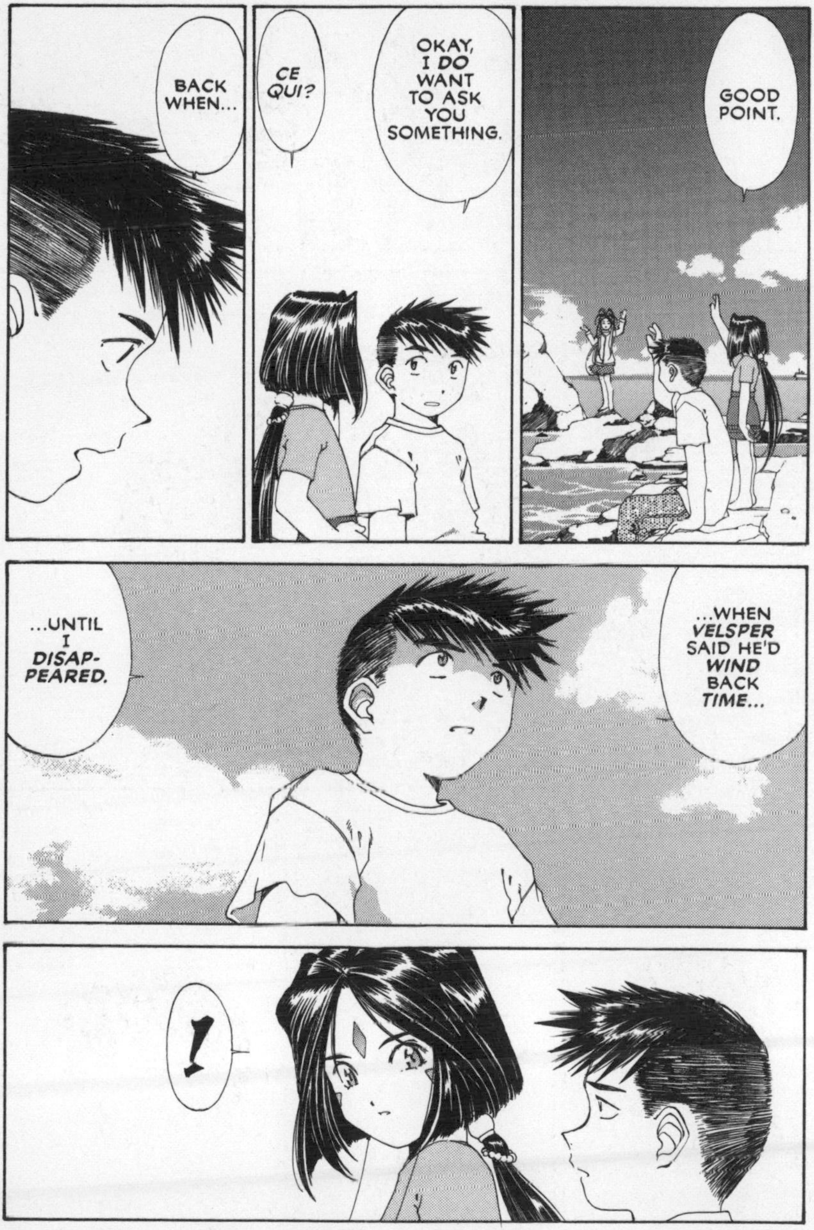
GOOD POINT.
OKAY, I DO WANT TO ASK YOU SOMETHING.
CE QUI?
BACK WHEN...
...WHEN VELSPER SAID HE'D WIND BACK TIME...
...UNTIL I DISAPPEARED.
!

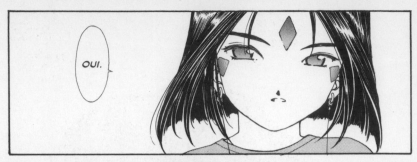

OUI.
BUT THE SPELL HIT *YOU* INSTEAD.
....
AND *YOU* DIDN'T DISAPPEAR.
WHICH MEANS YOU *CAN'T.*
C'EST EXACT.

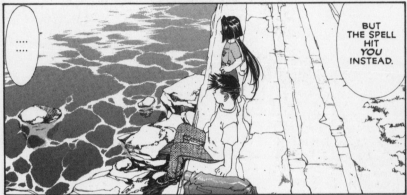

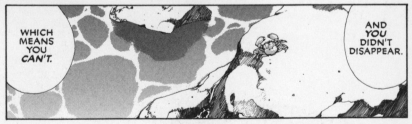

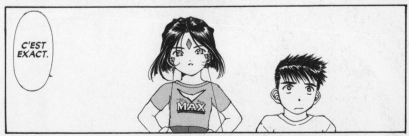

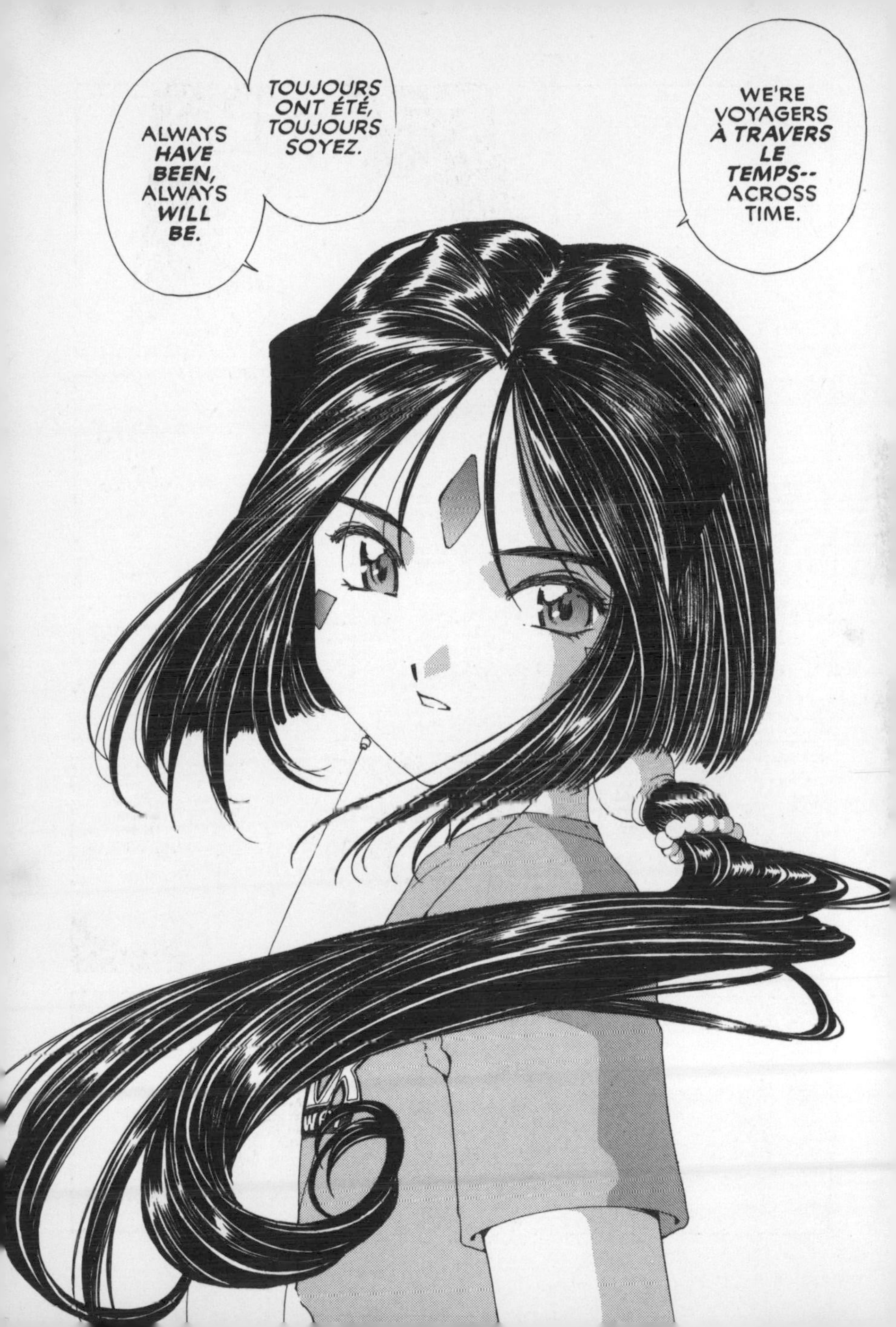
WE'RE VOYAGERS À *TRAVERS* *LE* *TEMPS*-- ACROSS TIME.
TOUJOURS ONT ÉTÉ, TOUJOURS SOYEZ.
ALWAYS *HAVE* BEEN, ALWAYS *WILL* BE.

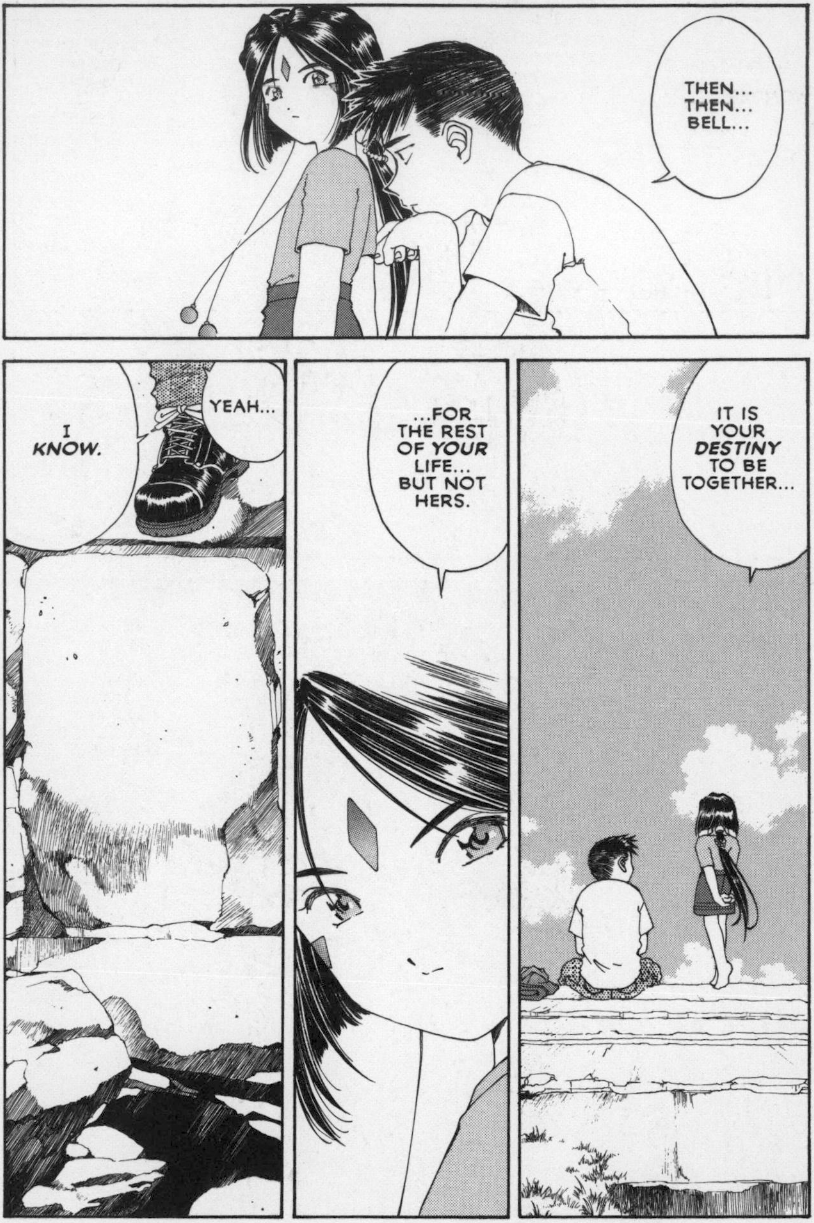
THEN... THEN... BELL...
IT IS YOUR *DESTINY* TO BE TOGETHER...
...FOR THE REST OF *YOUR* LIFE... BUT NOT HERS.
YEAH...
I *KNOW.*

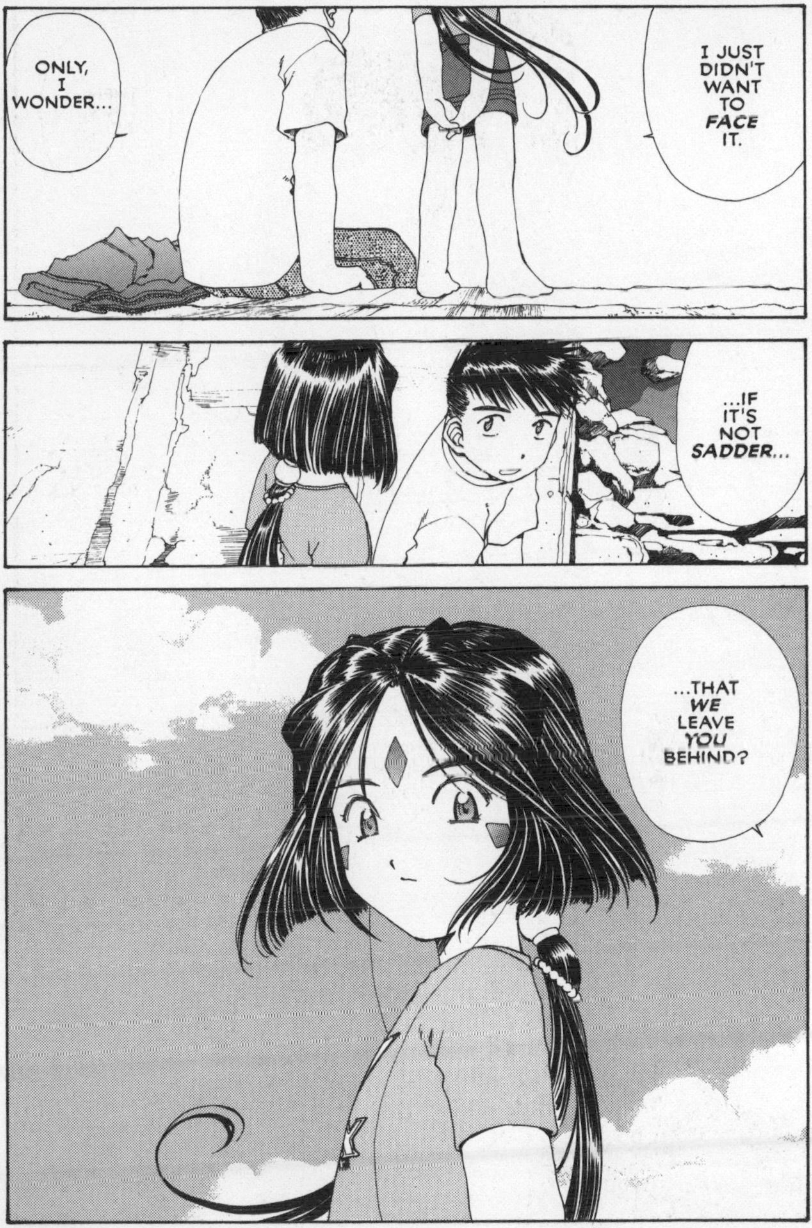
I JUST DIDN'T WANT TO *FACE* IT.
ONLY, I WONDER...
...IF IT'S NOT *SADDER*...
...THAT *WE* LEAVE *YOU* BEHIND?

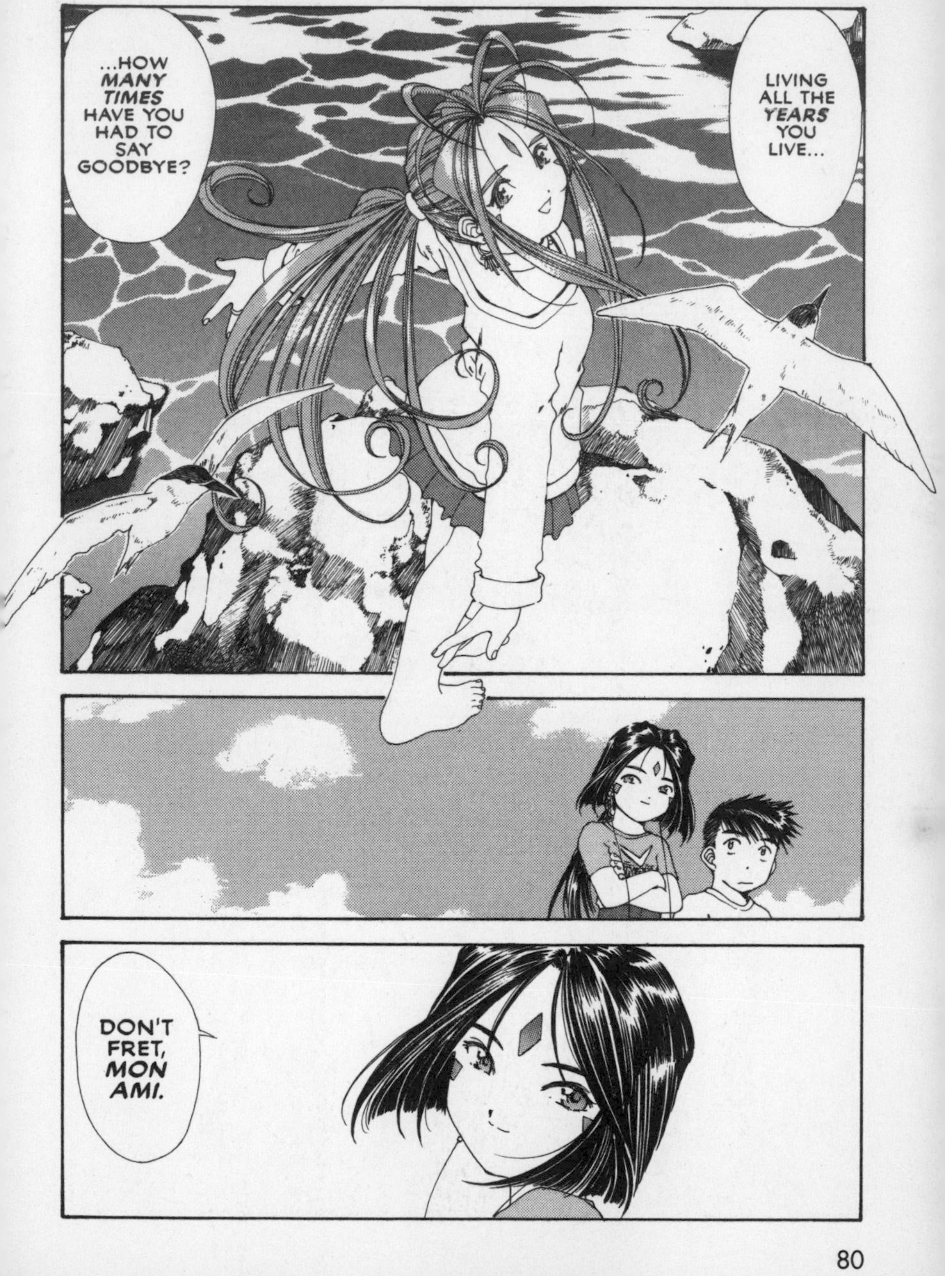
LIVING ALL THE YEARS YOU LIVE...
...HOW MANY TIMES HAVE YOU HAD TO SAY GOODBYE?
DON'T FRET, MON AMI.

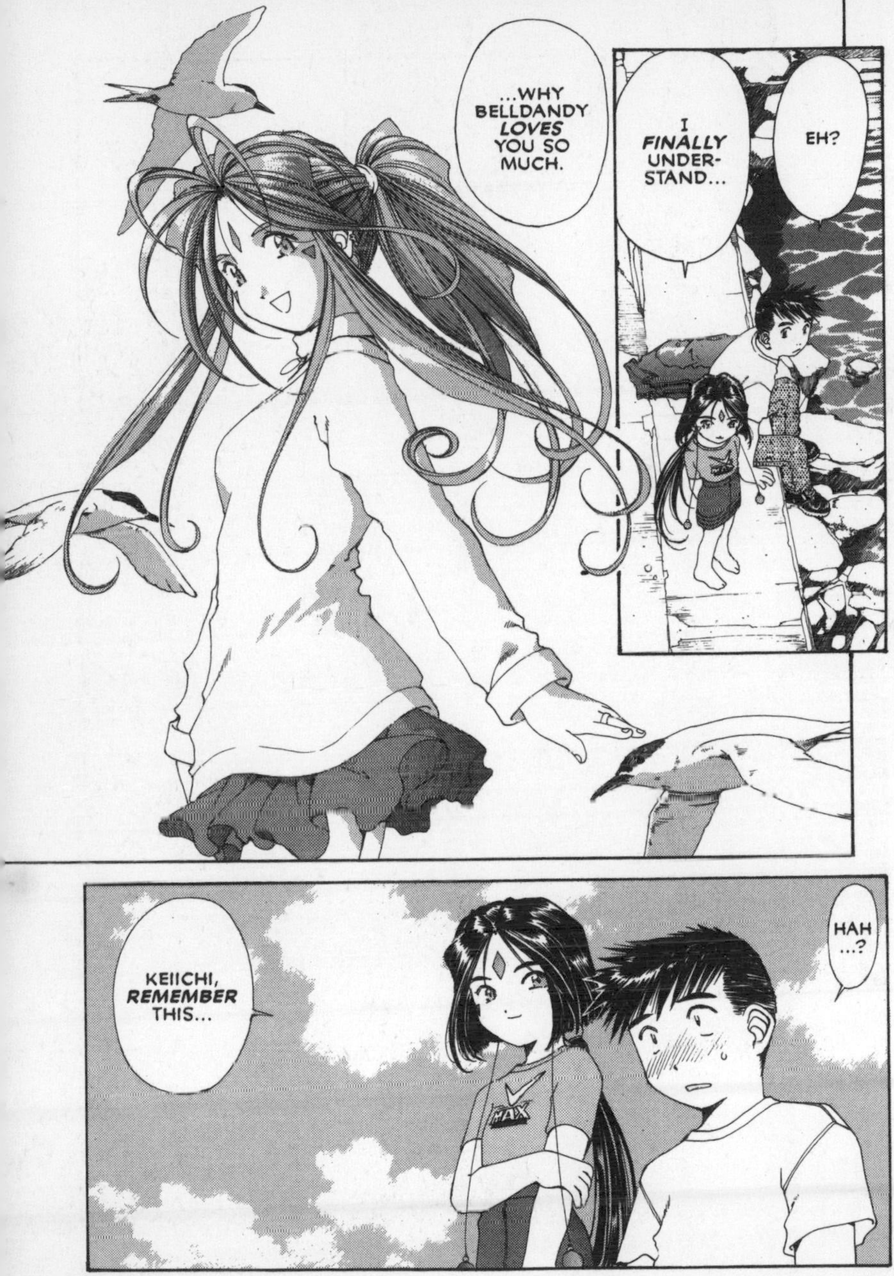
EH?
I *FINALLY* UNDER-STAND...
...WHY BELLDANDY *LOVES* YOU SO MUCH.
HAH ...?
KEIICHI, *REMEMBER* THIS...

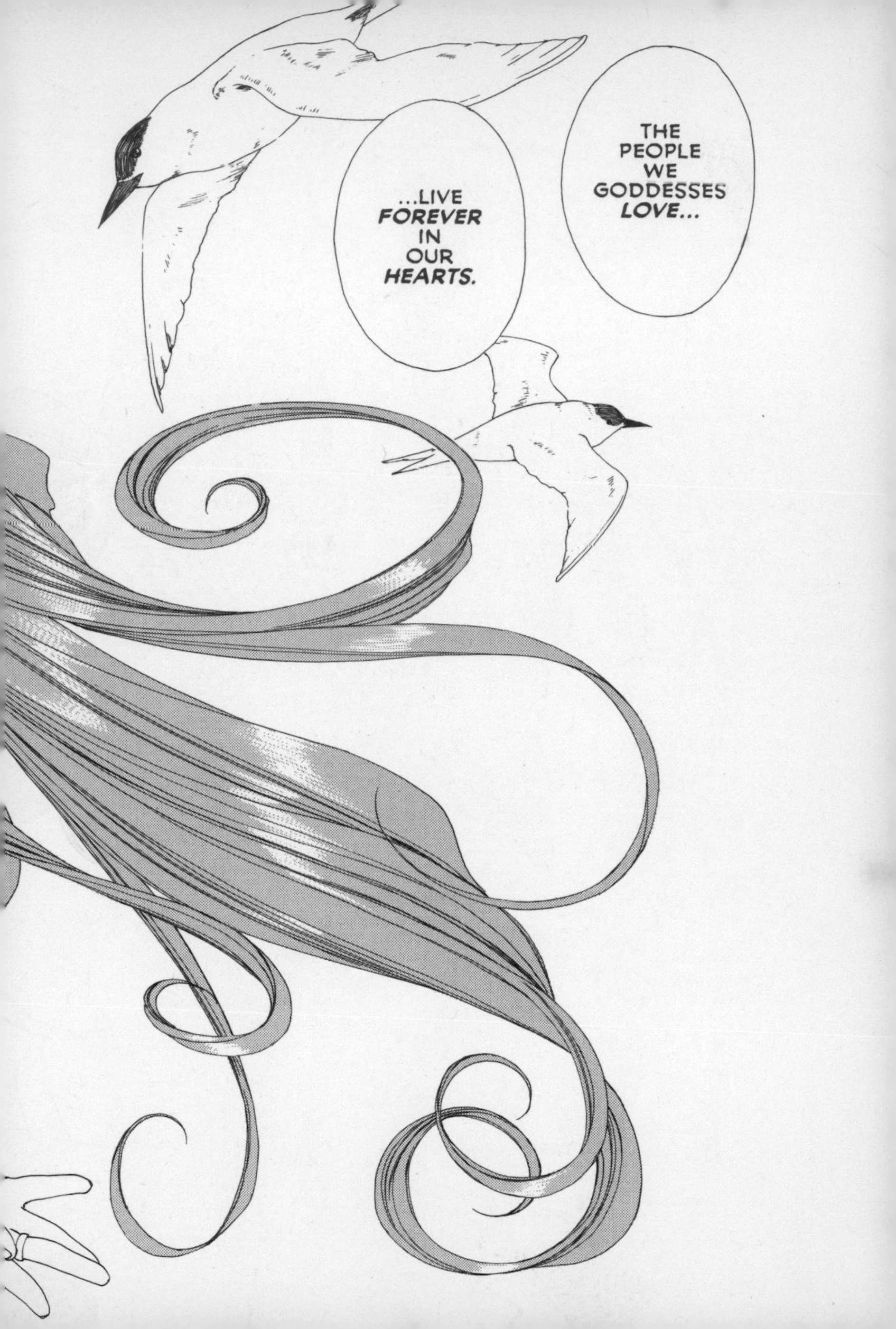
THE PEOPLE WE GODDESSES *LOVE...*
...LIVE ***FOREVER*** IN OUR ***HEARTS.***

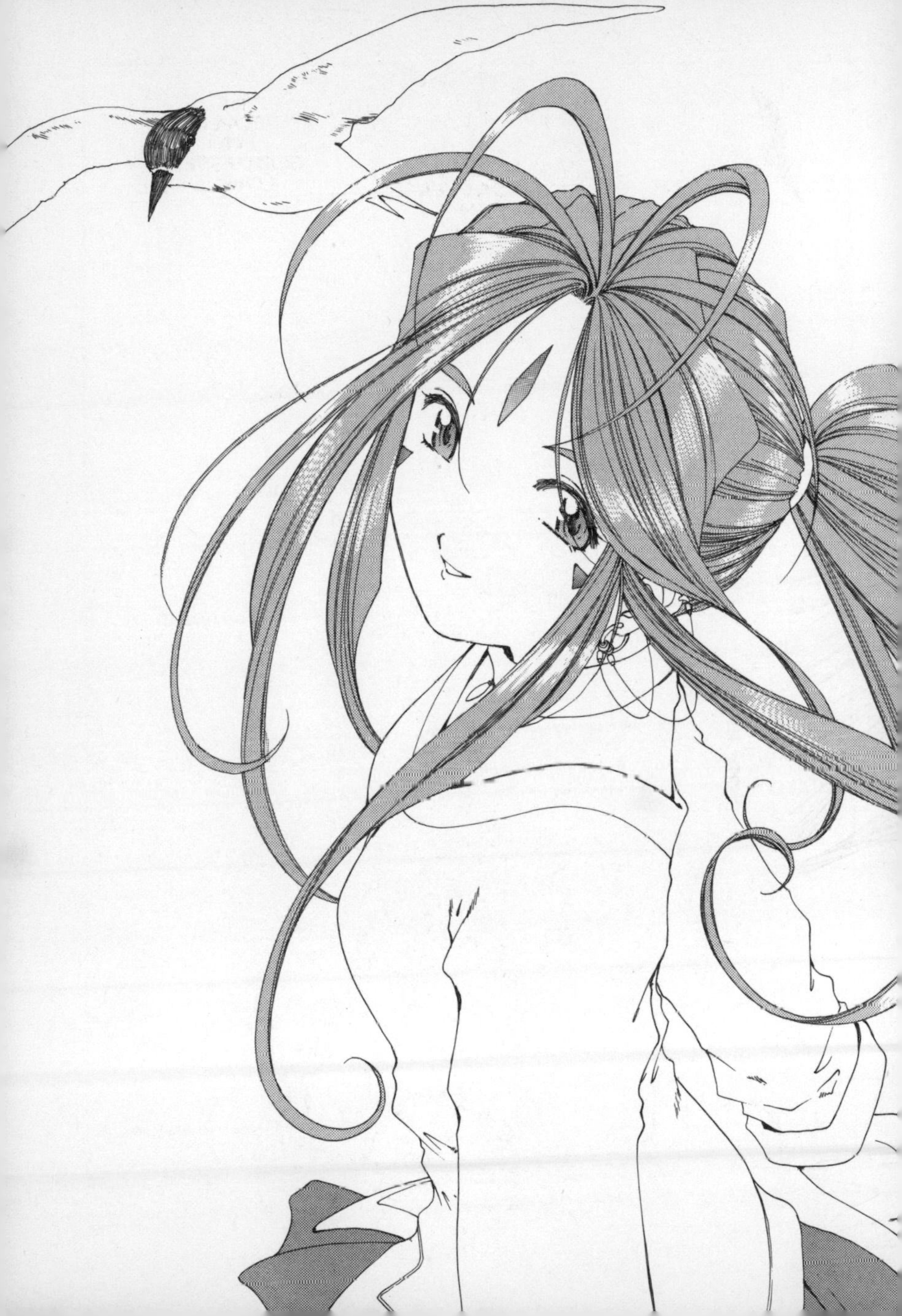

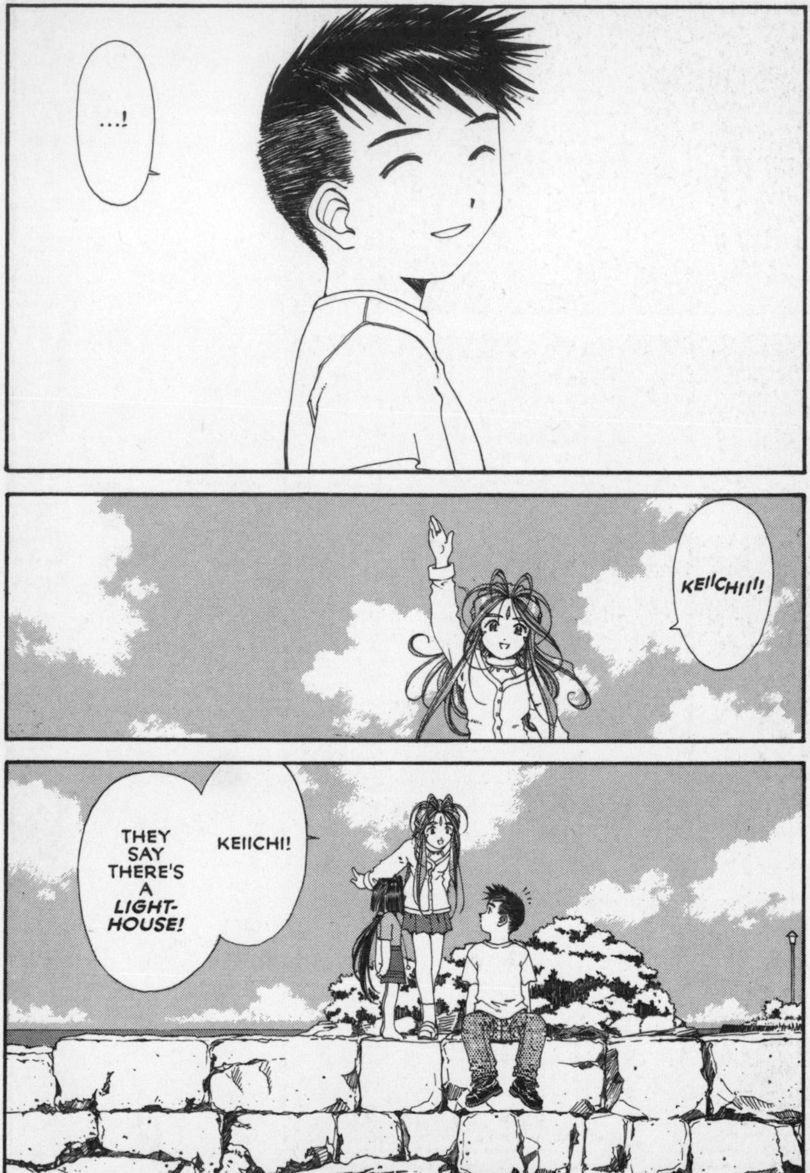
...!
KEIICHI!!
KEIICHI!
THEY SAY THERE'S A LIGHT-HOUSE!

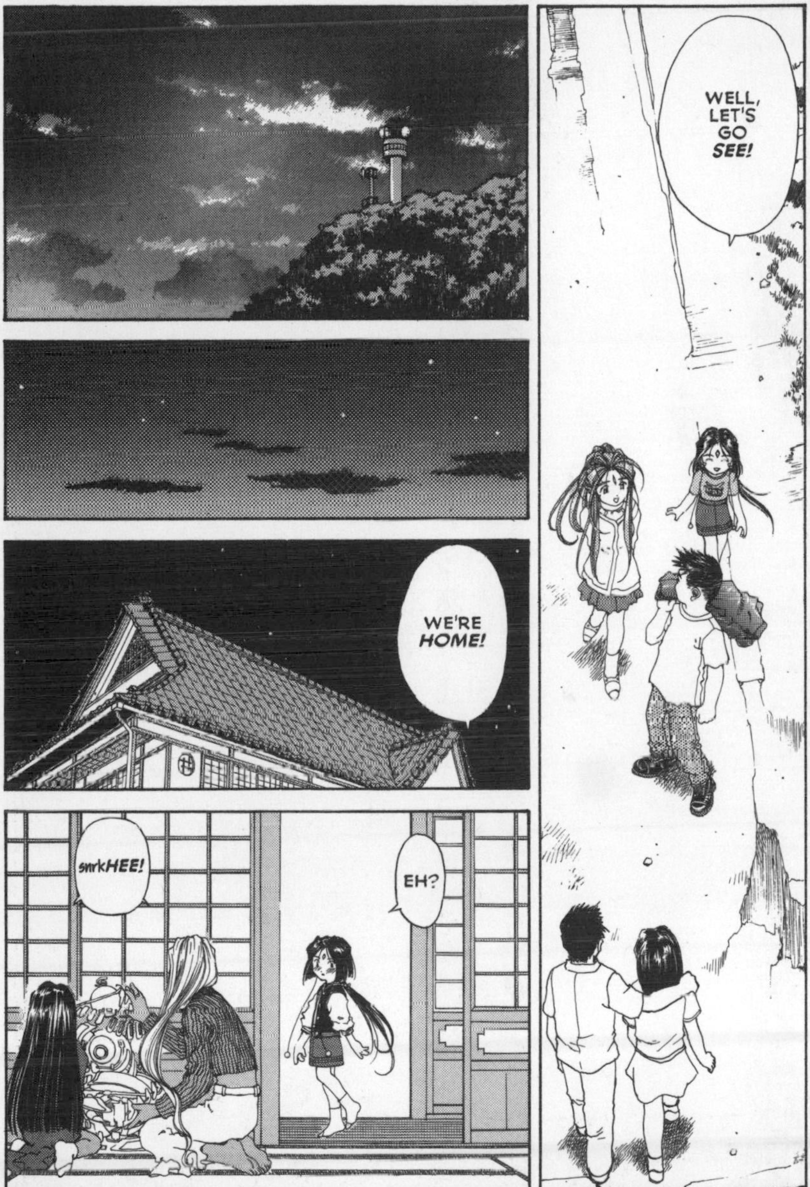
WELL, LET'S GO SEE!
WE'RE HOME!
EH?
snrkHEE!

END CHAPTER 132

OH MY GODDESS!
BELLDANDY

CHAPTER 133

The Cat That Stretched

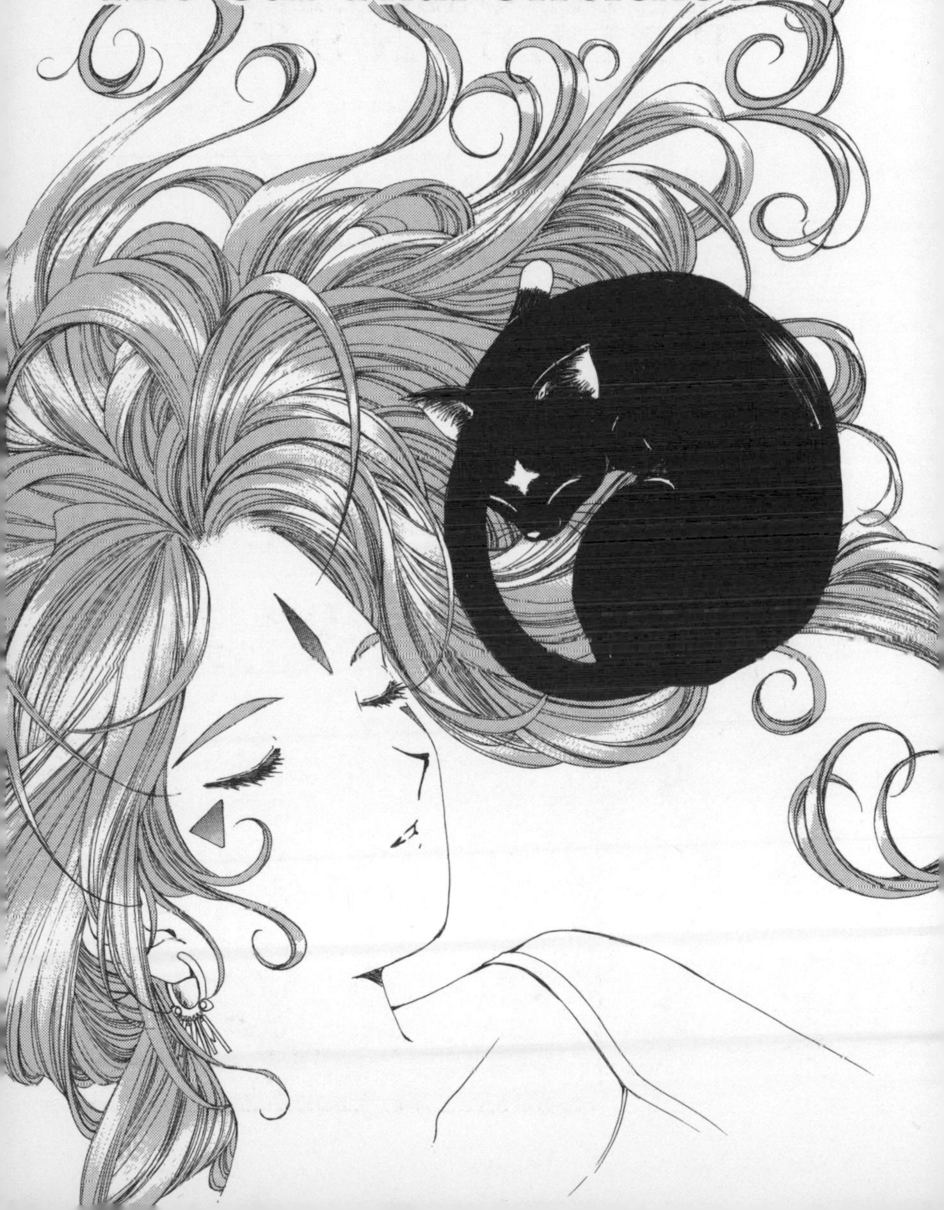

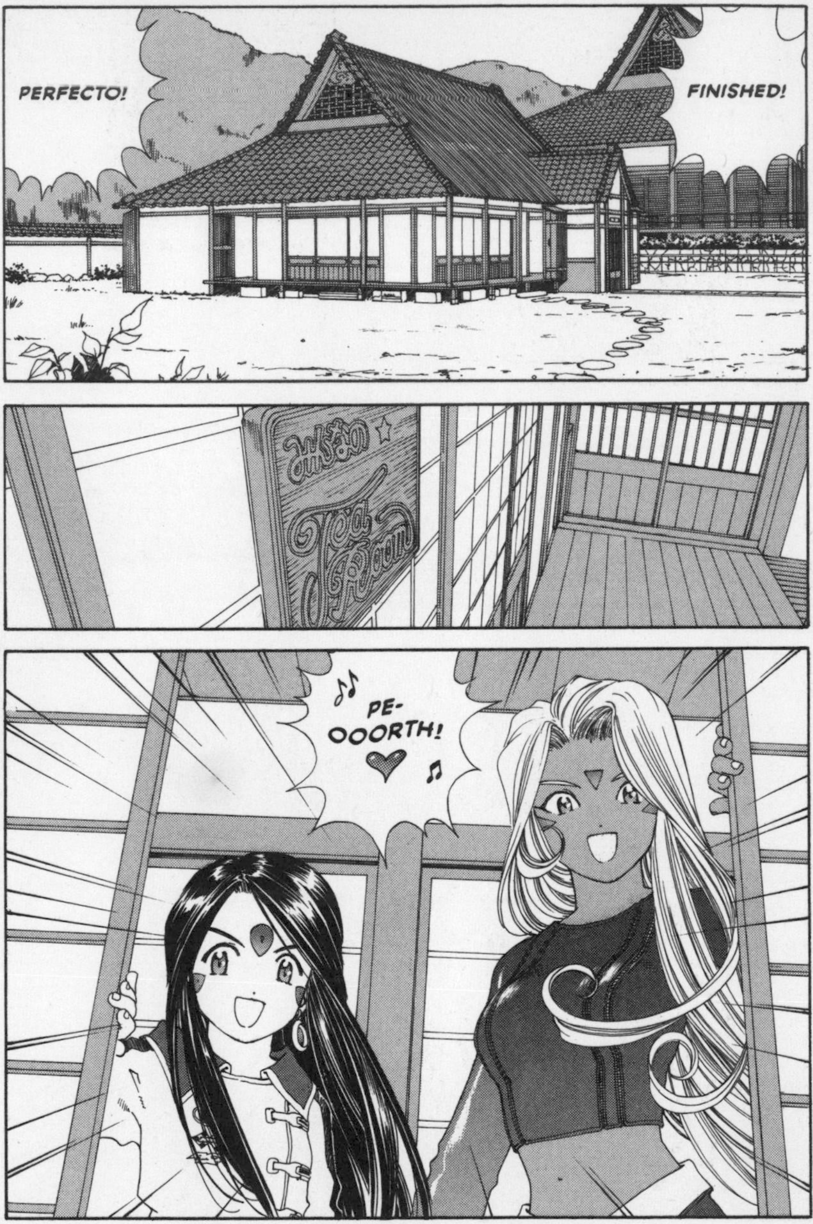
FINISHED!
PERFECTO!
Tea Room
PE- OOORTH!

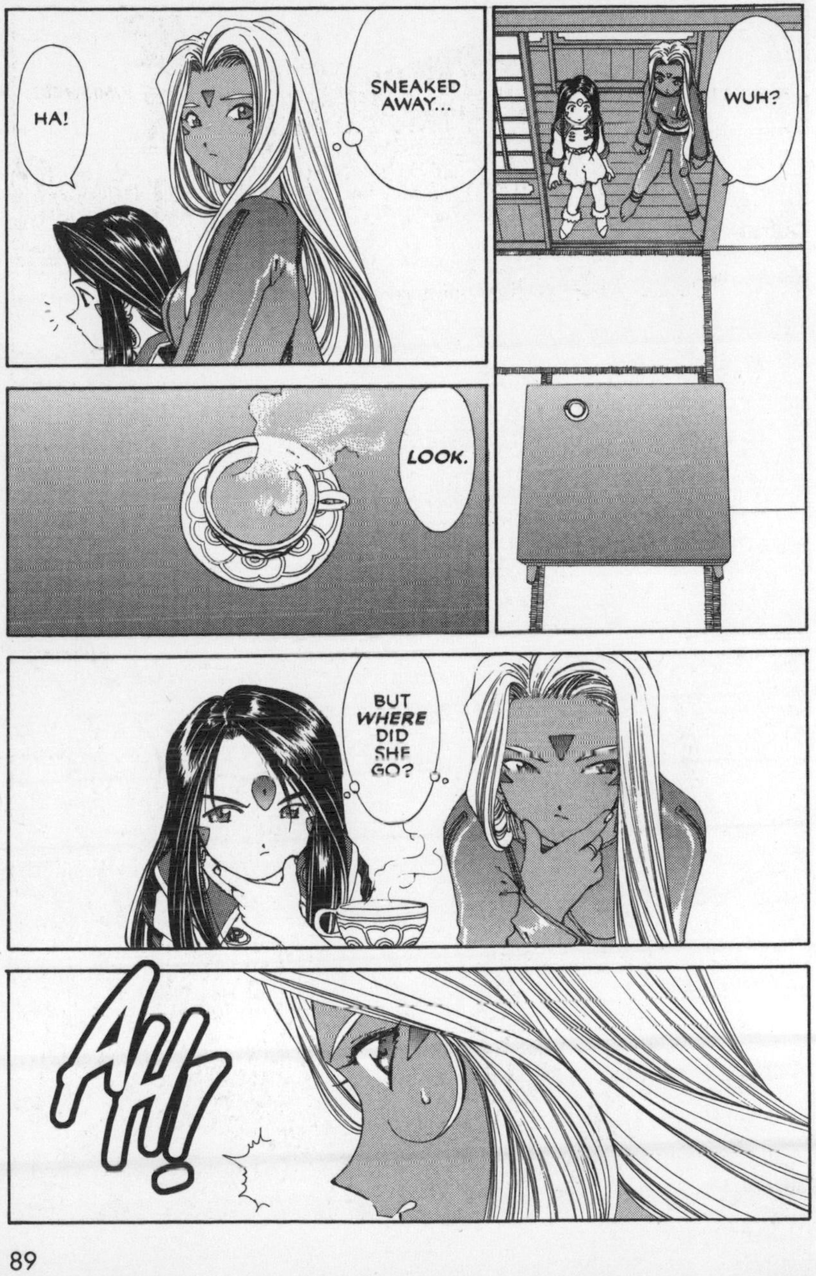
WUH?
SNEAKED AWAY...
HA!
LOOK.
BUT WHERE DID SHE GO?
AH!

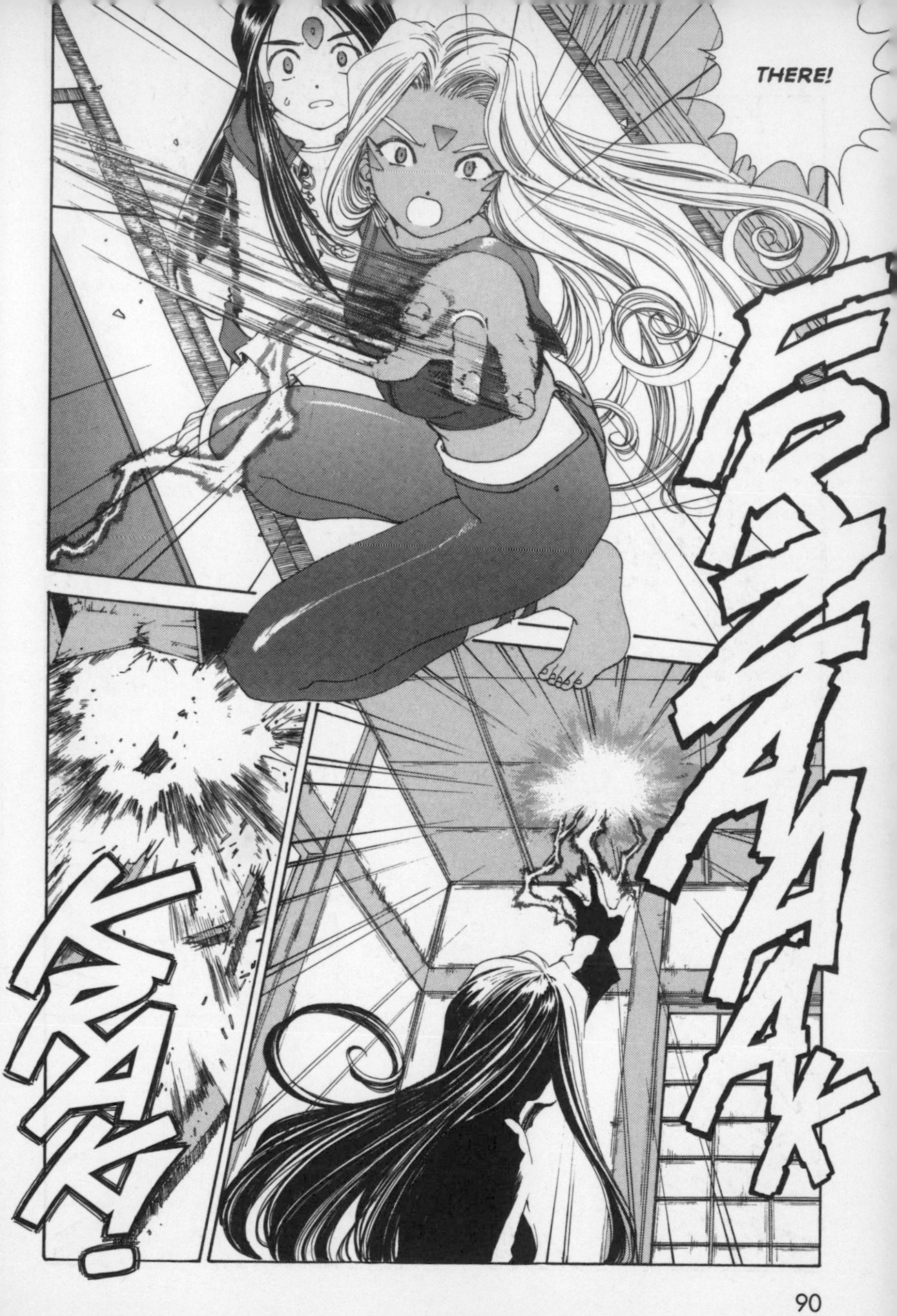
THERE!
KAKA!

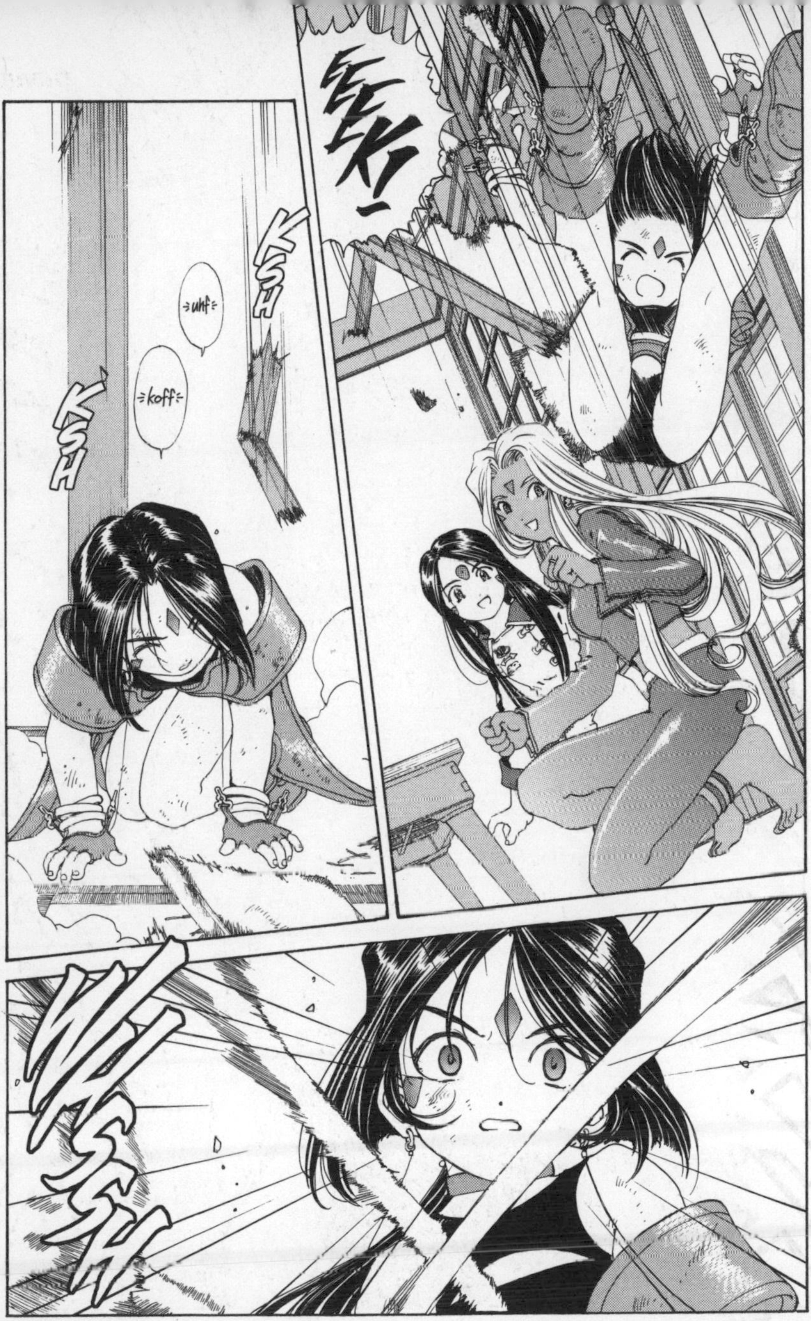
EEEK!
KSH
≈uhf≈
≈koff≈
KSH
WHSSH

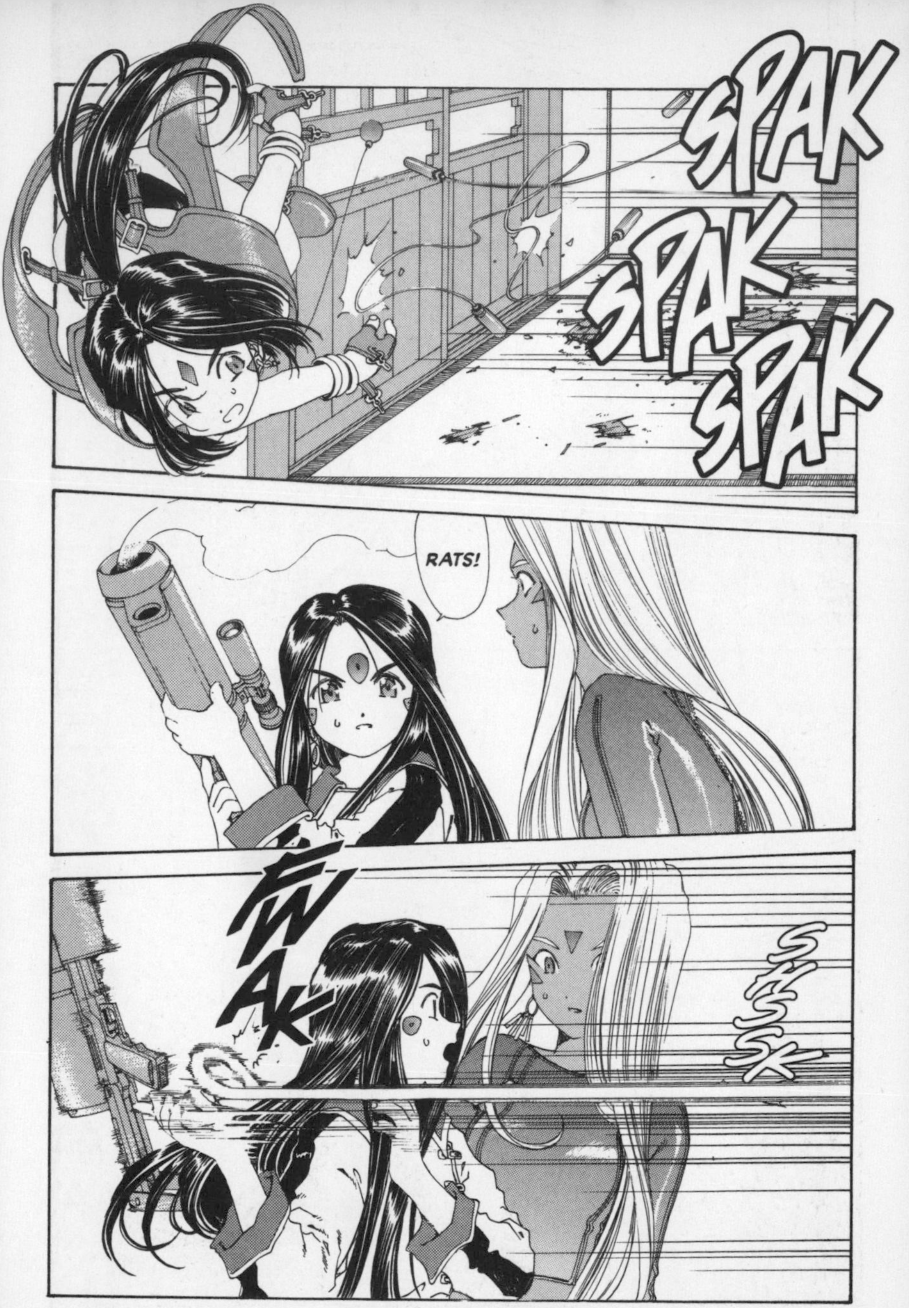
SPAK
SPAK
SPAK
SPAK
RATS!
SHSSK
FWAK

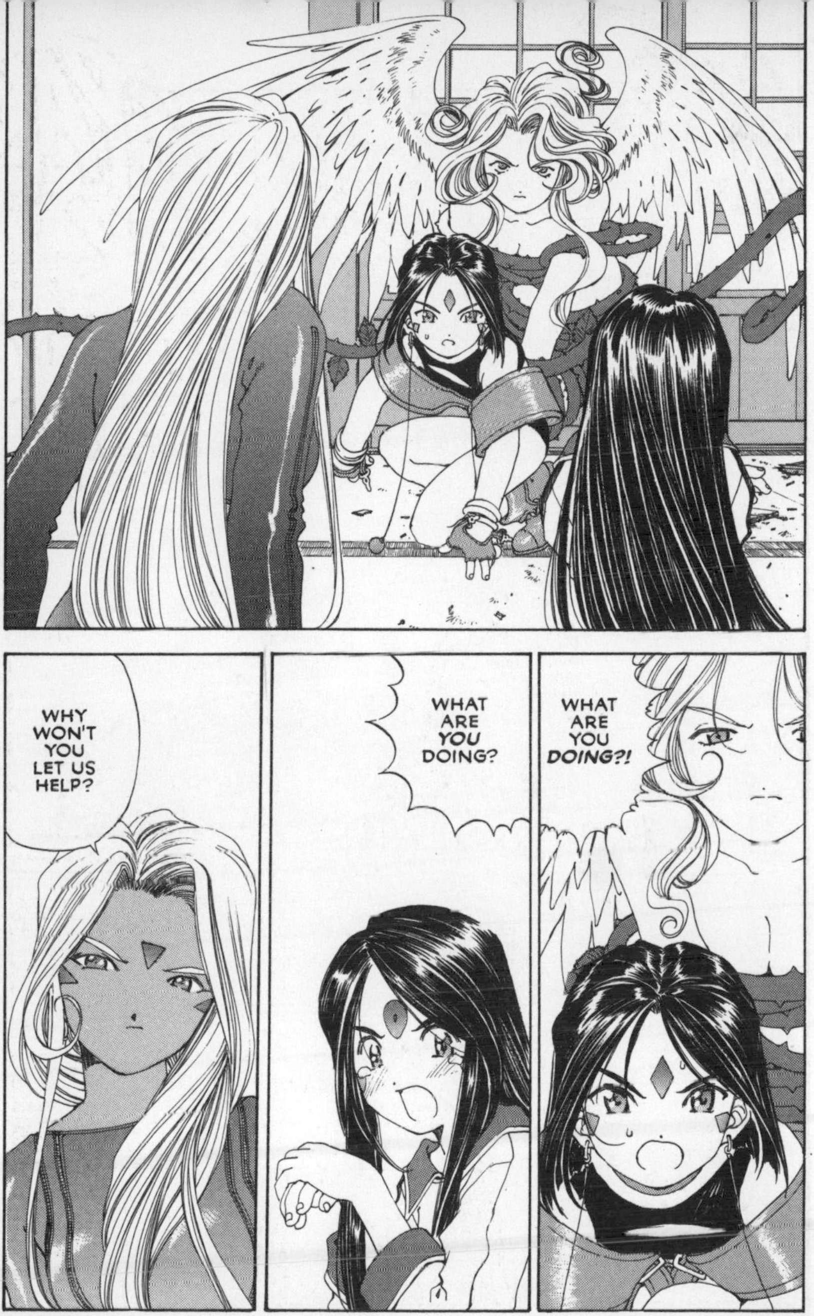
WHAT ARE YOU *DOING?!*
WHAT ARE *YOU* DOING?
WHY WON'T YOU LET US HELP?

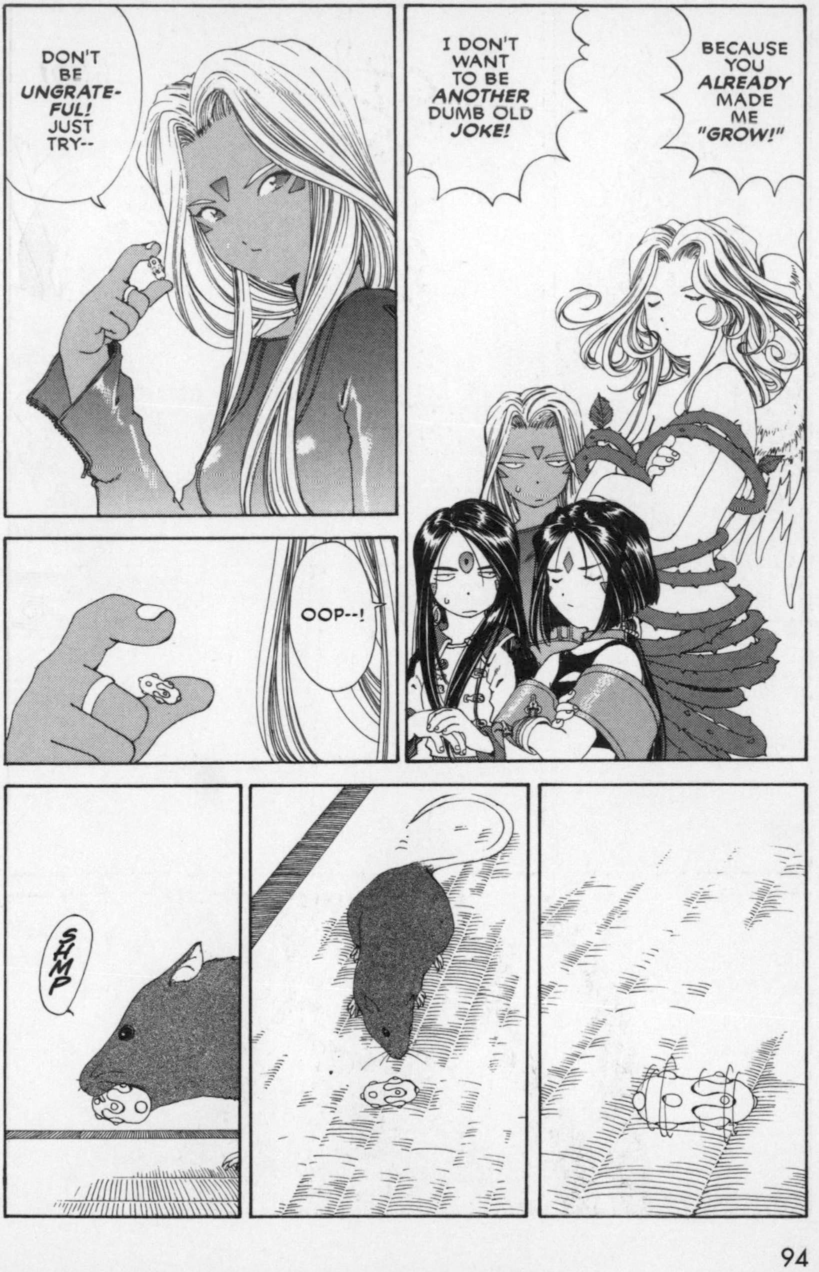
BECAUSE YOU *ALREADY* MADE ME *"GROW!"*
I DON'T WANT TO BE *ANOTHER* DUMB OLD *JOKE!*
DON'T BE *UNGRATE-FUL!* JUST TRY--
OOP--!
SHMP

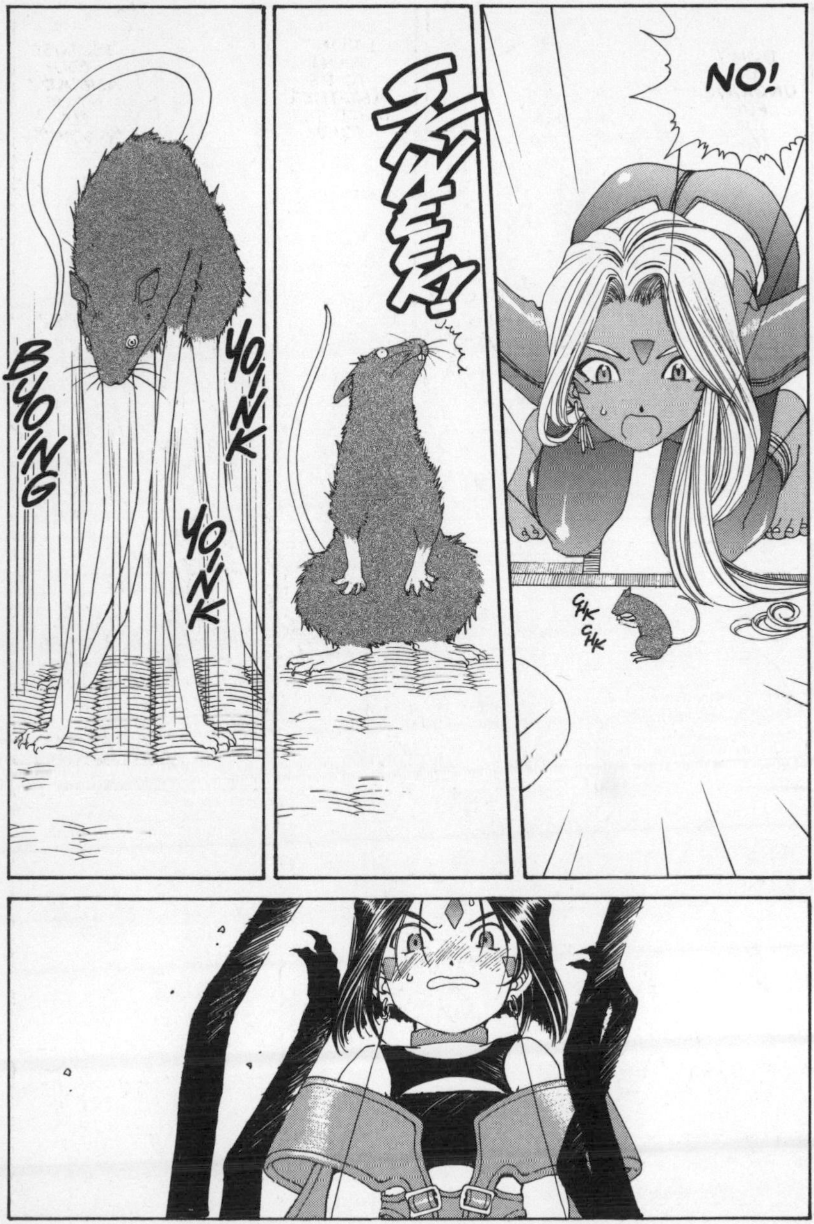
NO!
CHK
CHK
SKWEEK!
YOINK
YOINK
BYOING

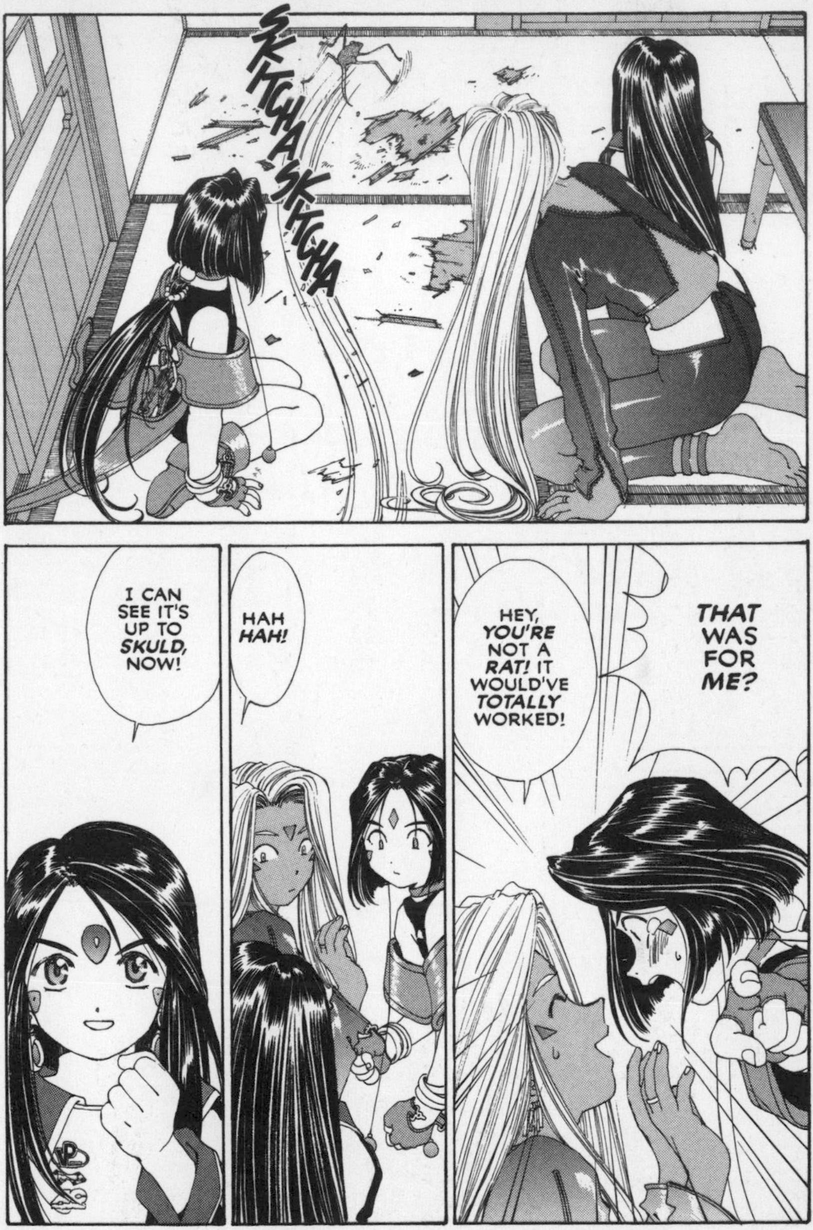
SKKTCHA SKKTCHA
THAT WAS FOR *ME?*
HEY, *YOU'RE* NOT A *RAT!* IT WOULD'VE *TOTALLY* WORKED!
HAH *HAH!*
I CAN SEE IT'S UP TO *SKULD,* NOW!

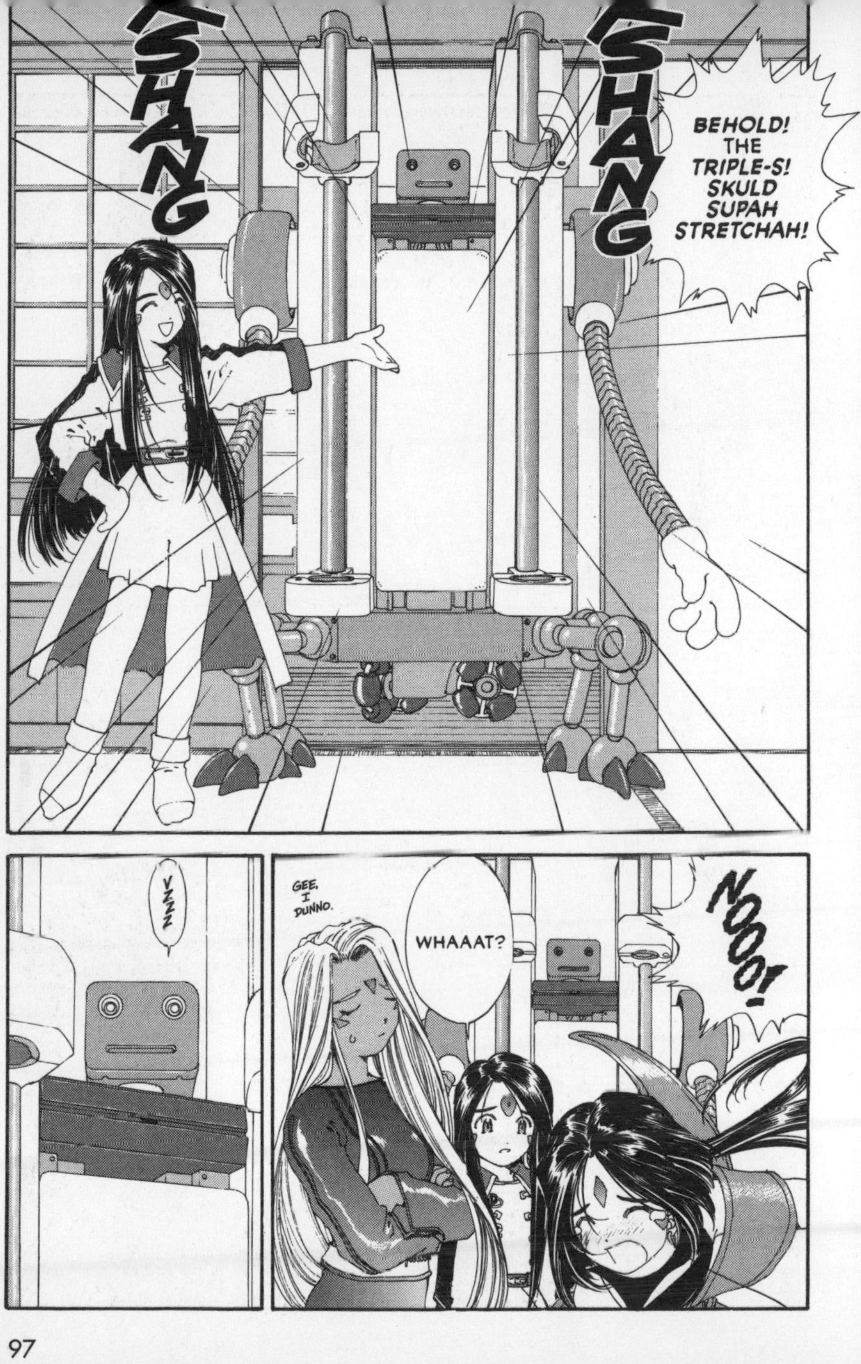
SHANG
SHANG
BEHOLD! THE TRIPLE-S! SKULD SUPAH STRETCHAH!
NOOO!
WHAAAT?
GEE, I DUNNO.
VZZZ

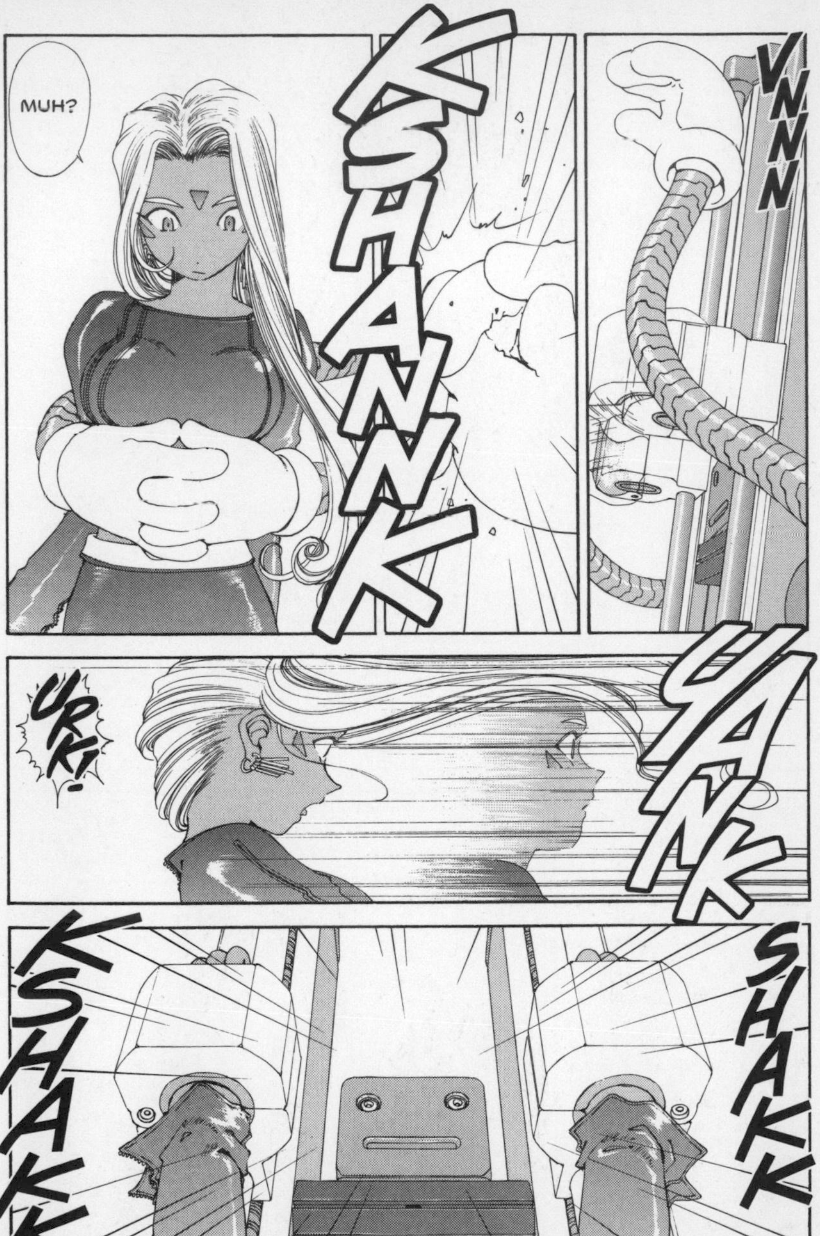
VNNN
KSHANNK
MUH?
YANK
URK!
SHAKK
KSHAKK

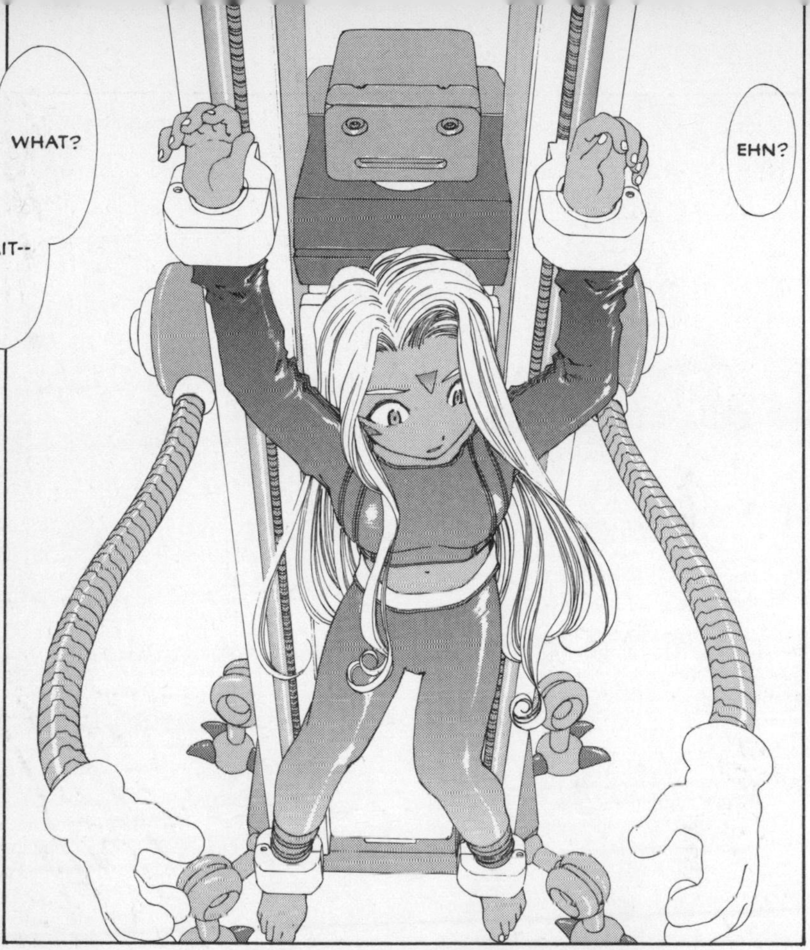
EHN?
WHAT?
WAIT--
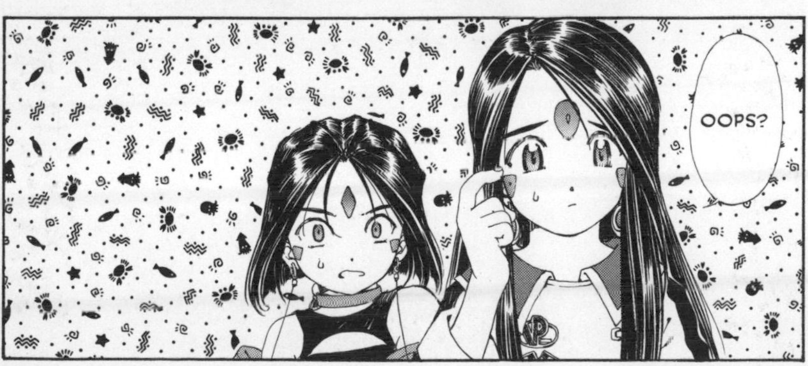
OOPS?

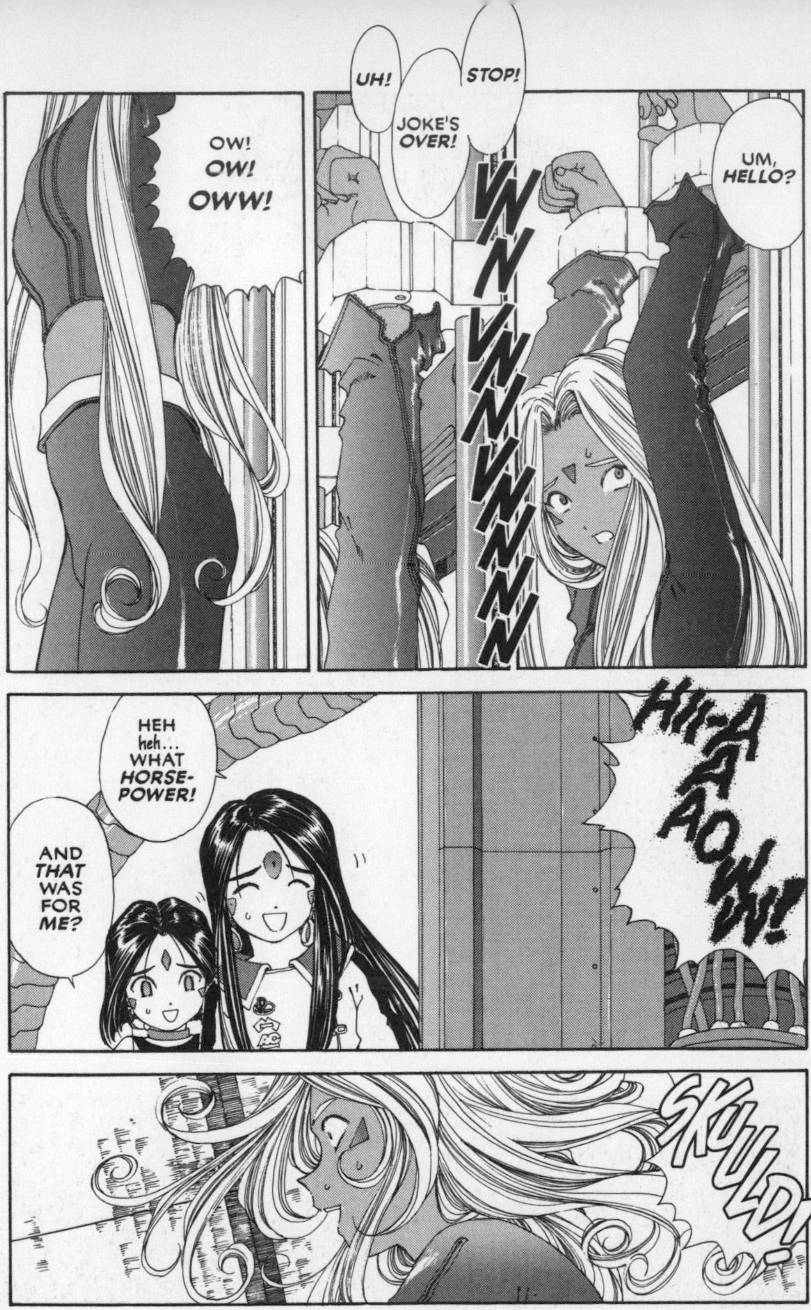
UM, HELLO?
STOP!
JOKE'S OVER!
UH!
VNNNNNNNNN
OW! OW! OWW!
HII-AAAOWW!
HEH heh... WHAT HORSE-POWER!
AND THAT WAS FOR ME?
SKULLD!

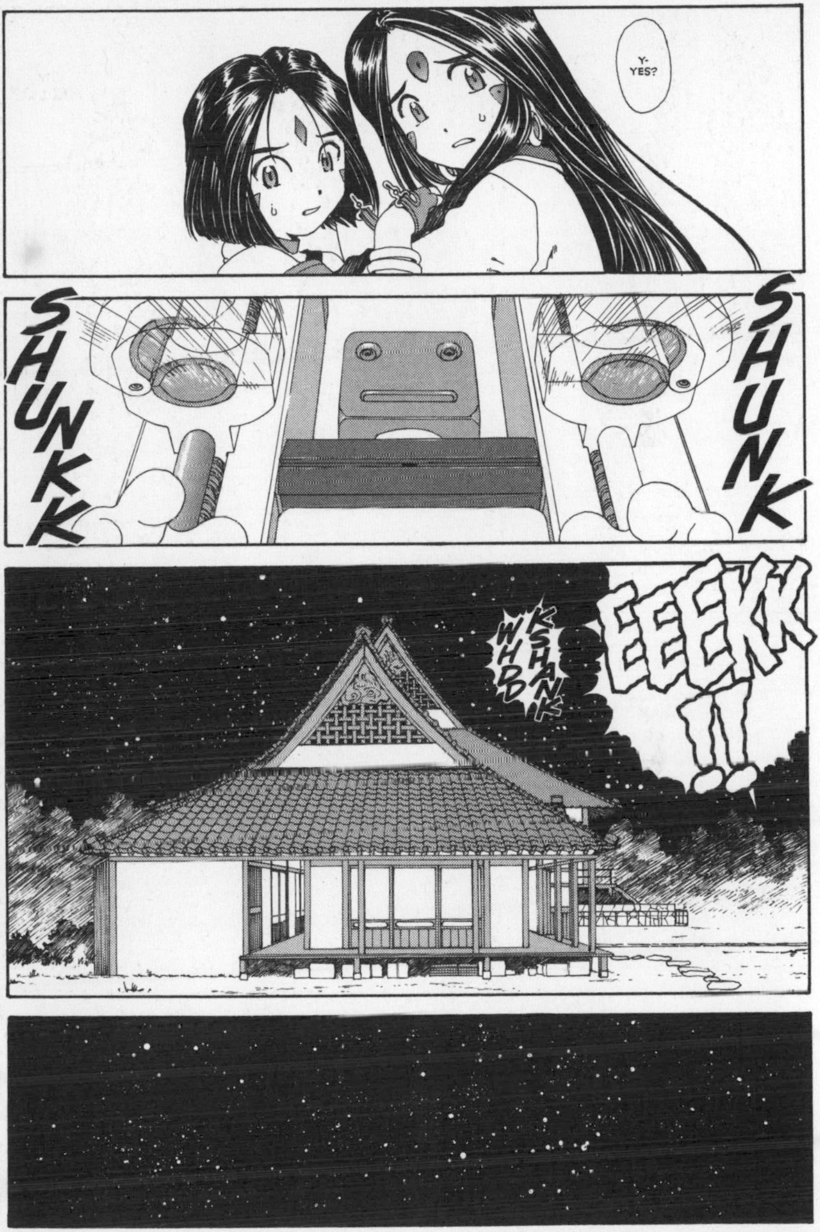
Y-YES?
SHUNK
SHUNKK
EEEKK!!
KSHANK
WHDD

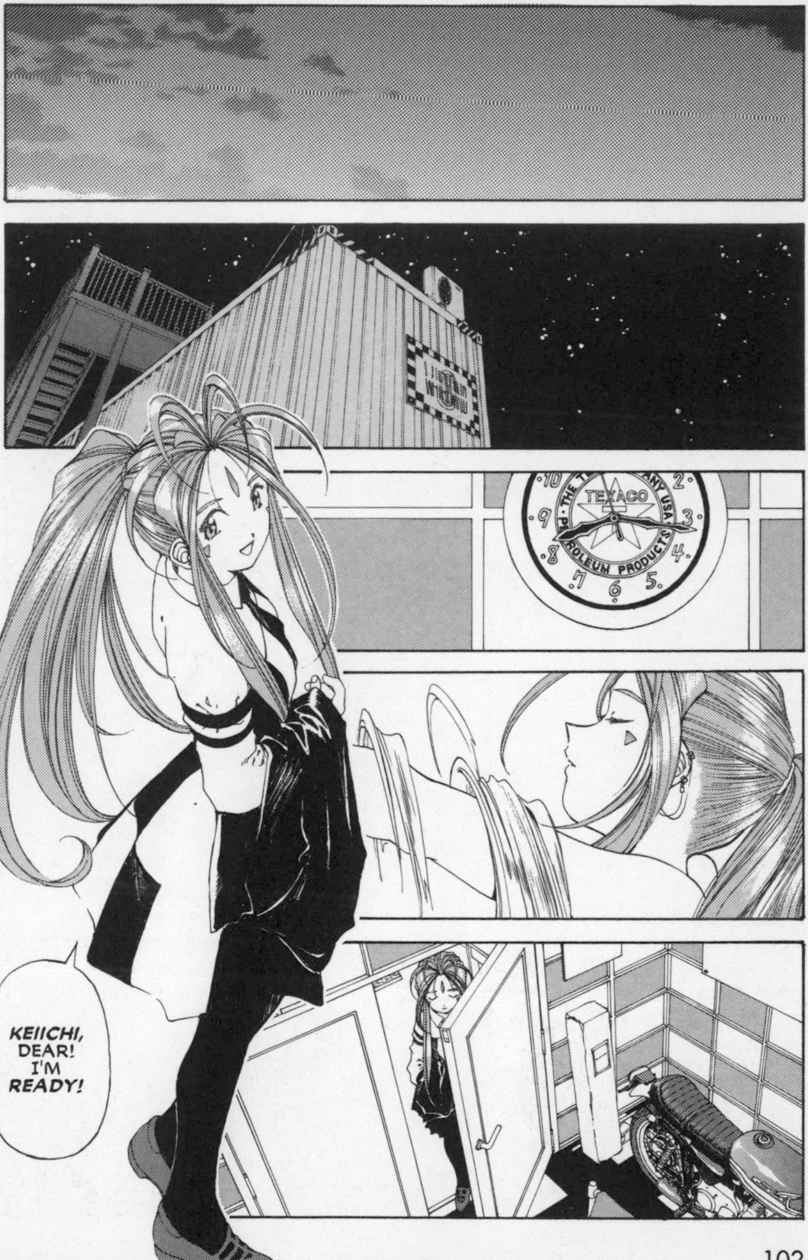
TEXACO
THE TEXAS COMPANY USA
PETROLEUM PRODUCTS
KEIICHI, DEAR! I'M *READY!*

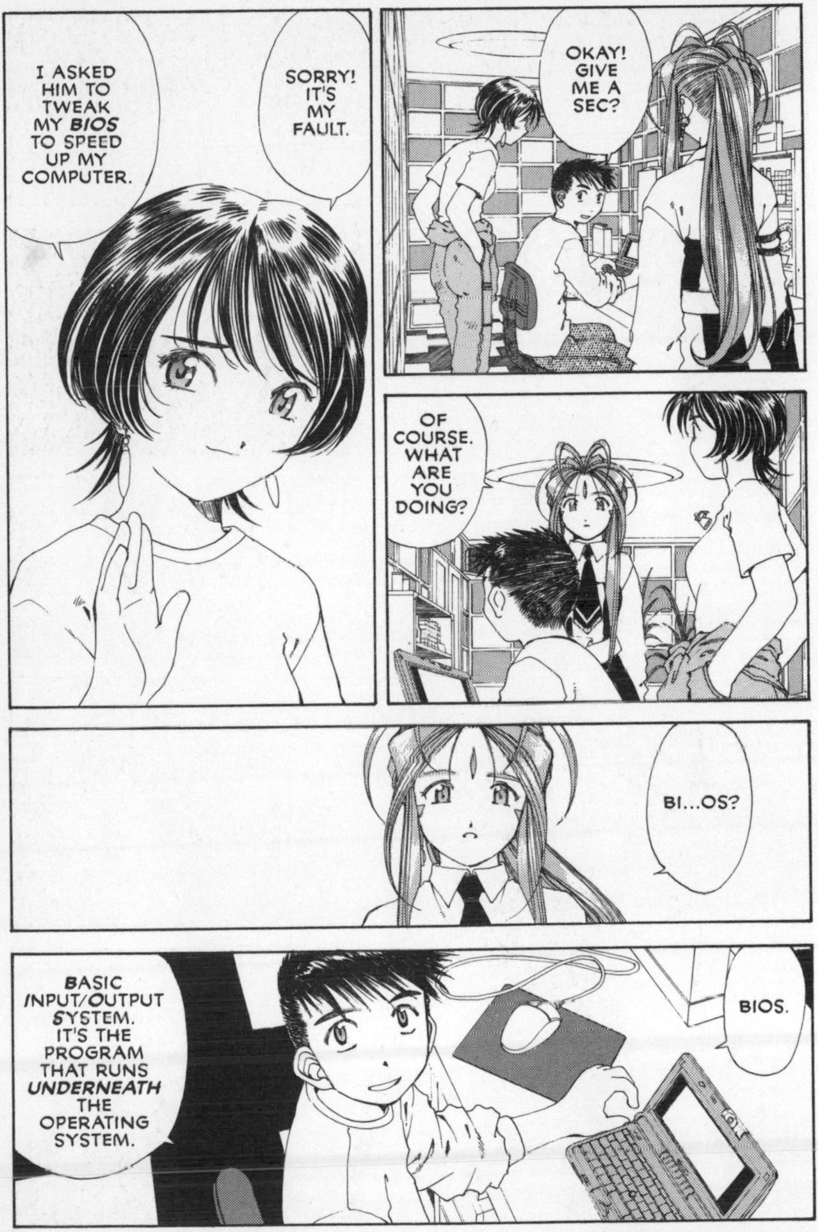

OKAY! GIVE ME A SEC?
OF COURSE. WHAT ARE YOU DOING?
SORRY! IT'S MY FAULT.
I ASKED HIM TO TWEAK MY *BIOS* TO SPEED UP MY COMPUTER.
BI...OS?
BIOS.
BASIC INPUT/OUTPUT SYSTEM. IT'S THE PROGRAM THAT RUNS *UNDERNEATH* THE OPERATING SYSTEM.

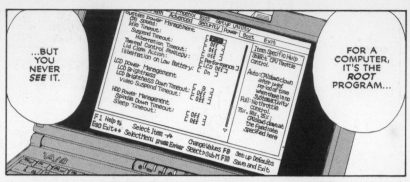

FOR A COMPUTER, IT'S THE ROOT PROGRAM...
Phoenix BIOS Setup Utility
Main Advanced Security Power Boot Exit
System Power Management
CPU Speed:
Idle Timeout:
Suspend Timeout:
Hibernation Timeout:
Thermal Control Strategy:
Lid Close Action:
Hibernation on Low Battery:
[Off]
[Off]
[Performance]
[LCD Off]
[On]
LCD Power Management
LCD Brightness
LCD Brightness Down Timeout:
Video Suspend Timeout:
[9]
[Off]
[Off]
HDD Power Management
Spindle Down Timeout:
Sleep Timeout:
[Off]
[Off]
Item Specific Help
Select CPU Throttle control.
Auto: CPU slows down after brief period of time when there is no System activity
Full: No throttle control.
75%, 50%, 25%: CPU slows down at the fixed rate Specified here
F1 Help
Esc Exit
Select Item
SelectMenu
Change Values F9
Setup Defaults
Select ▷ Sub-M F10
Save and Exit
...BUT YOU NEVER SEE IT.
ROOT...
THERE.
CHK
THAT'LL SPEED THINGS UP.
THANKS!

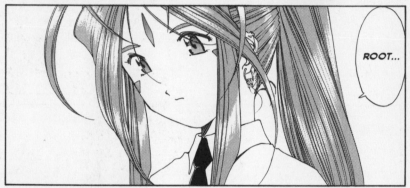

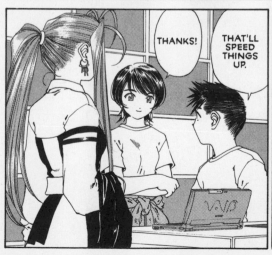

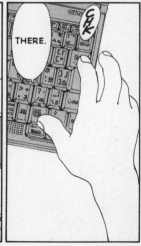

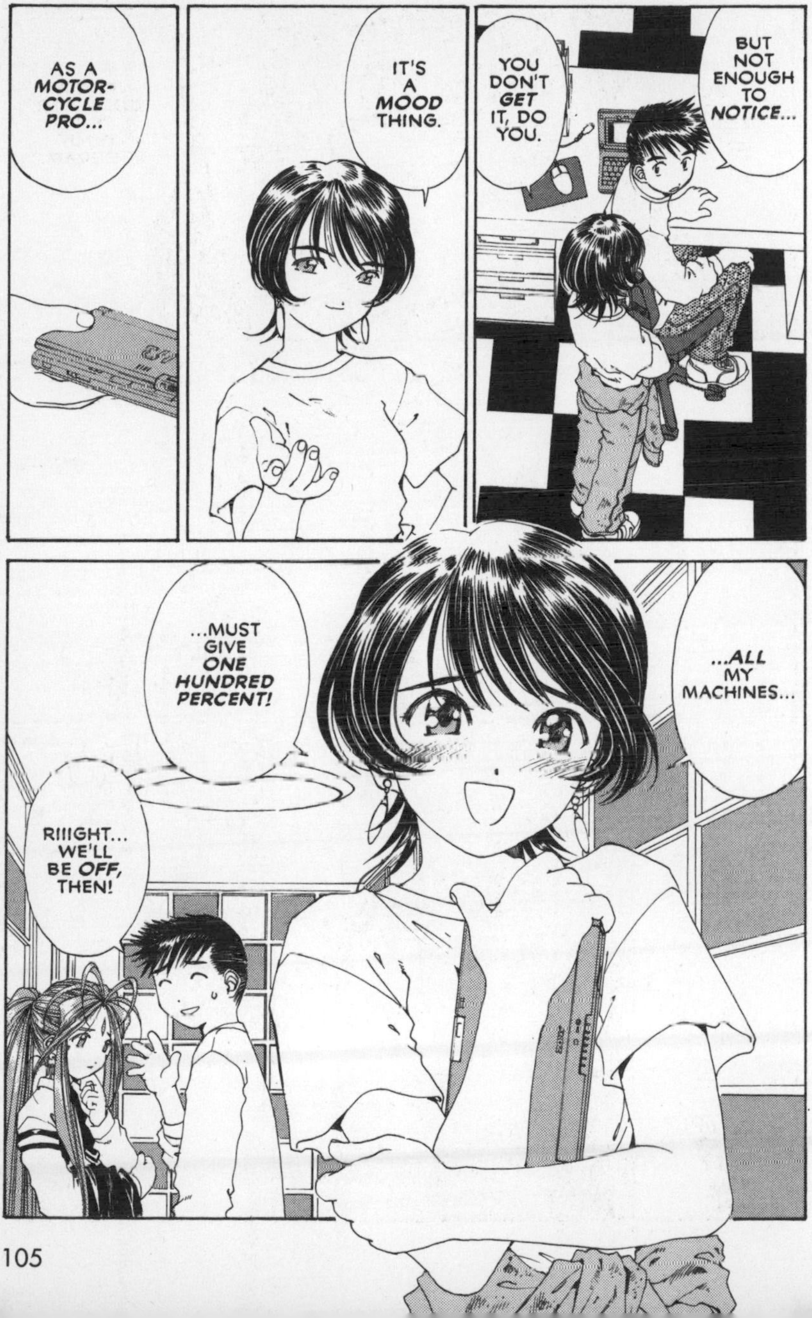
BUT NOT ENOUGH TO NOTICE...
YOU DON'T GET IT, DO YOU.
IT'S A MOOD THING.
AS A MOTOR-CYCLE PRO...
...ALL MY MACHINES...
...MUST GIVE ONE HUNDRED PERCENT!
RIIIGHT... WE'LL BE OFF, THEN!

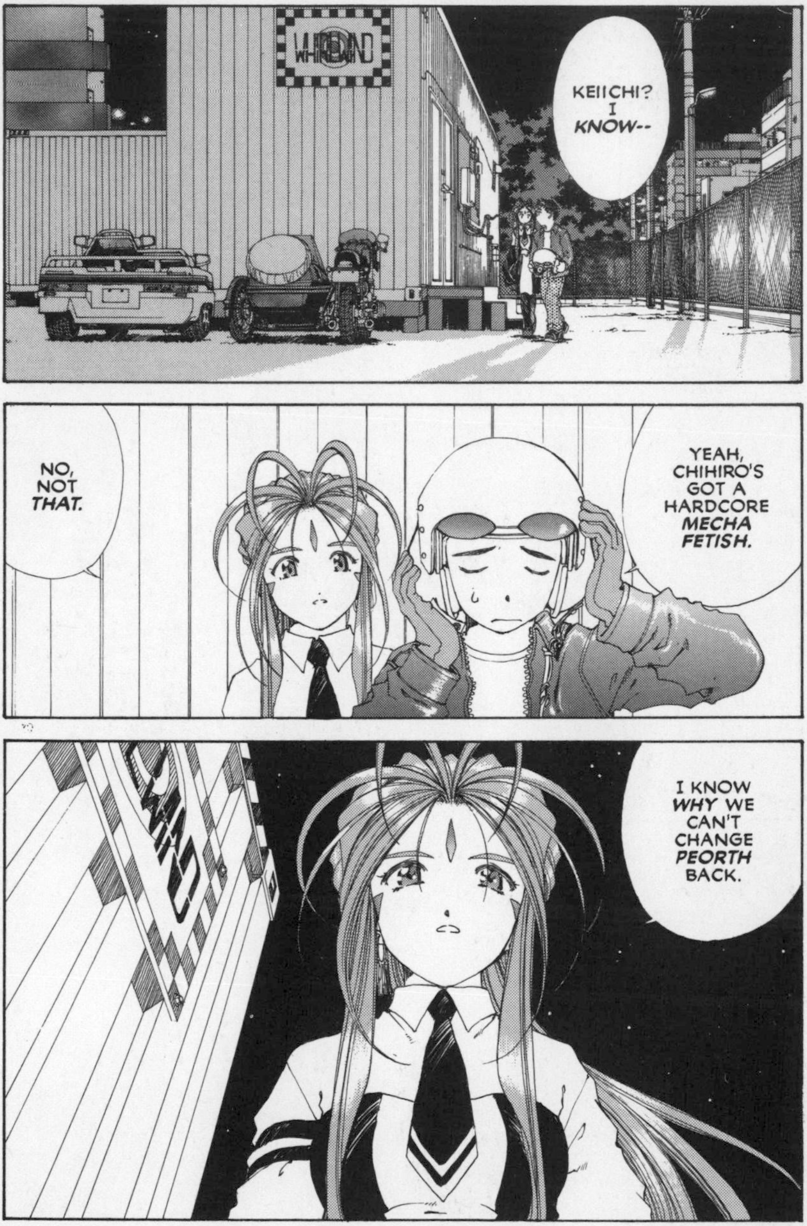
WHIRLWIND
KEIICHI? I KNOW--
YEAH, CHIHIRO'S GOT A HARDCORE MECHA FETISH.
NO, NOT THAT.
I KNOW WHY WE CAN'T CHANGE PEORTH BACK.

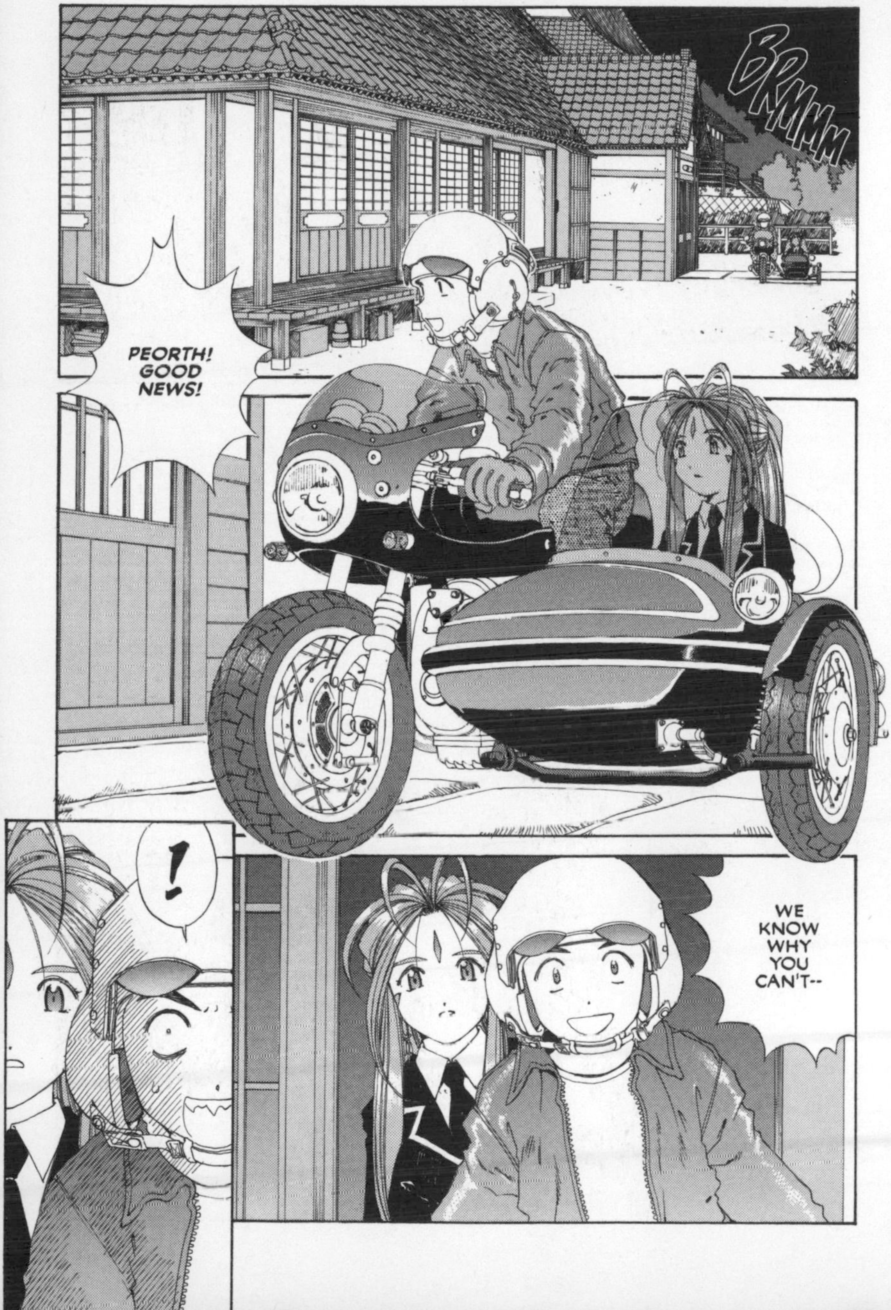
BRMMMM
PEORTH! GOOD NEWS!
WE KNOW WHY YOU CAN'T--
!

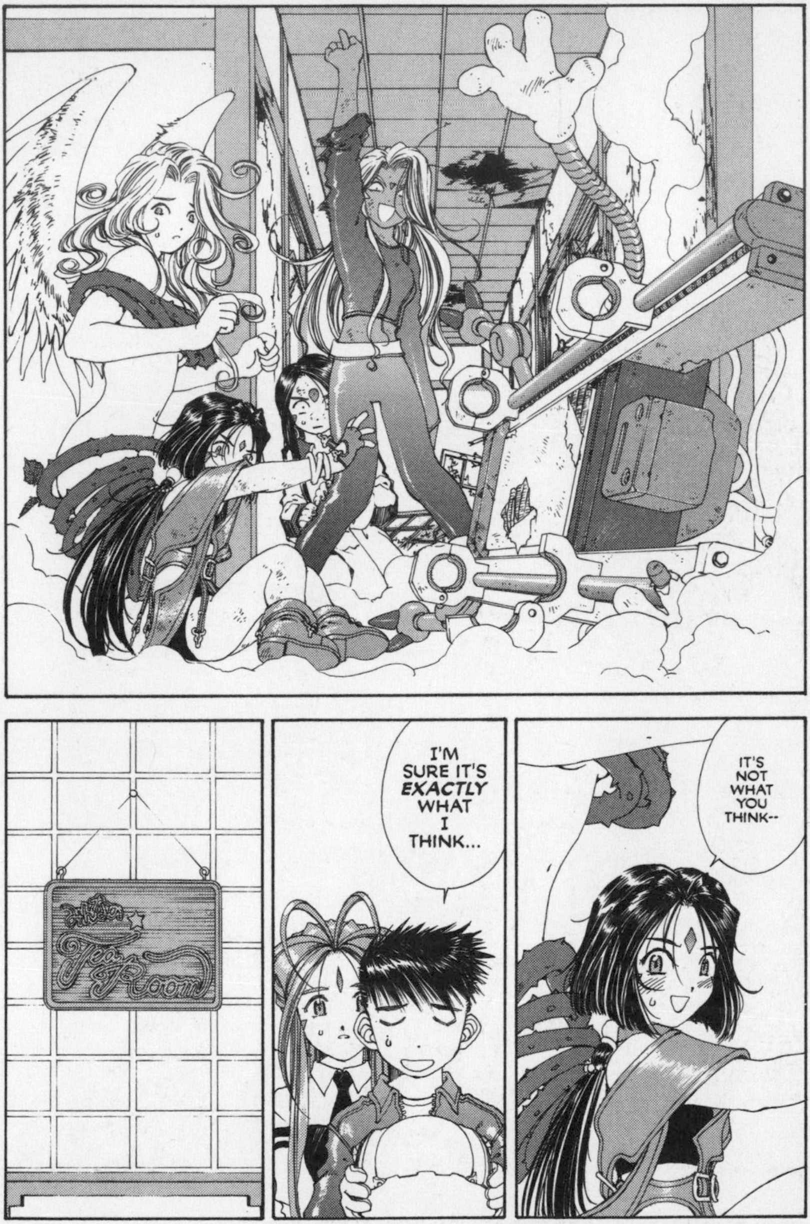
IT'S NOT WHAT YOU THINK--
I'M SURE IT'S *EXACTLY* WHAT I THINK...

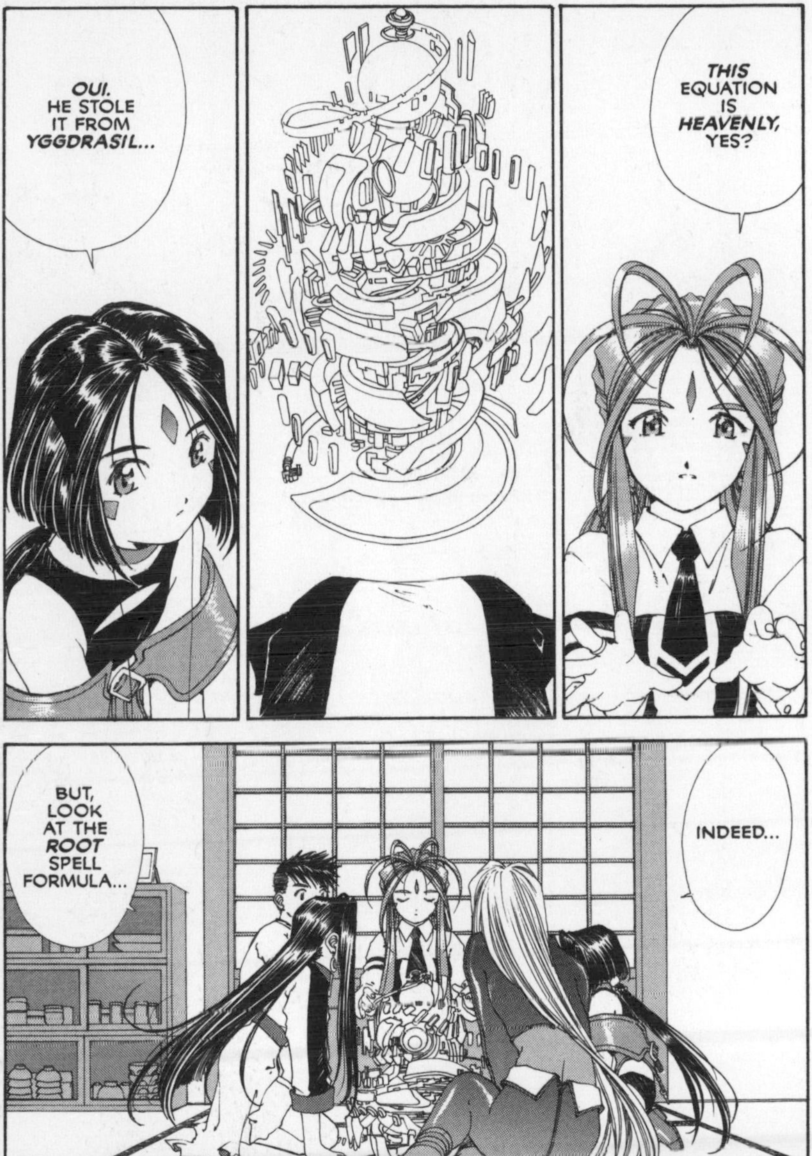
THIS EQUATION IS HEAVENLY, YES?
OUI. HE STOLE IT FROM YGGDRASIL...
INDEED...
BUT, LOOK AT THE ROOT SPELL FORMULA...

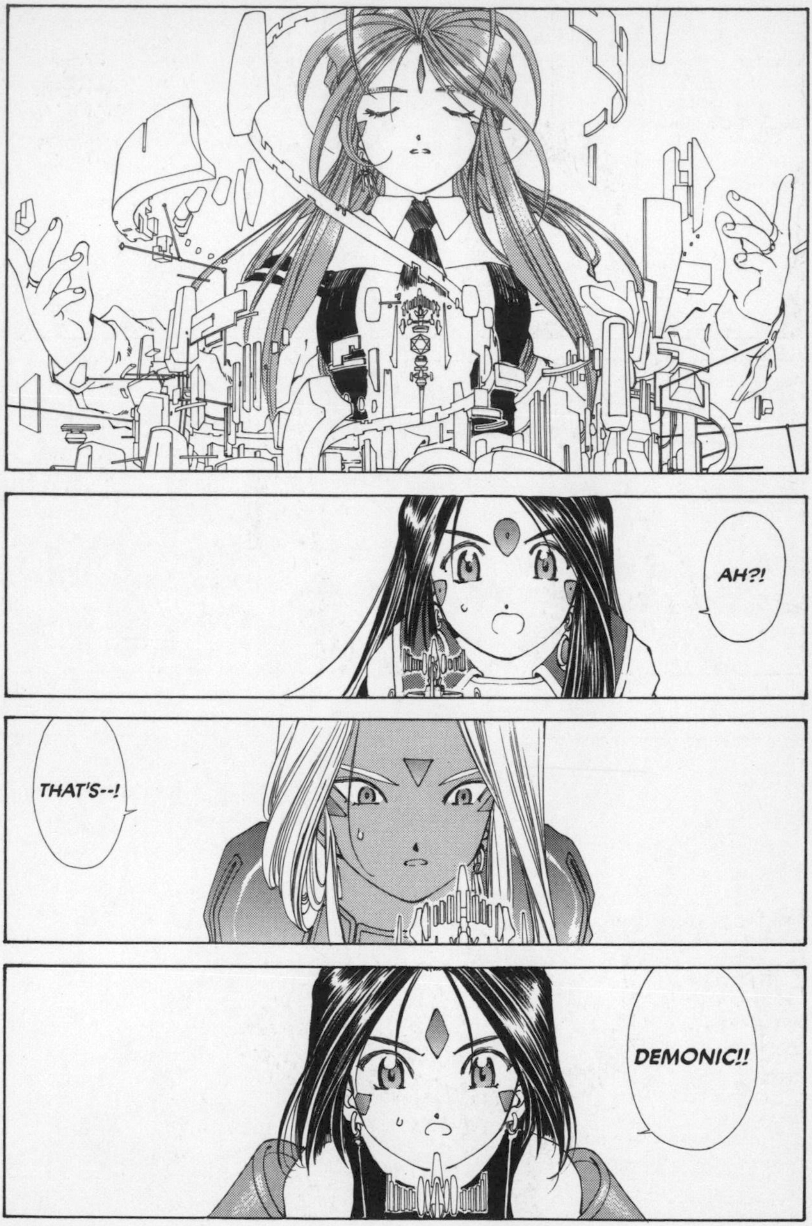
AH?!
THAT'S--!
DEMONIC!!

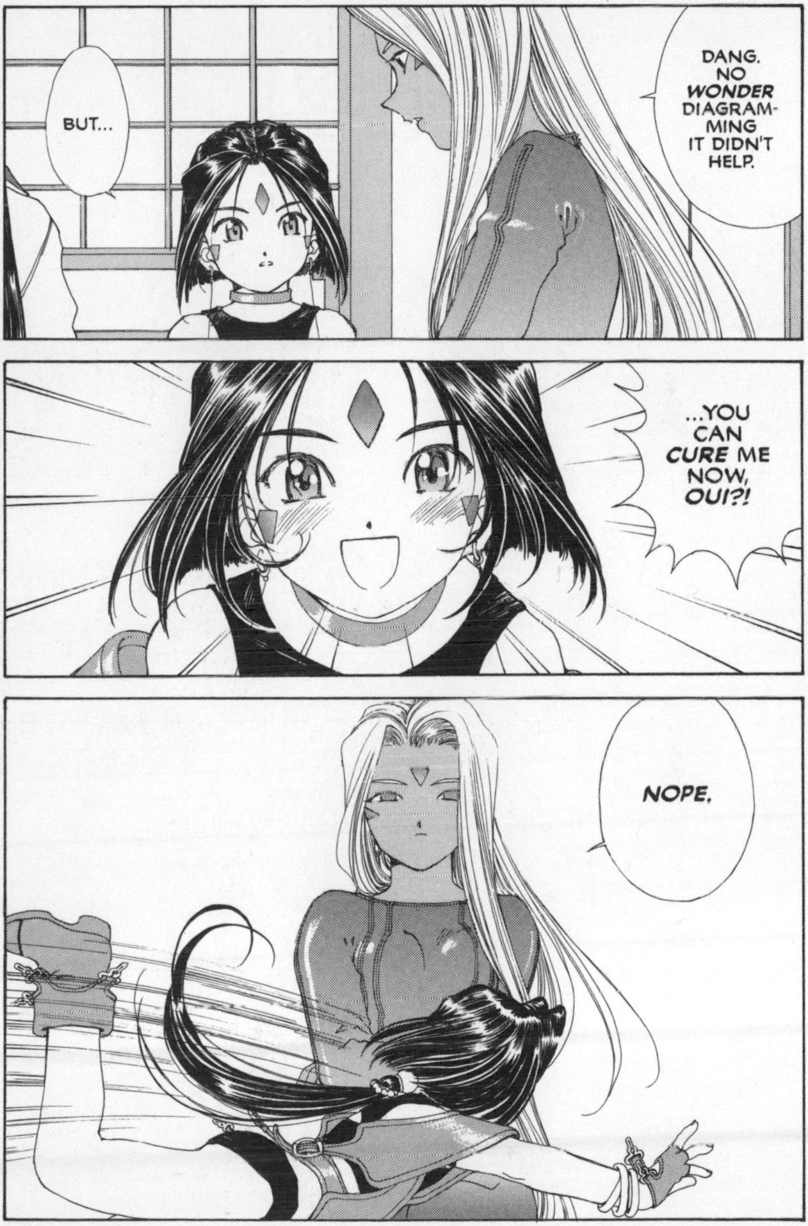
DANG. NO WONDER DIAGRAMMING IT DIDN'T HELP.
BUT...
...YOU CAN CURE ME NOW, OUI?!
NOPE.

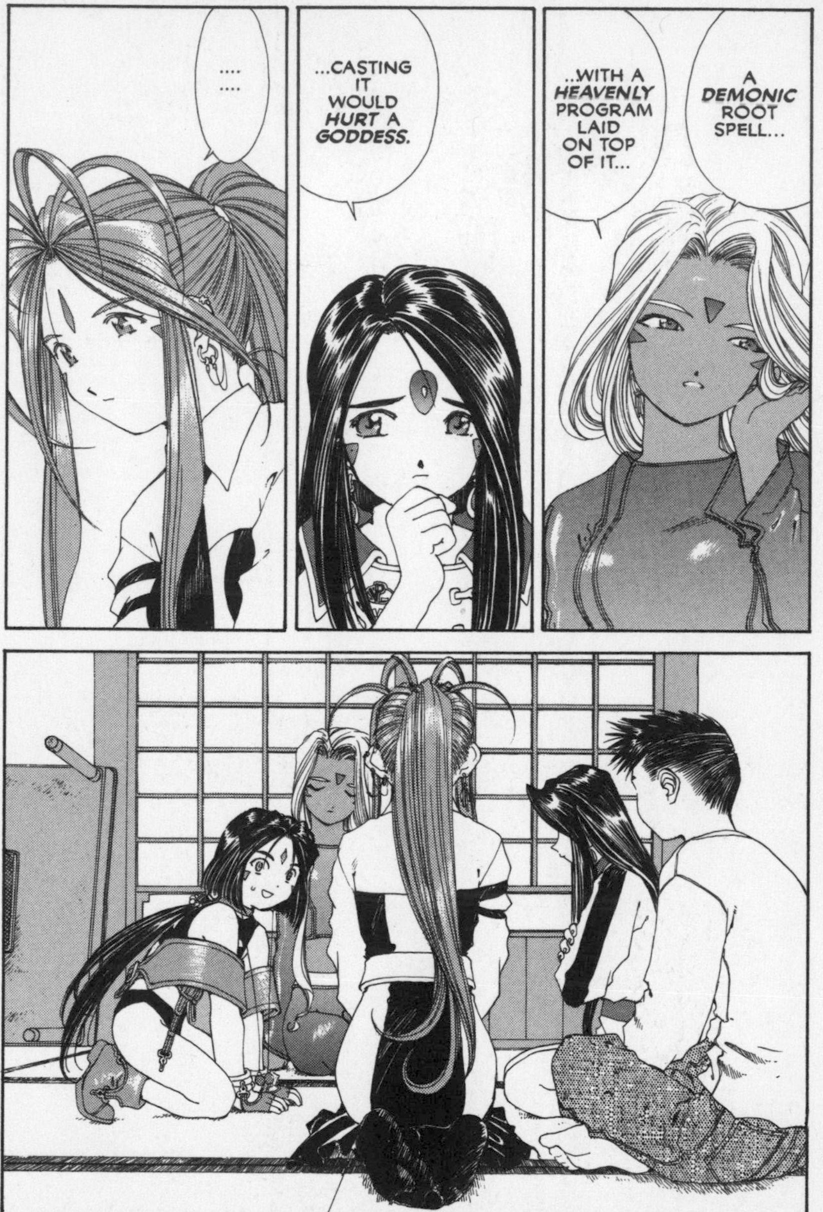
A DEMONIC ROOT SPELL...
...WITH A HEAVENLY PROGRAM LAID ON TOP OF IT...
...CASTING IT WOULD HURT A GODDESS.
....
....

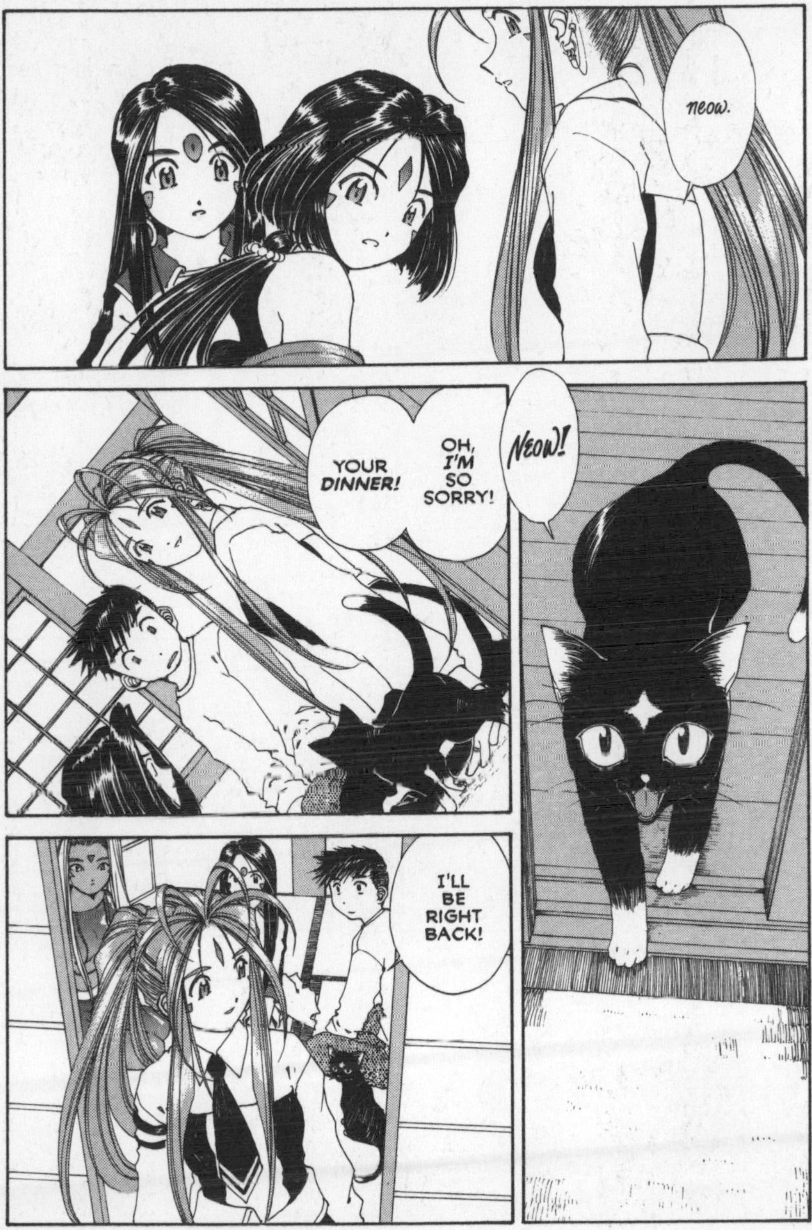
neow.
NEOW!
OH, I'M SO SORRY!
YOUR DINNER!
I'LL BE RIGHT BACK!

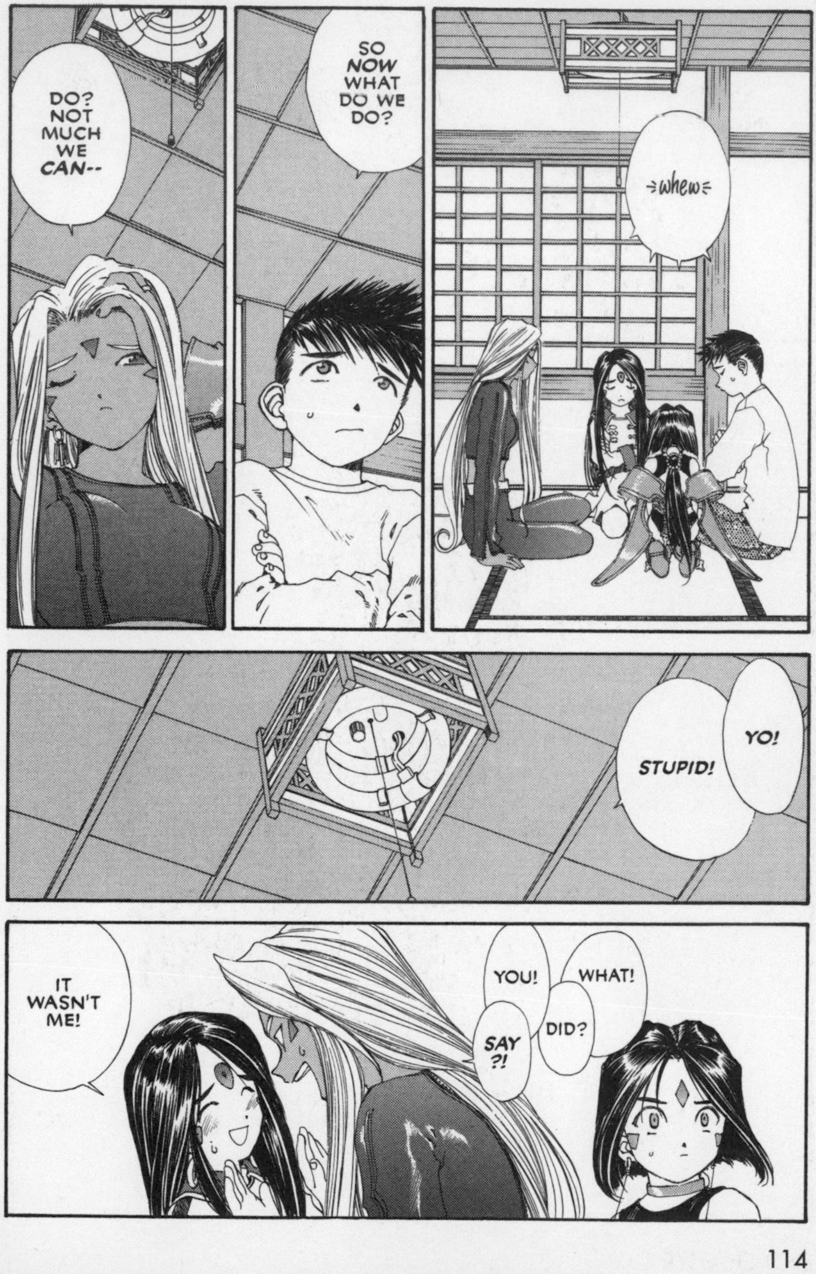
whew
SO NOW WHAT DO WE DO?
DO? NOT MUCH WE CAN--
YO!
STUPID!
WHAT!
YOU!
DID?
SAY?!
IT WASN'T ME!

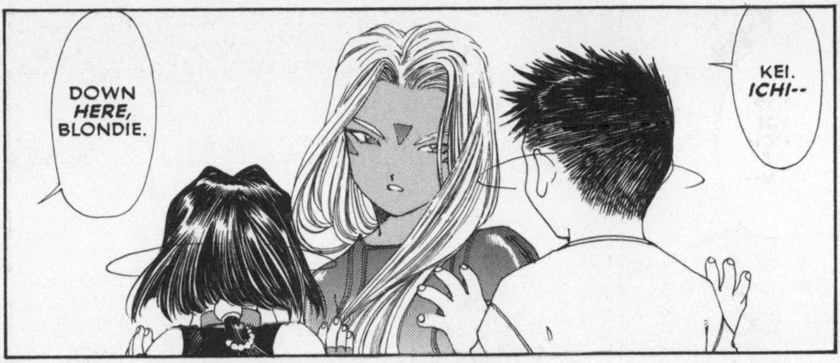
KEI. *ICHI--*
DOWN *HERE,* BLONDIE.

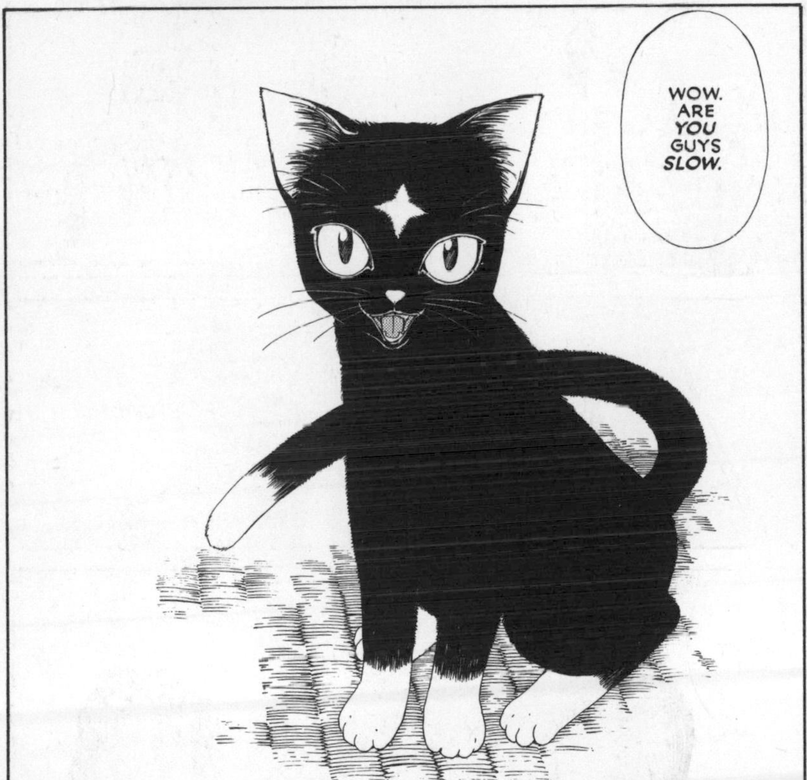
WOW. ARE *YOU* GUYS *SLOW.*

END CHAPTER 133

OH MY GODDESS!
V E L S P E R

CHAPTER 134

The Final Option

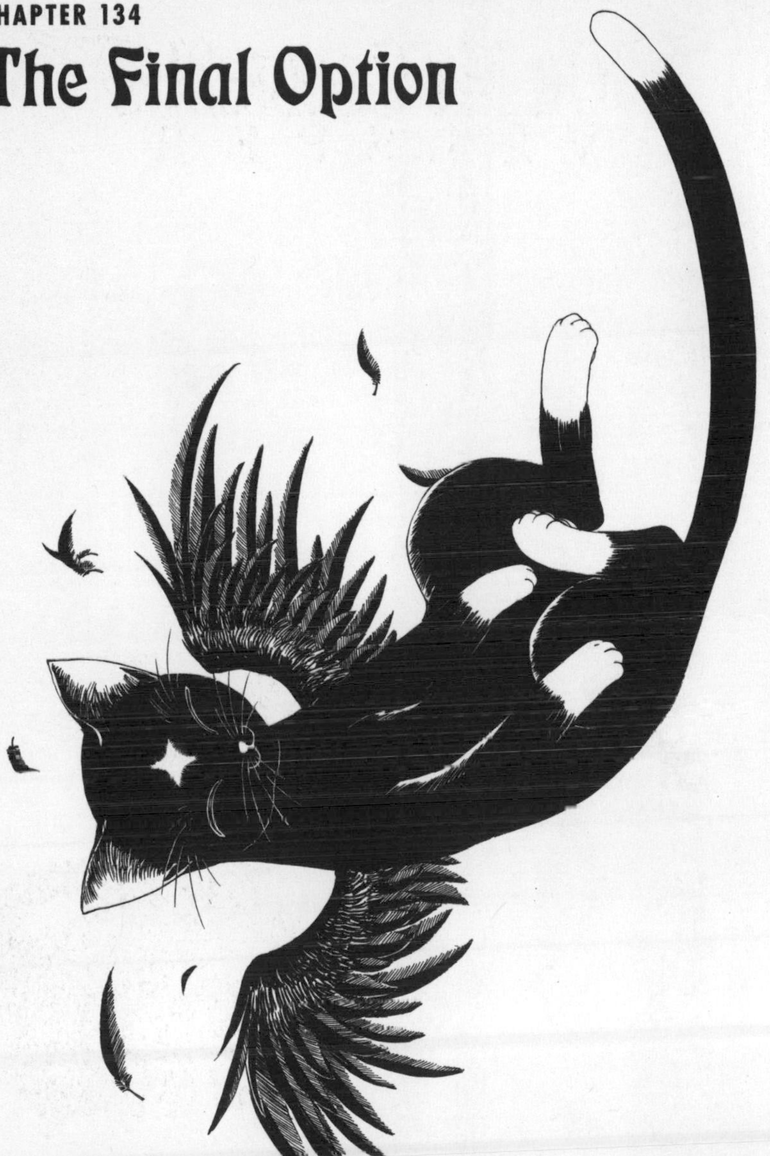

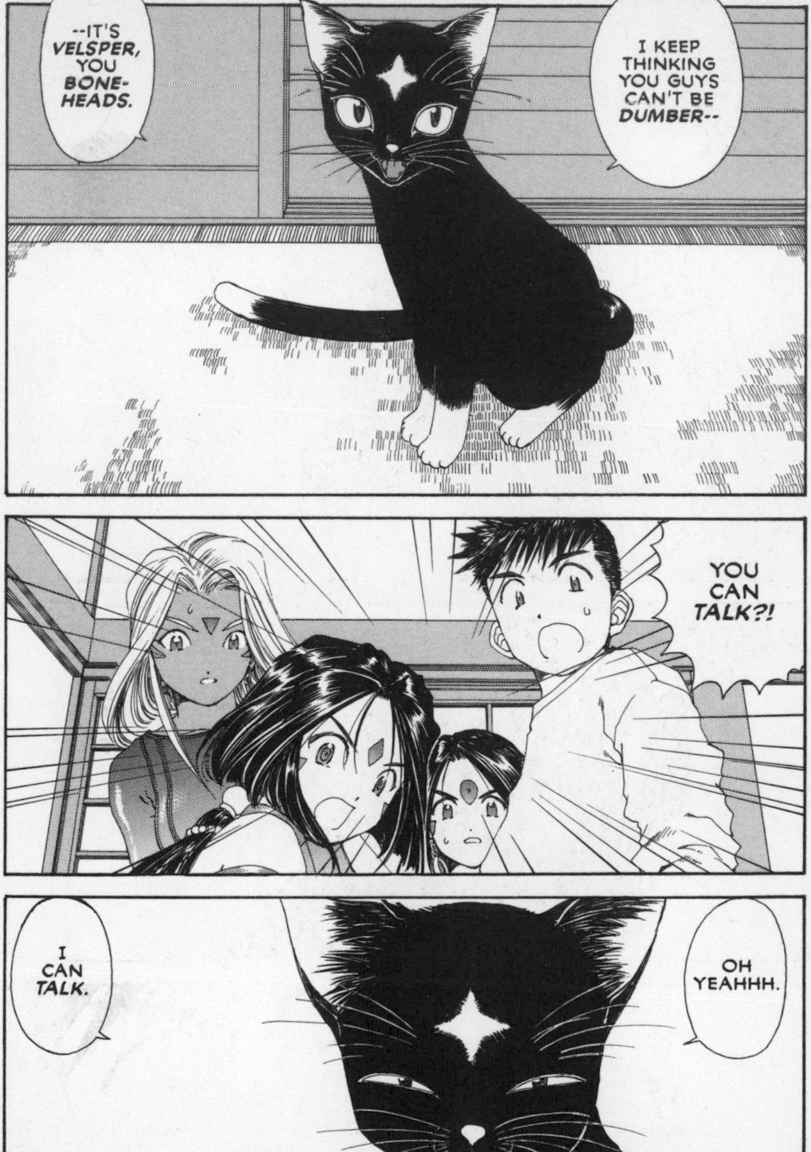
I KEEP THINKING YOU GUYS CAN'T BE *DUMBER*--
--IT'S *VELSPER,* YOU *BONE-HEADS.*
YOU CAN *TALK?!*
OH YEAHHH.
I CAN *TALK.*

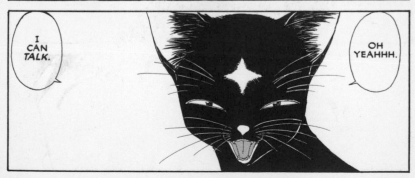

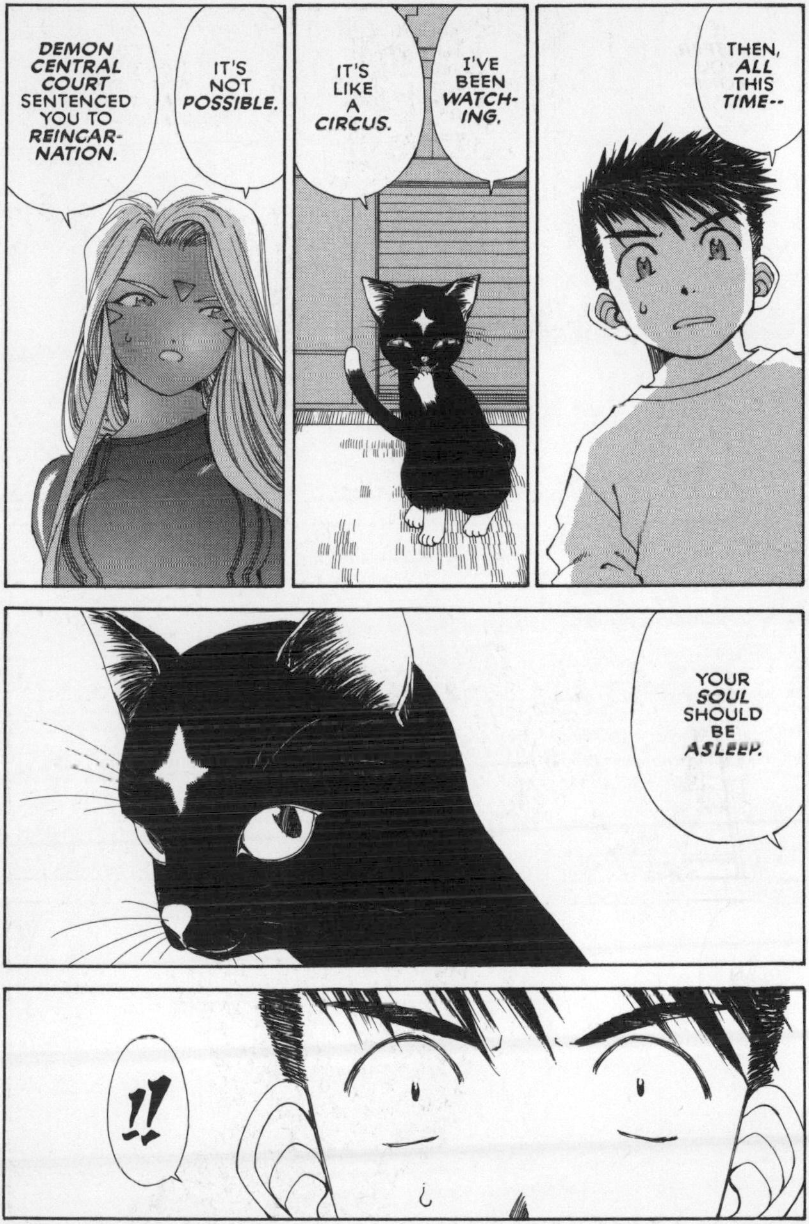
THEN, ALL THIS TIME--
I'VE BEEN WATCHING.
IT'S LIKE A CIRCUS.
IT'S NOT POSSIBLE.
DEMON CENTRAL COURT SENTENCED YOU TO REINCARNATION.
YOUR SOUL SHOULD BE ASLEEP.
!!

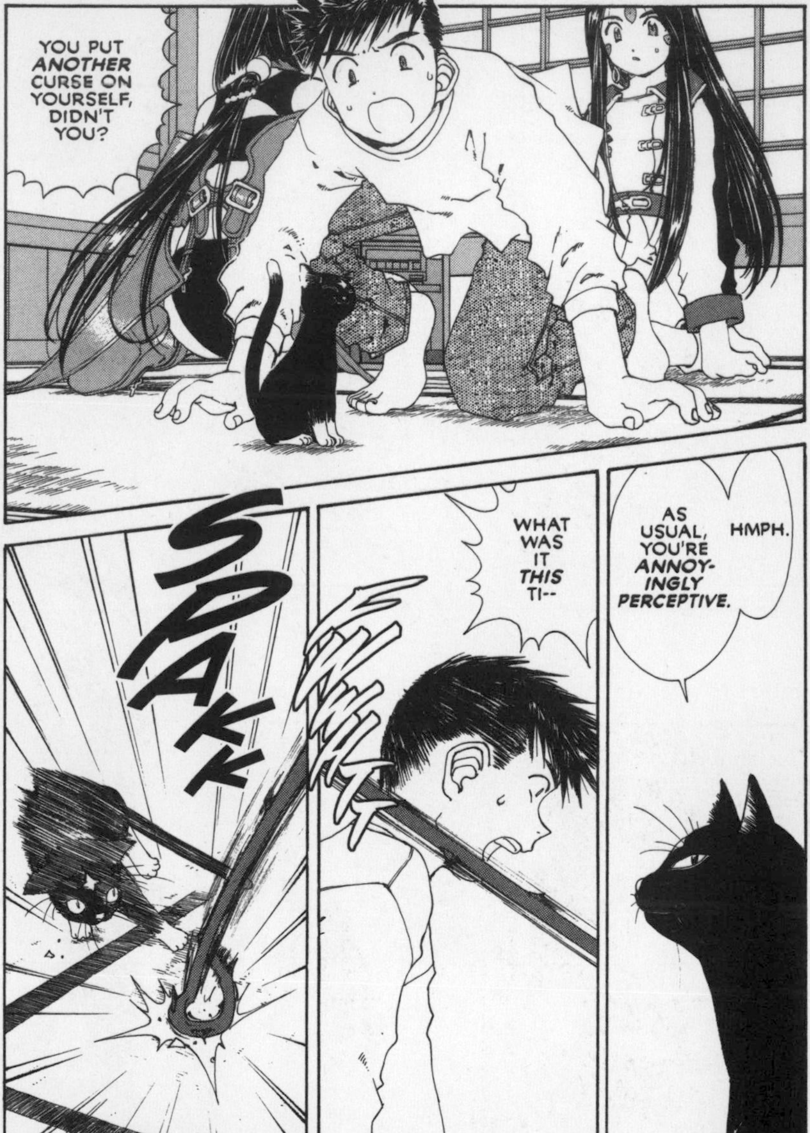
YOU PUT ANOTHER CURSE ON YOURSELF, DIDN'T YOU?
HMPH.
AS USUAL, YOU'RE ANNOY-INGLY PERCEPTIVE.
WHAT WAS IT THIS TI--
SPAKK

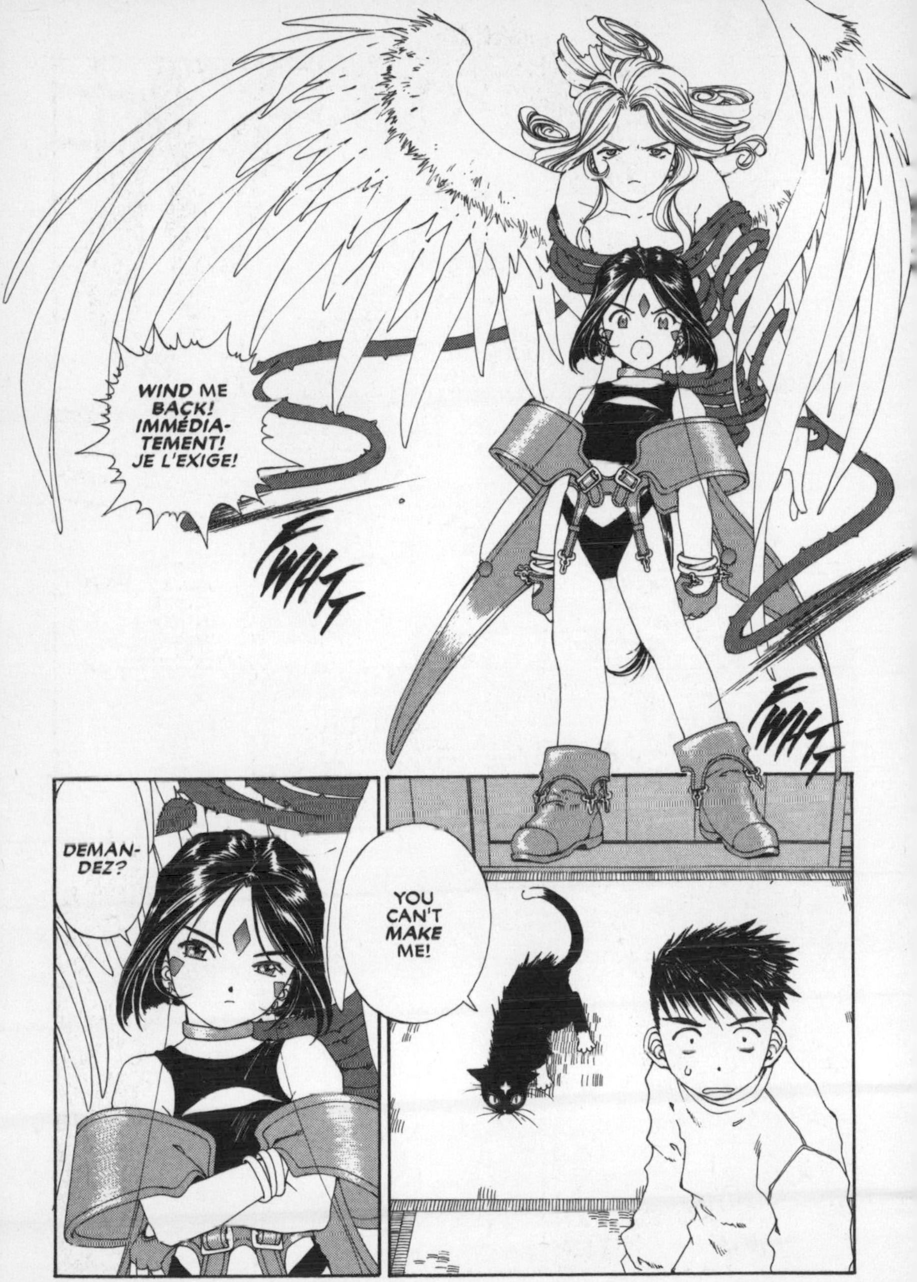
WIND ME BACK! IMMÉDIATEMENT! JE L'EXIGE!
YOU CAN'T MAKE ME!
DEMANDEZ?

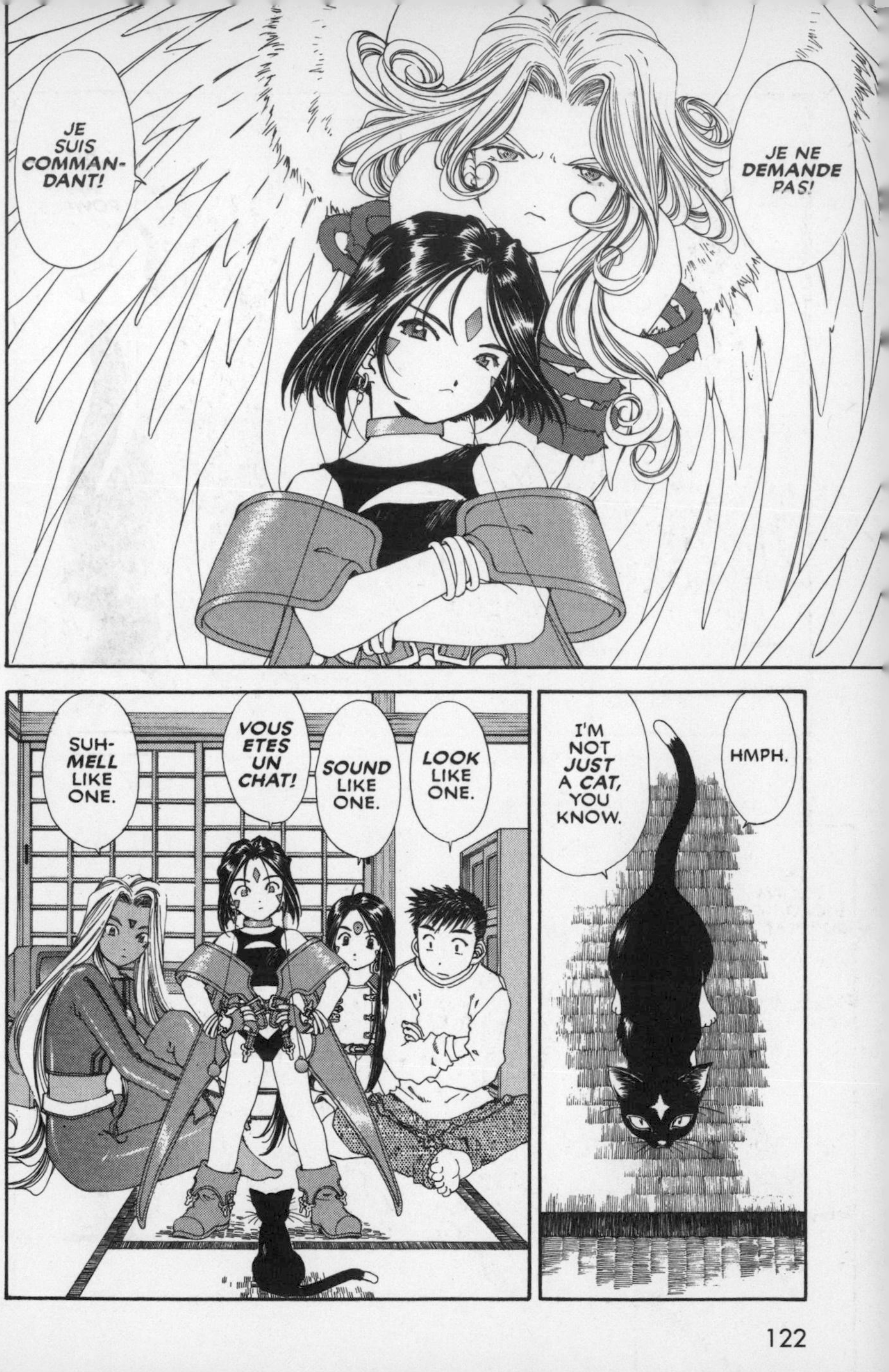
JE NE DEMANDE PAS!
JE SUIS COMMANDANT!
HMPH.
I'M NOT JUST A CAT, YOU KNOW.
LOOK LIKE ONE.
SOUND LIKE ONE.
VOUS ETES UN CHAT!
SUH-MELL LIKE ONE.

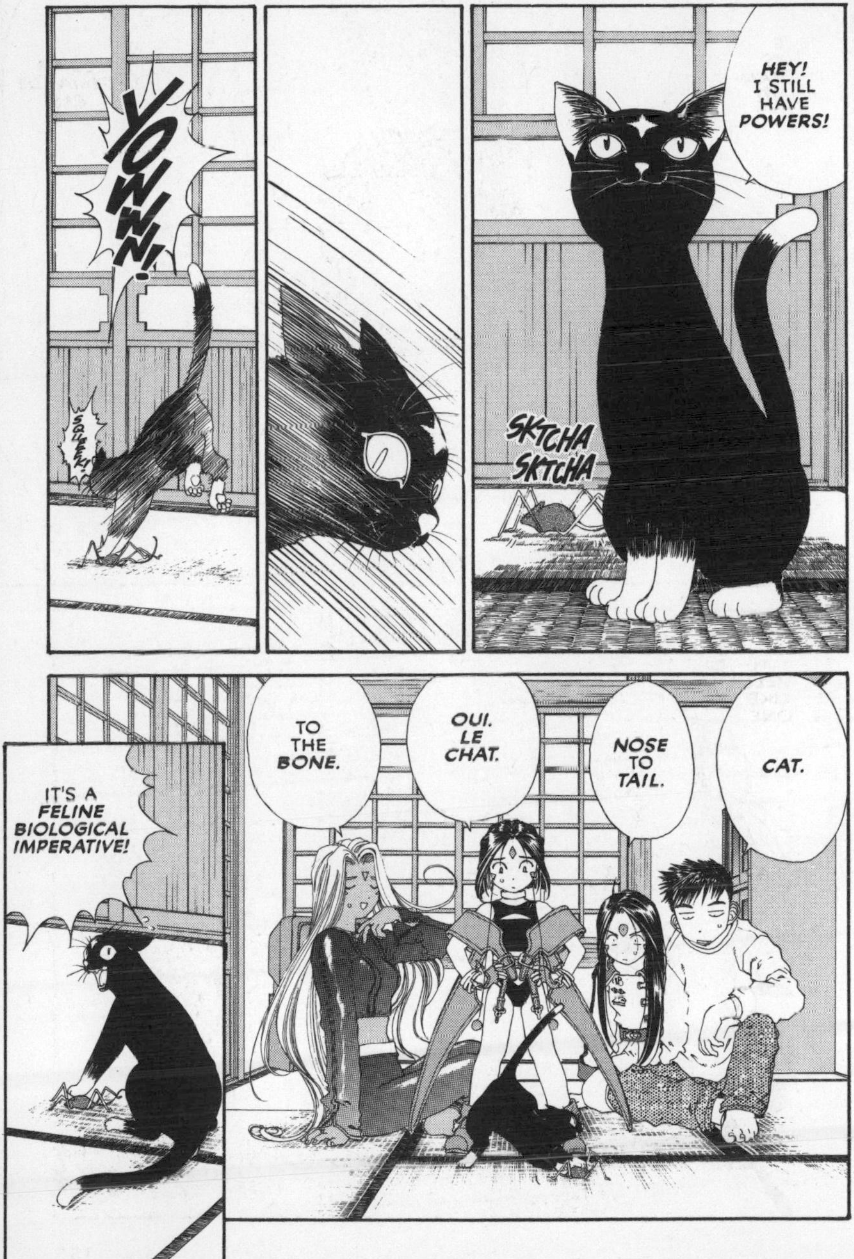
HEY! I STILL HAVE POWERS!
SKTCHA SKTCHA
YOWWN!
SQUEEK!
CAT.
NOSE TO TAIL.
OUI. LE CHAT.
TO THE BONE.
IT'S A FELINE BIOLOGICAL IMPERATIVE!

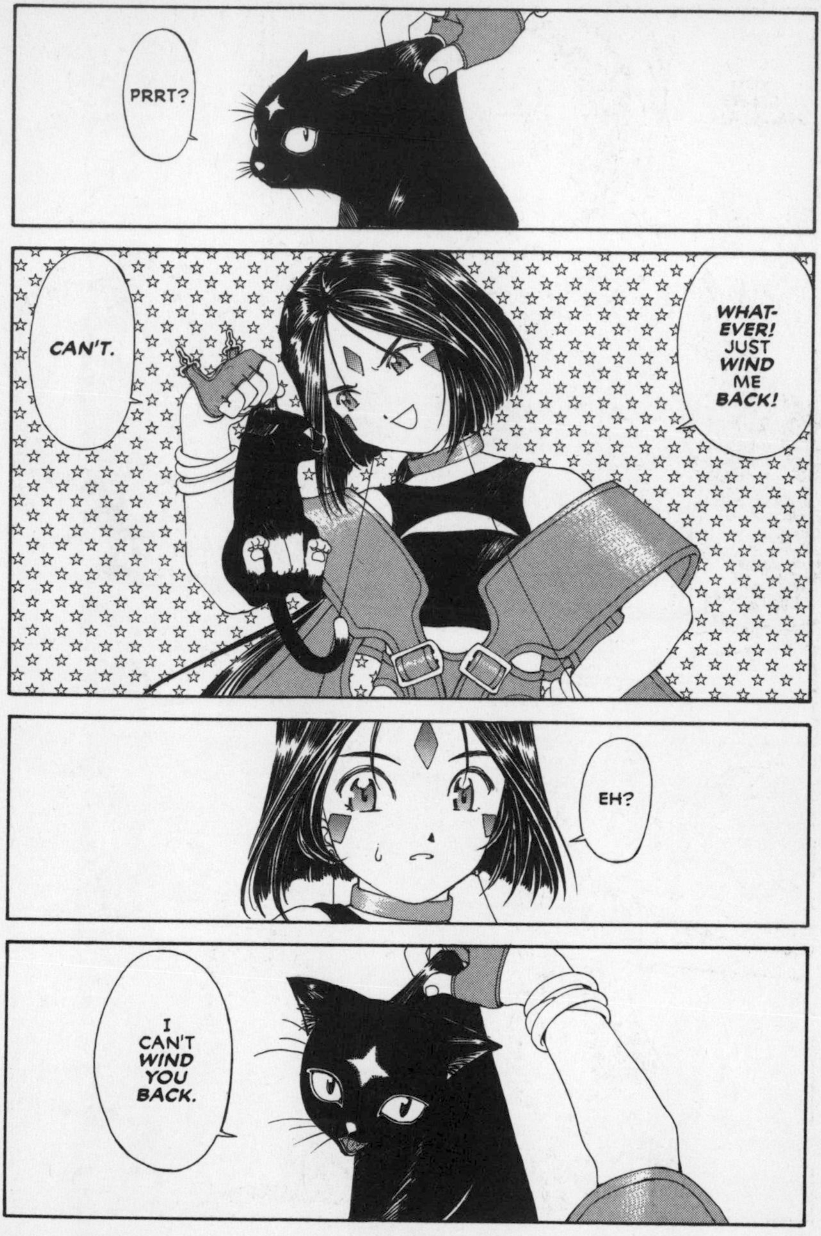
PRRT?
WHAT-EVER! JUST WIND ME BACK!
CAN'T.
EH?
I CAN'T WIND YOU BACK.

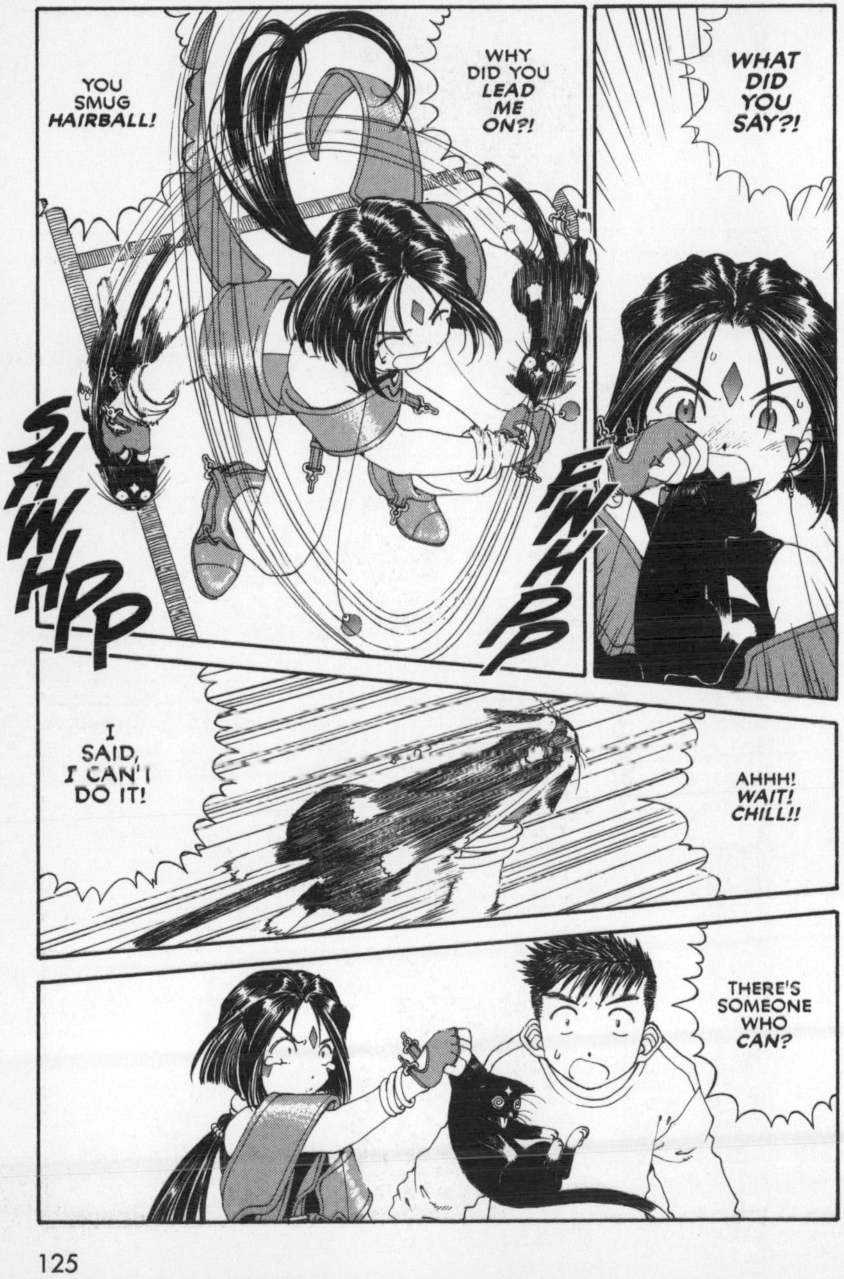
WHAT DID YOU SAY?!
WHY DID YOU LEAD ME ON?!
YOU SMUG HAIRBALL!
FWHPP
SHWHPP
AHHH! WAIT! CHILL!!
I SAID, I CAN'T DO IT!
THERE'S SOMEONE WHO CAN?

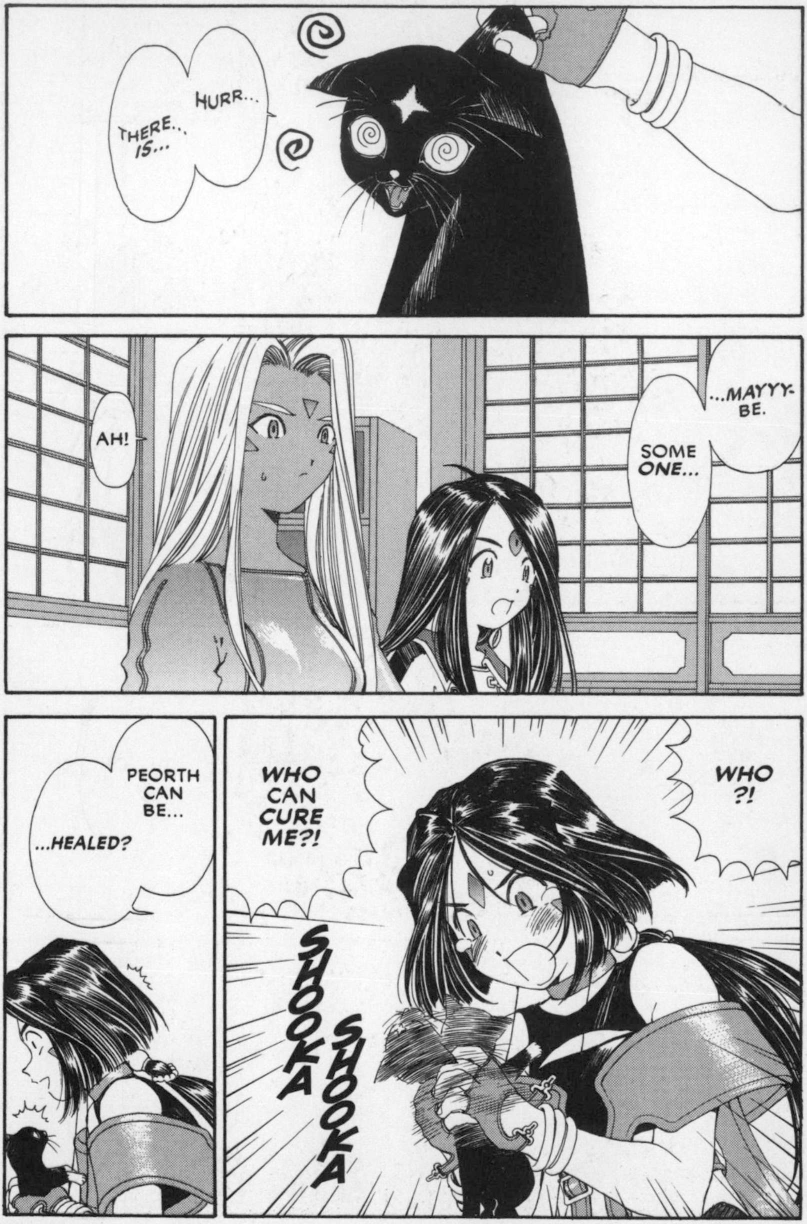
HURR...
THERE... IS...
...MAYYY-BE.
SOME ONE...
AH!
WHO ?!
WHO CAN CURE ME?!
SHOOKA SHOOKA
PEORTH CAN BE...
...HEALED?

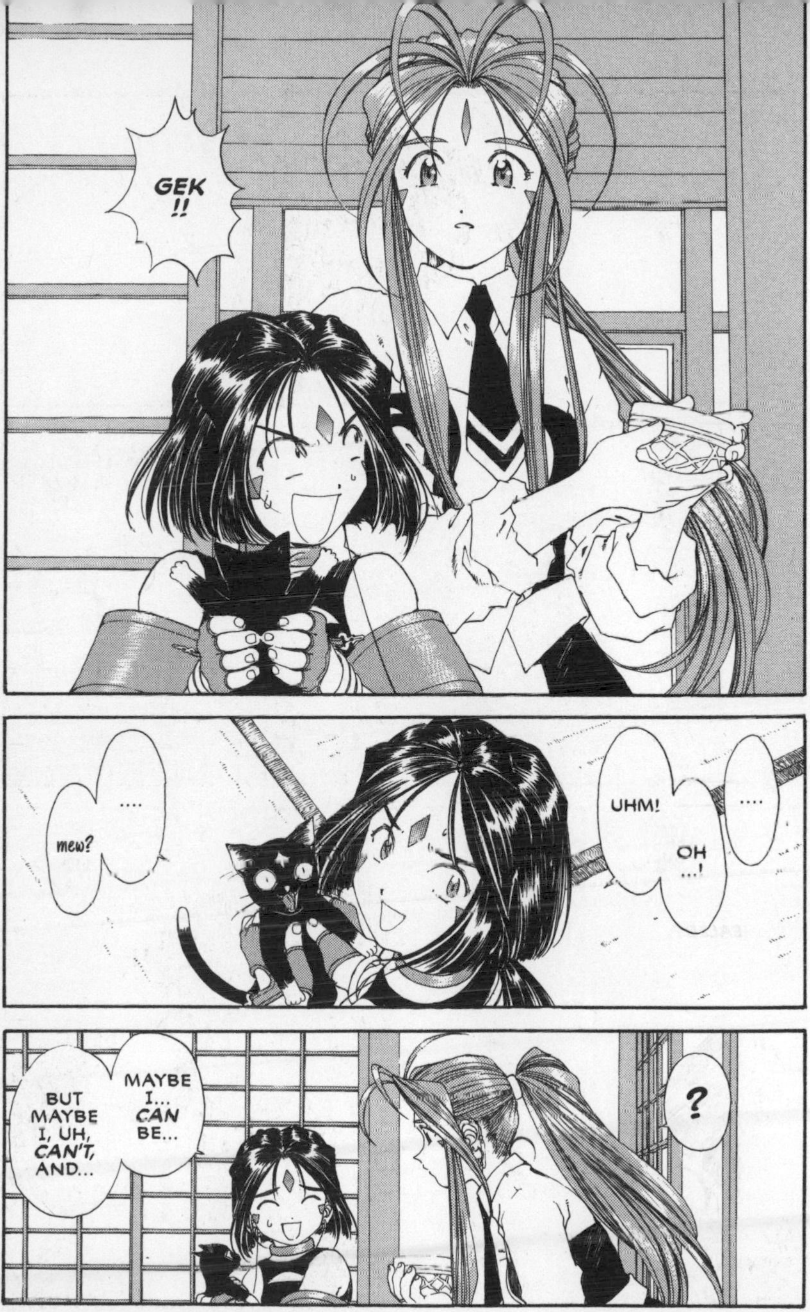
GEK !!
....
UHM! OH ...!
.... mew?
?
MAYBE I... *CAN* BE...
BUT MAYBE I, UH, *CAN'T*, AND...

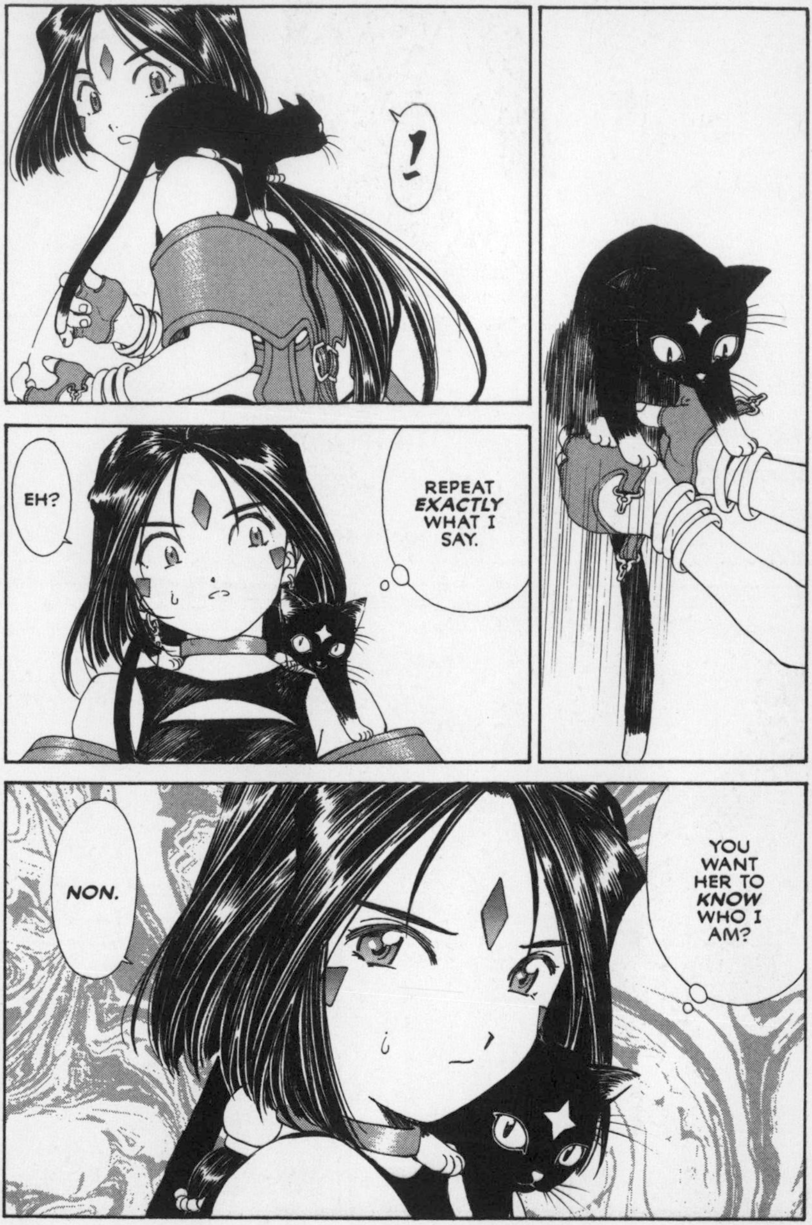
!
REPEAT *EXACTLY* WHAT I SAY.
EH?
YOU WANT HER TO *KNOW* WHO I AM?
NON.

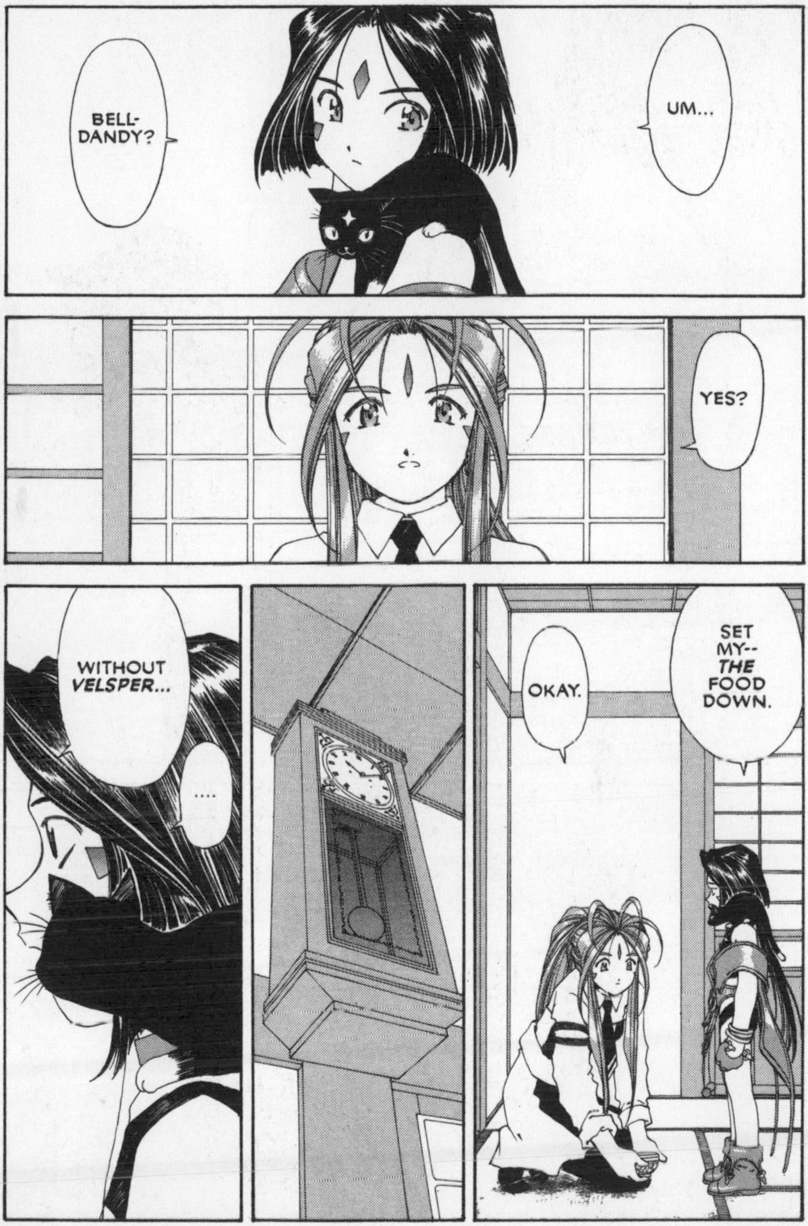
UM...
BELL-DANDY?
YES?
SET MY-- *THE* FOOD DOWN.
OKAY.
WITHOUT *VELSPER*...
....

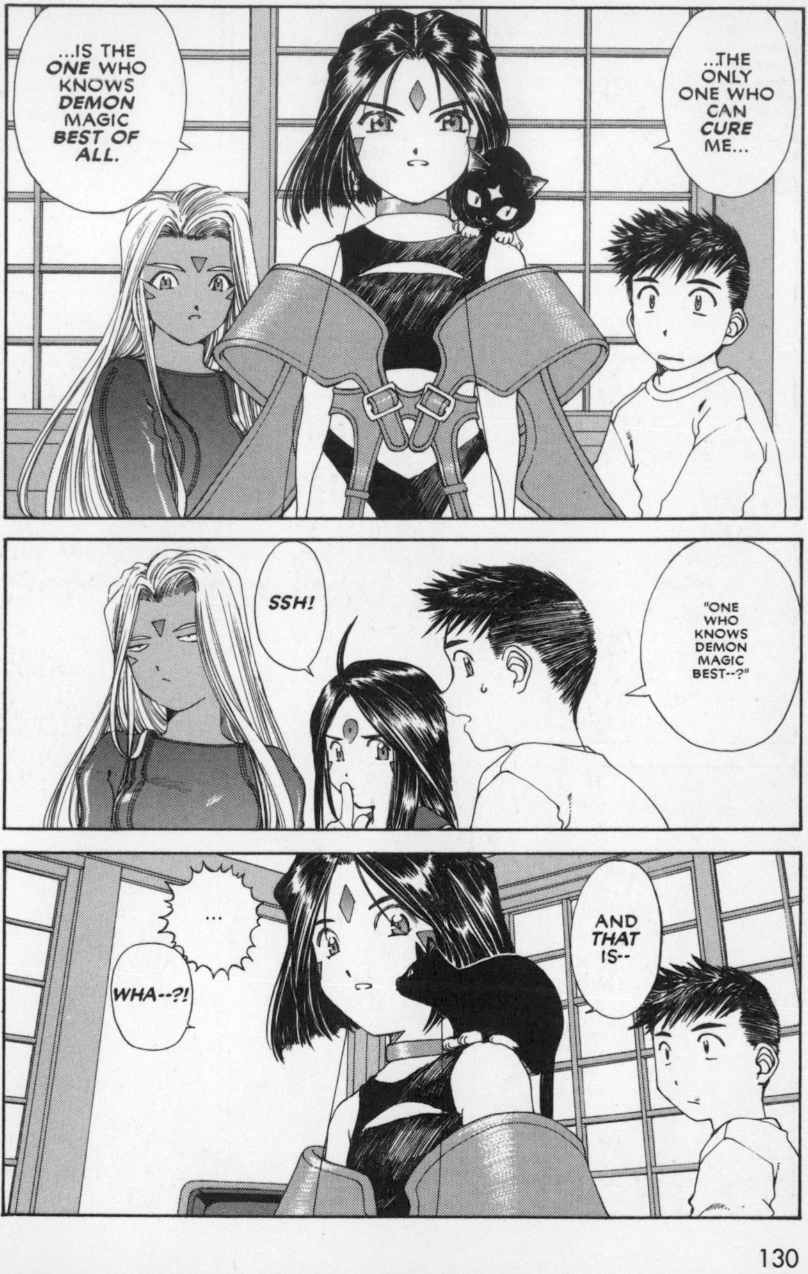
...THE ONLY ONE WHO CAN CURE ME...
...IS THE ONE WHO KNOWS DEMON MAGIC BEST OF ALL.
"ONE WHO KNOWS DEMON MAGIC BEST--?"
SSH!
AND THAT IS--
...
WHA--?!

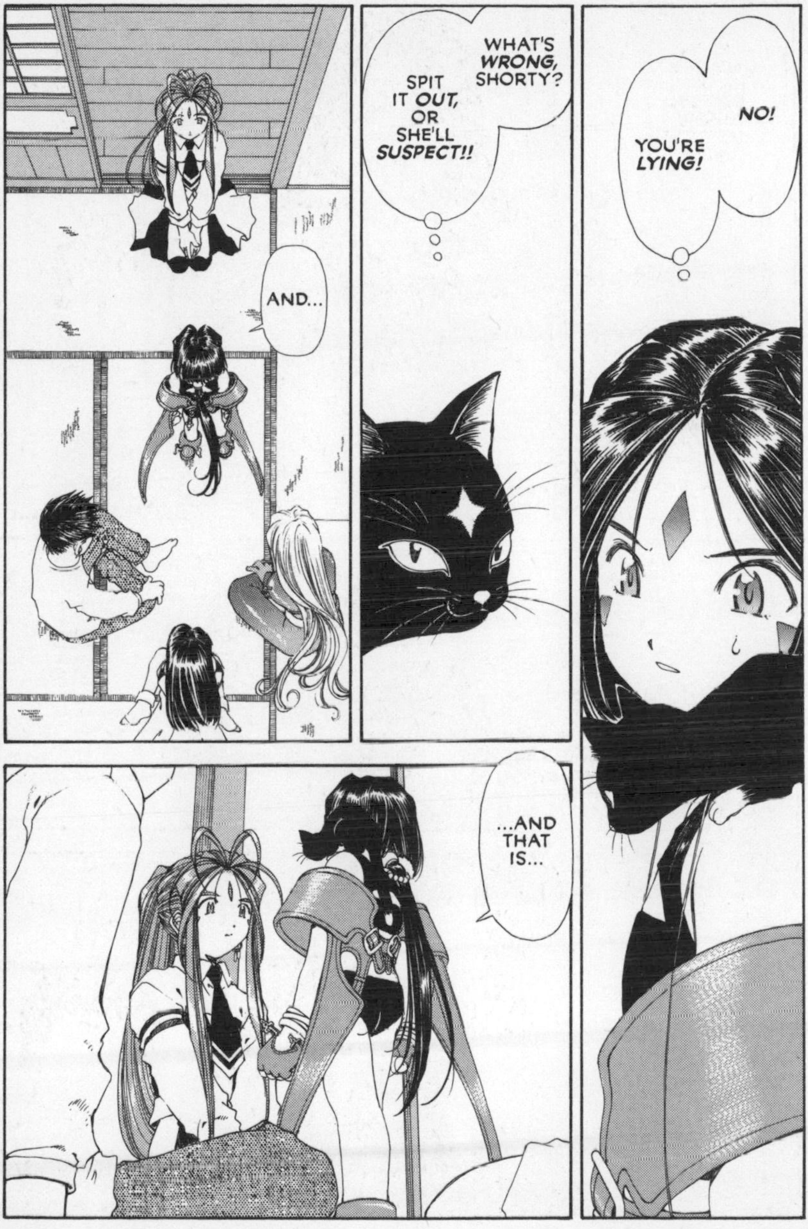

NO!
YOU'RE LYING!
WHAT'S WRONG, SHORTY?
SPIT IT OUT, OR SHE'LL SUSPECT!!
AND...
...AND THAT IS...

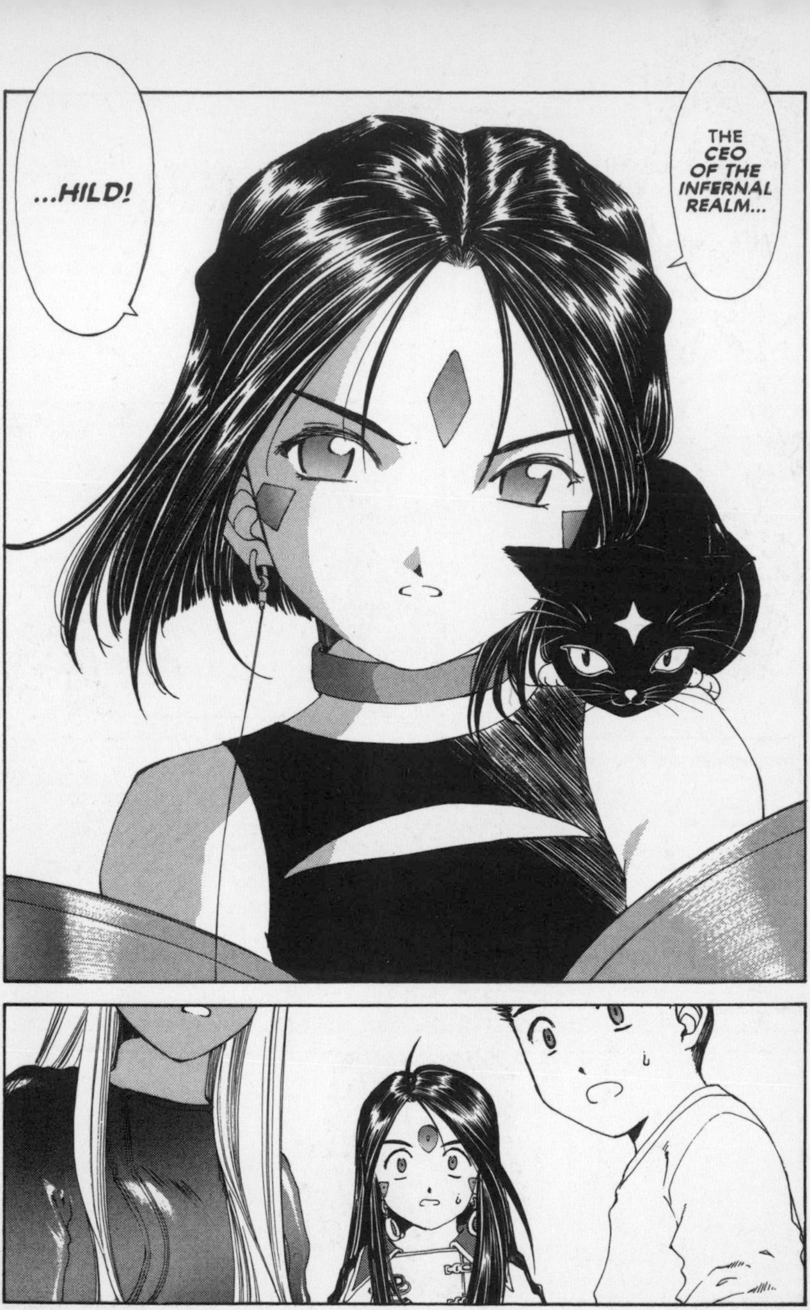
THE CEO OF THE INFERNAL REALM...
...HILD!

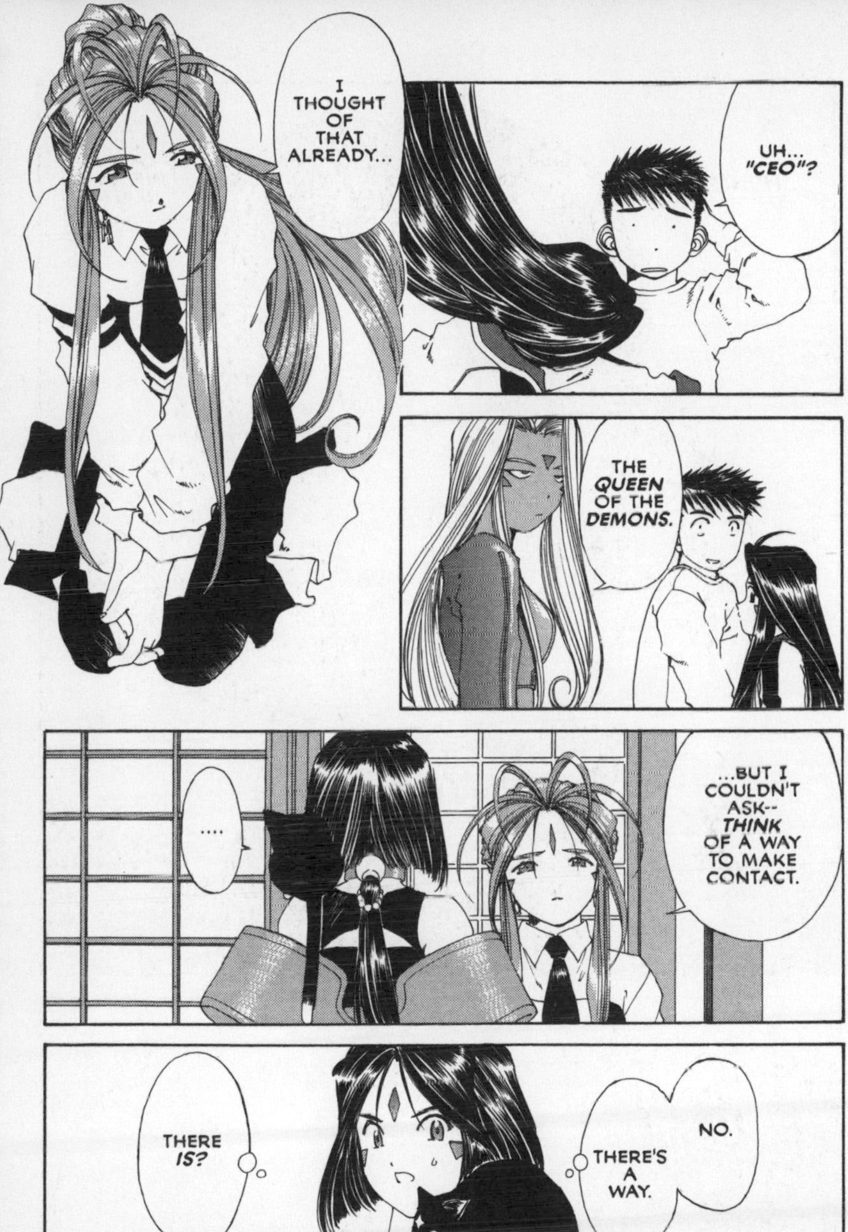
UH... "CEO"?
THE QUEEN OF THE DEMONS.
I THOUGHT OF THAT ALREADY...
...BUT I COULDN'T ASK-- THINK OF A WAY TO MAKE CONTACT.
....
NO. THERE'S A WAY.
THERE IS?

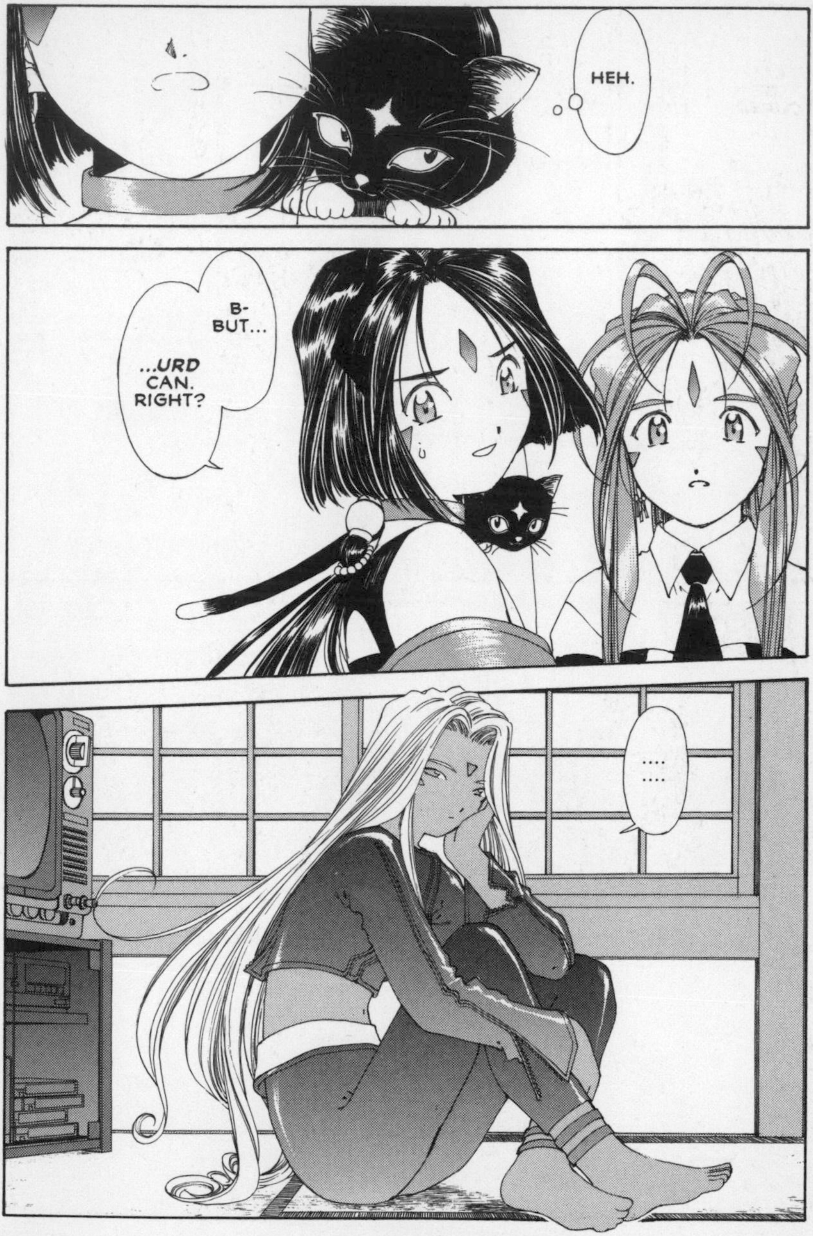
HEH.
B-BUT...
...URD CAN. RIGHT?
....
....

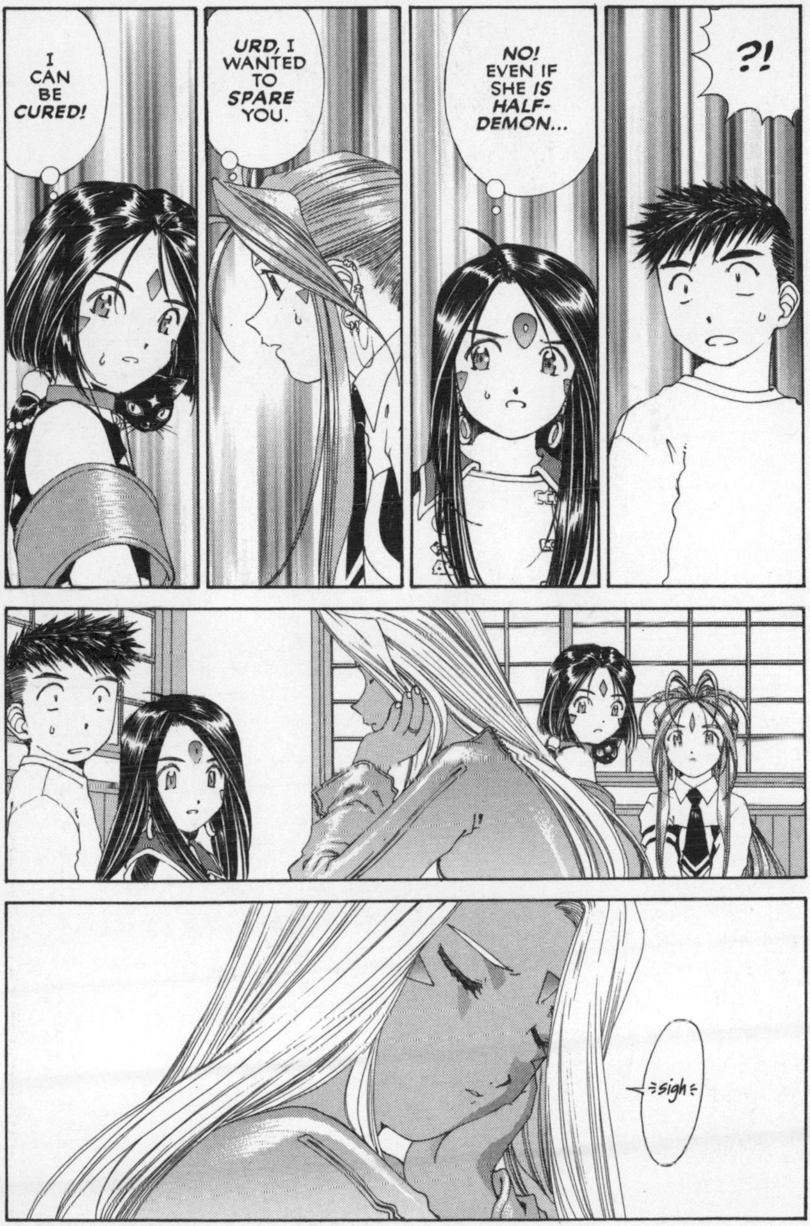
?!
NO! EVEN IF SHE IS HALF-DEMON...
URD, I WANTED TO SPARE YOU.
I CAN BE CURED!
≡sigh≡

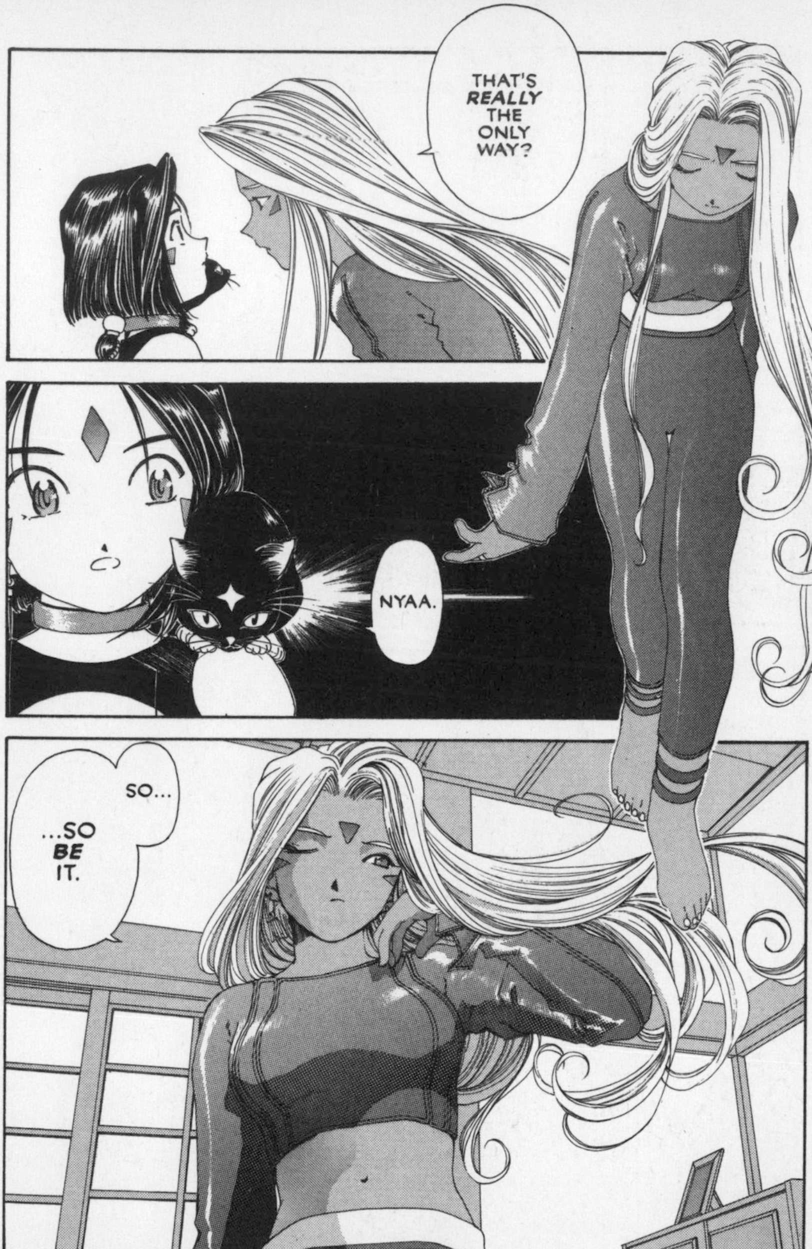
THAT'S *REALLY* THE ONLY WAY?
NYAA.
SO...
...SO *BE* IT.

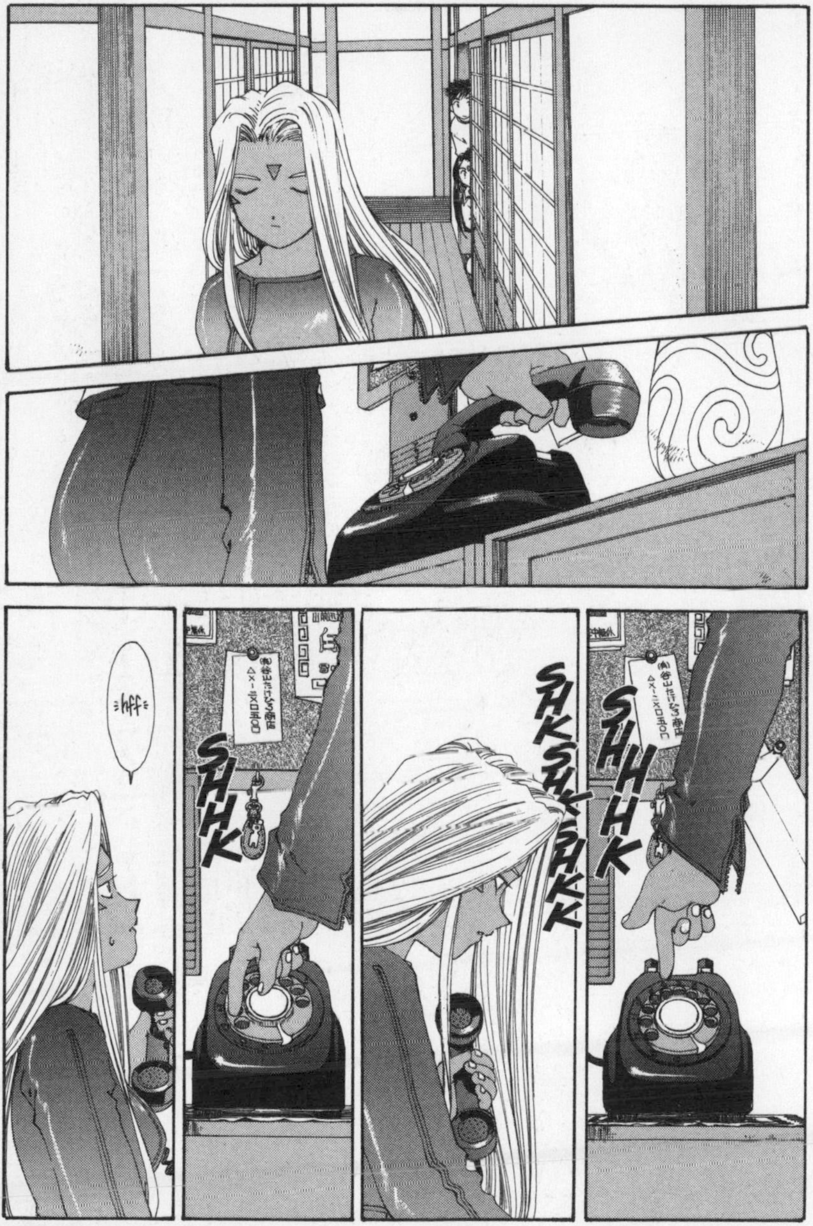
SHHHHK
SHKSHKSHKK
SHHK
hff

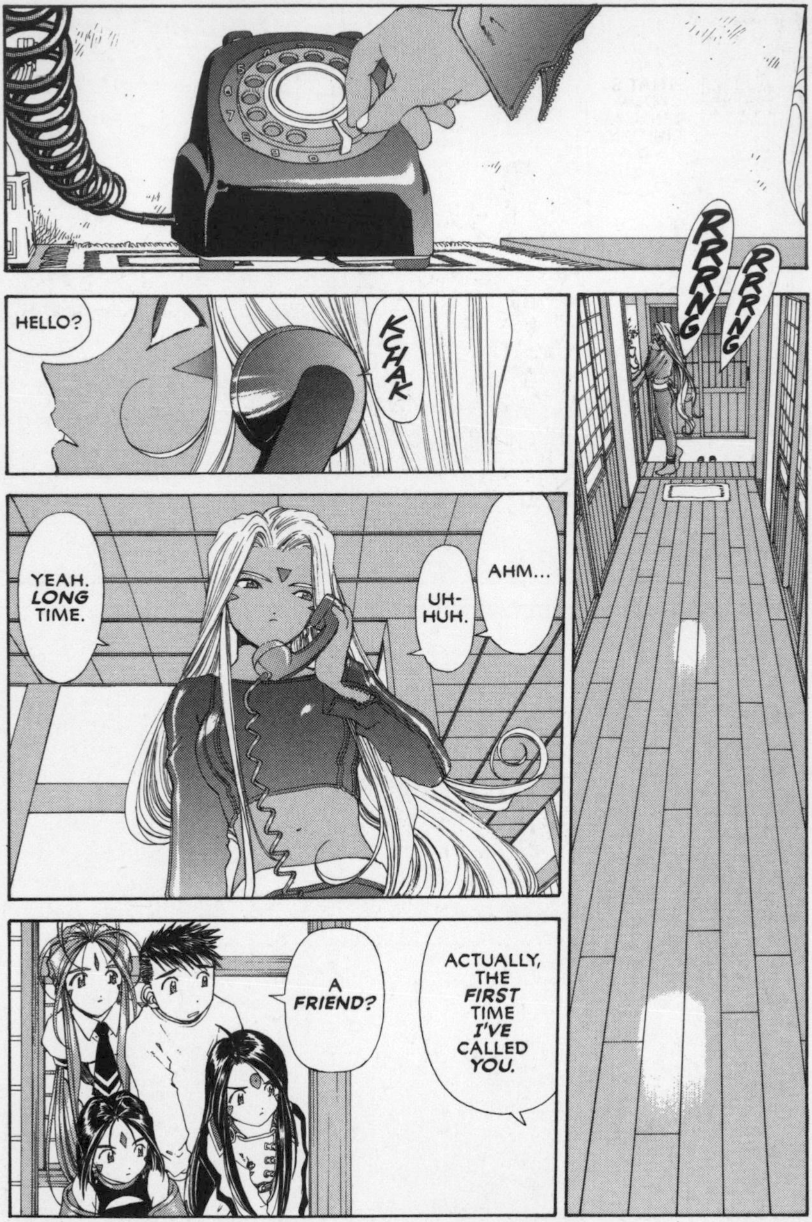
RRRNG
RRRNG
KCHAK
HELLO?
AHM...
UH-HUH.
YEAH. LONG TIME.
ACTUALLY, THE FIRST TIME I'VE CALLED YOU.
A FRIEND?

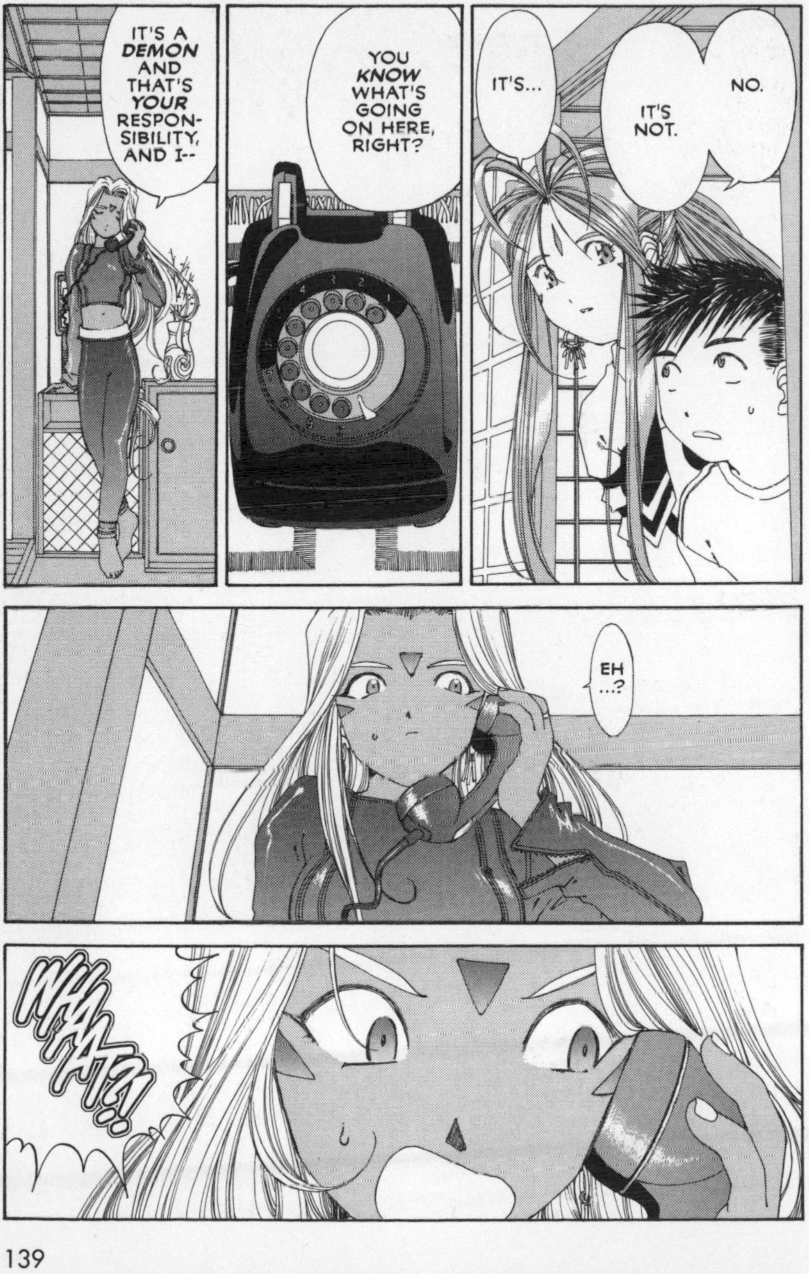
IT'S A DEMON AND THAT'S YOUR RESPONSIBILITY, AND I--
YOU KNOW WHAT'S GOING ON HERE, RIGHT?
IT'S...
NO.
IT'S NOT.
EH ...?
WHAAAT?!

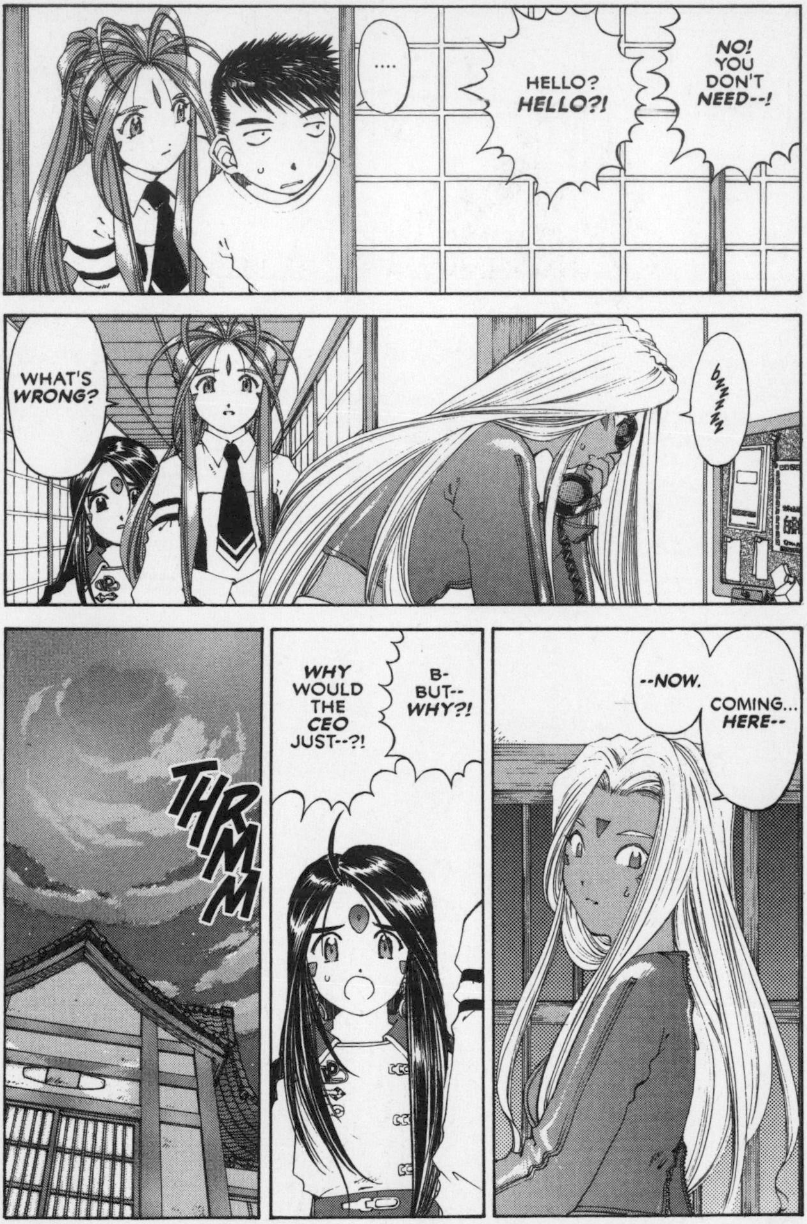
NO! YOU DON'T NEED--!
HELLO? HELLO?!
....
bzzzzz
WHAT'S WRONG?
COMING... HERE--
--NOW.
B-BUT--WHY?!
WHY WOULD THE CEO JUST--?!
THRMM

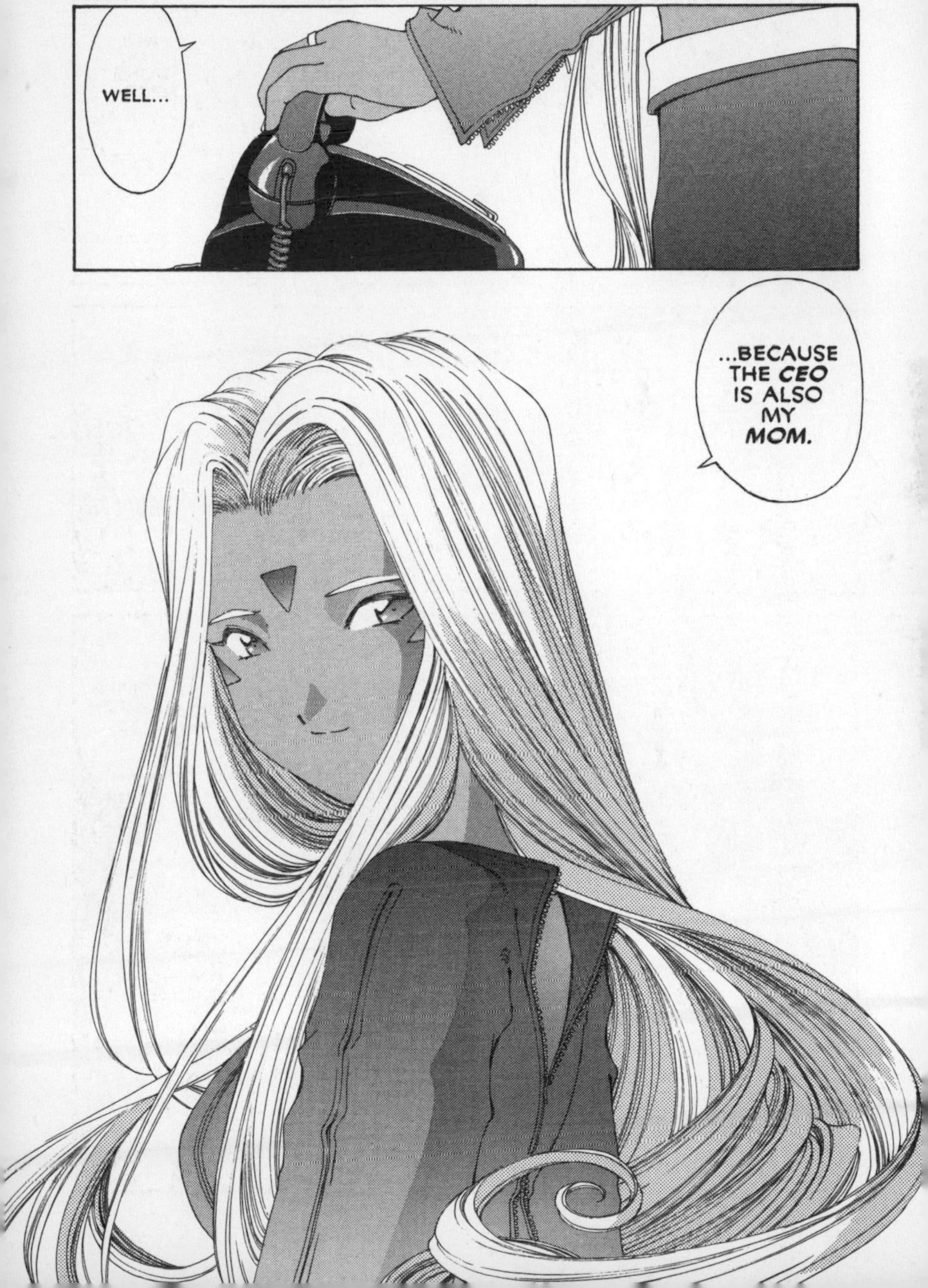
WELL...
...BECAUSE THE *CEO* IS ALSO MY *MOM.*

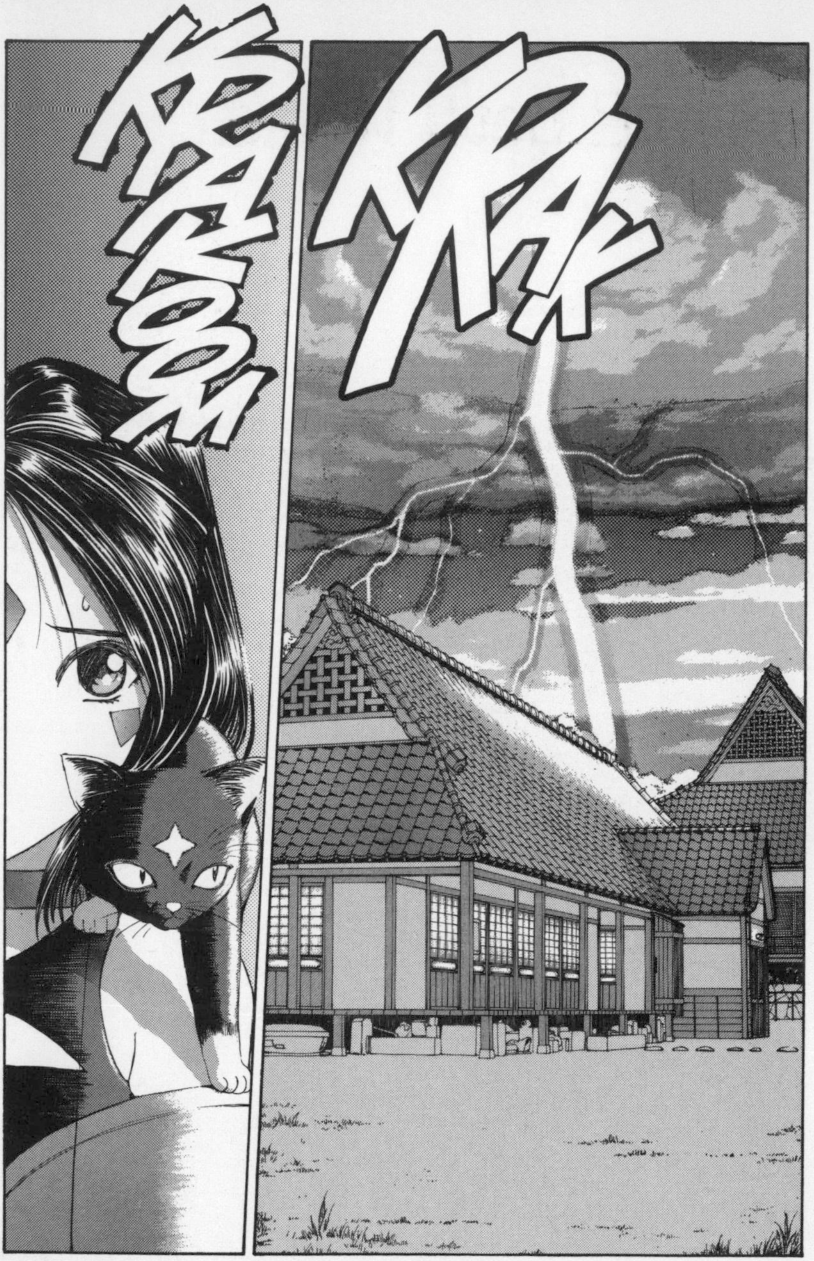
KRAK!
KRAKOOM

END CHAPTER 134

CHAPTER 135

She's A Devil Woman

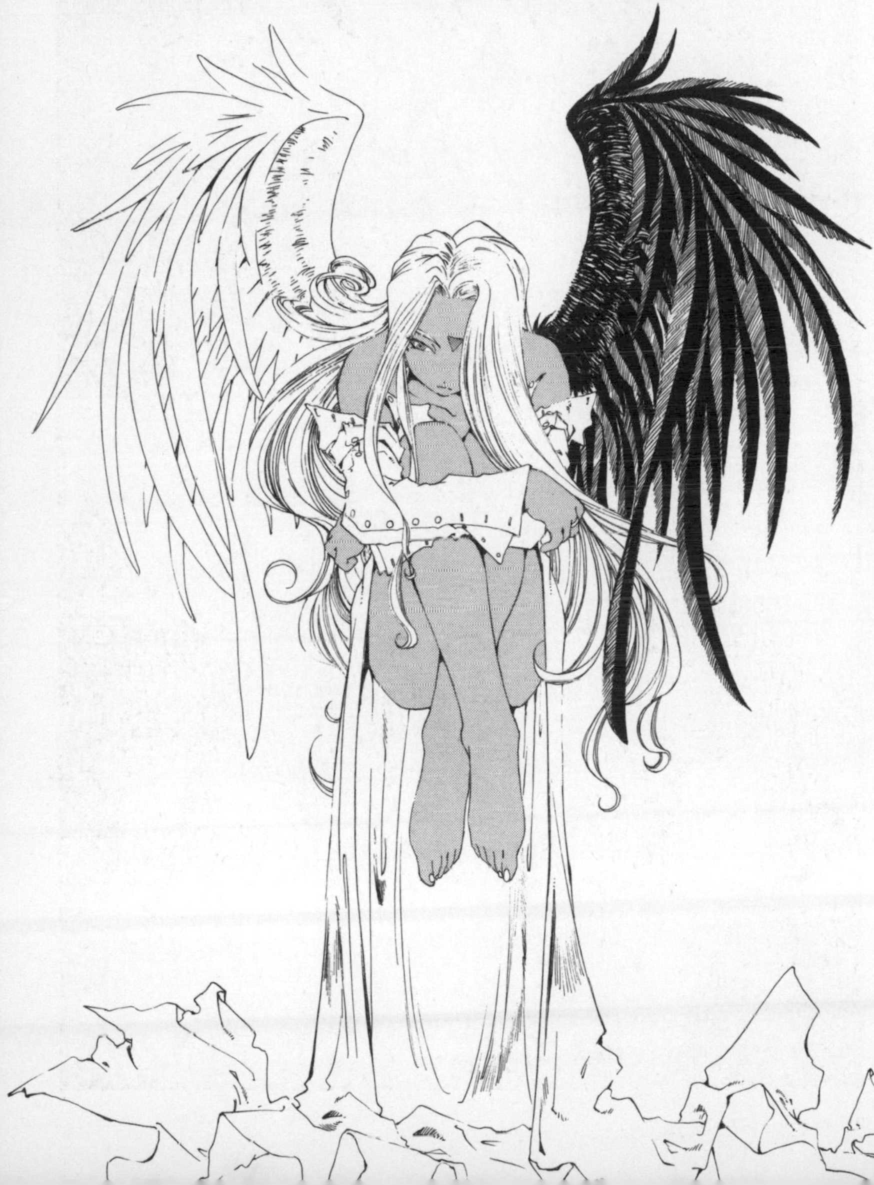

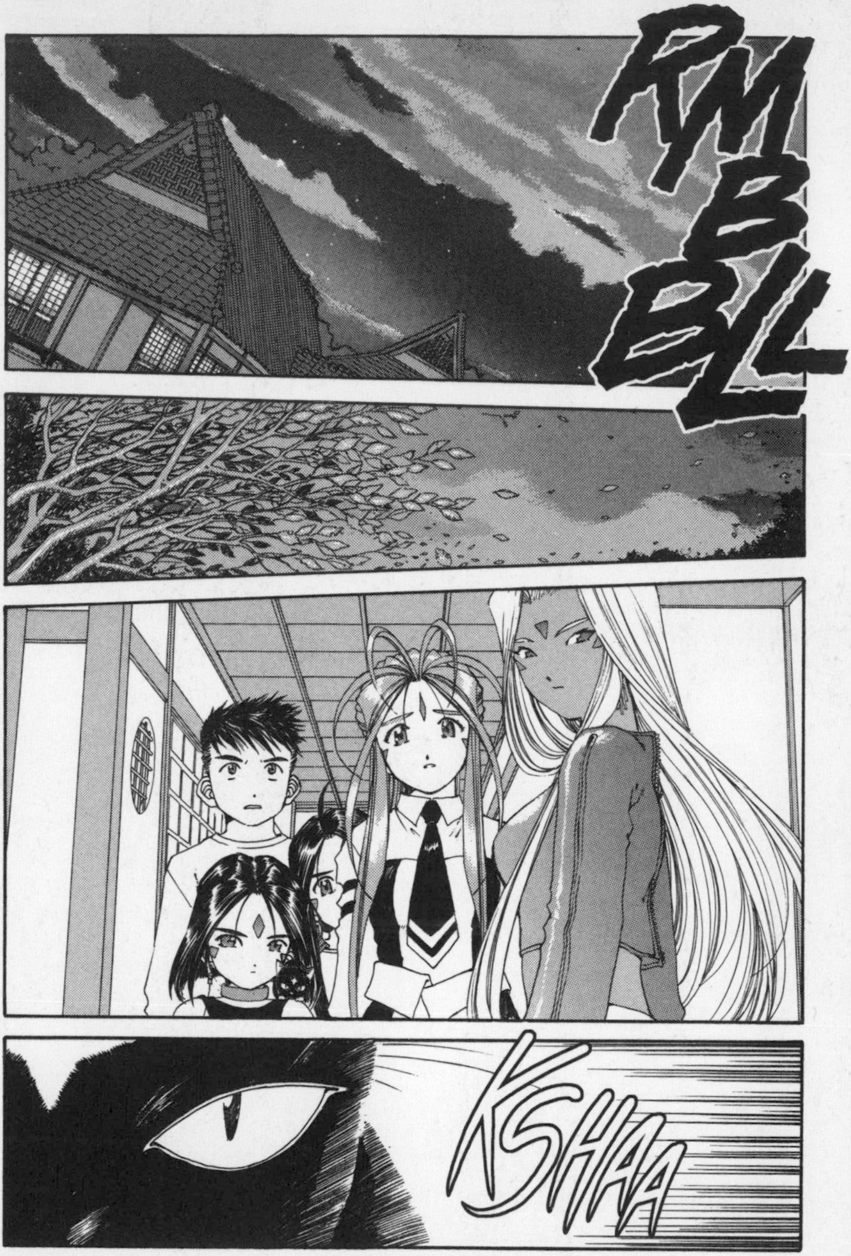
RMBBL
KSHAA

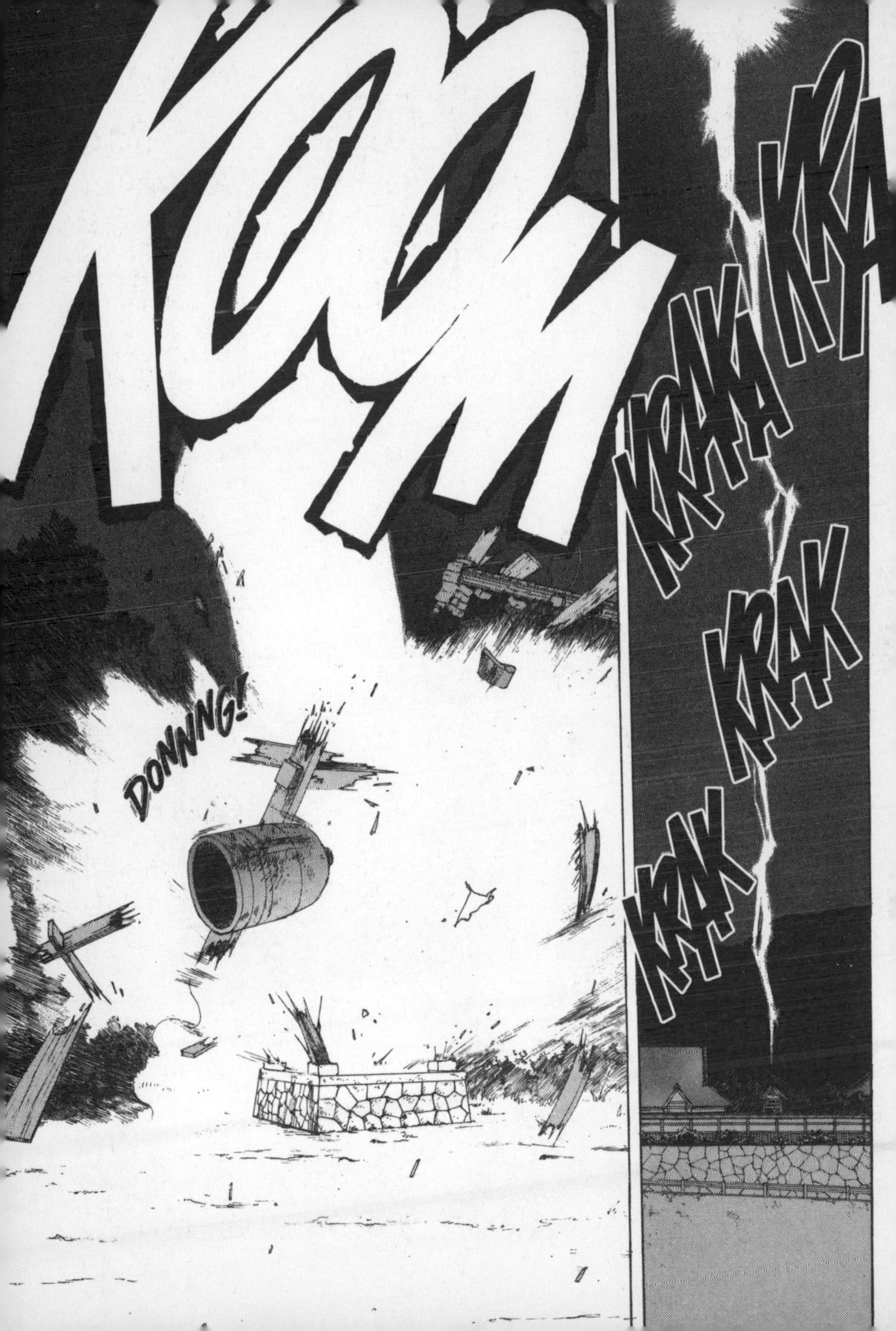
KRAKA KRA
KRAK
KRAK
KOOM
DONNNG!

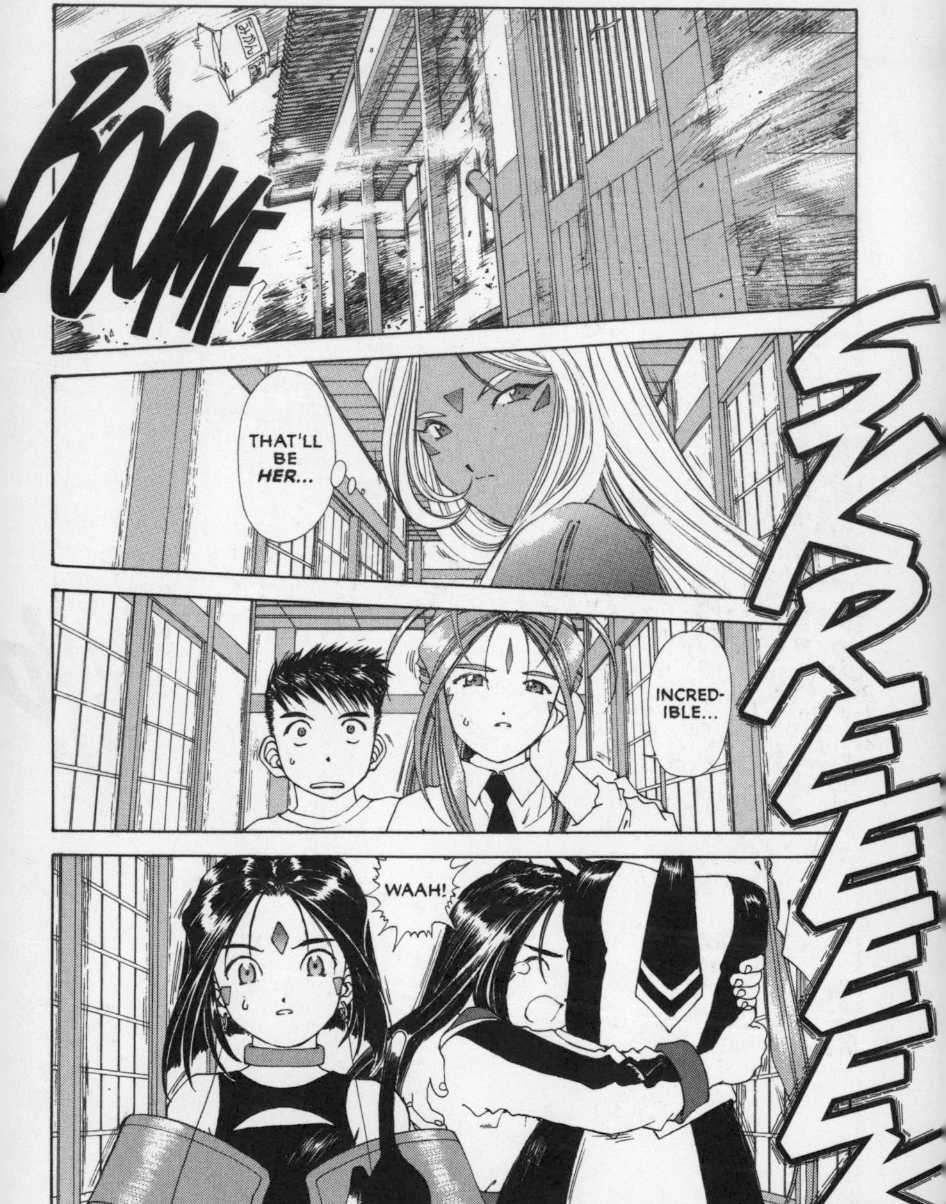
BOOMF
SKREEEEK
THAT'LL BE *HER*...
INCRED-IBLE...
WAAH!

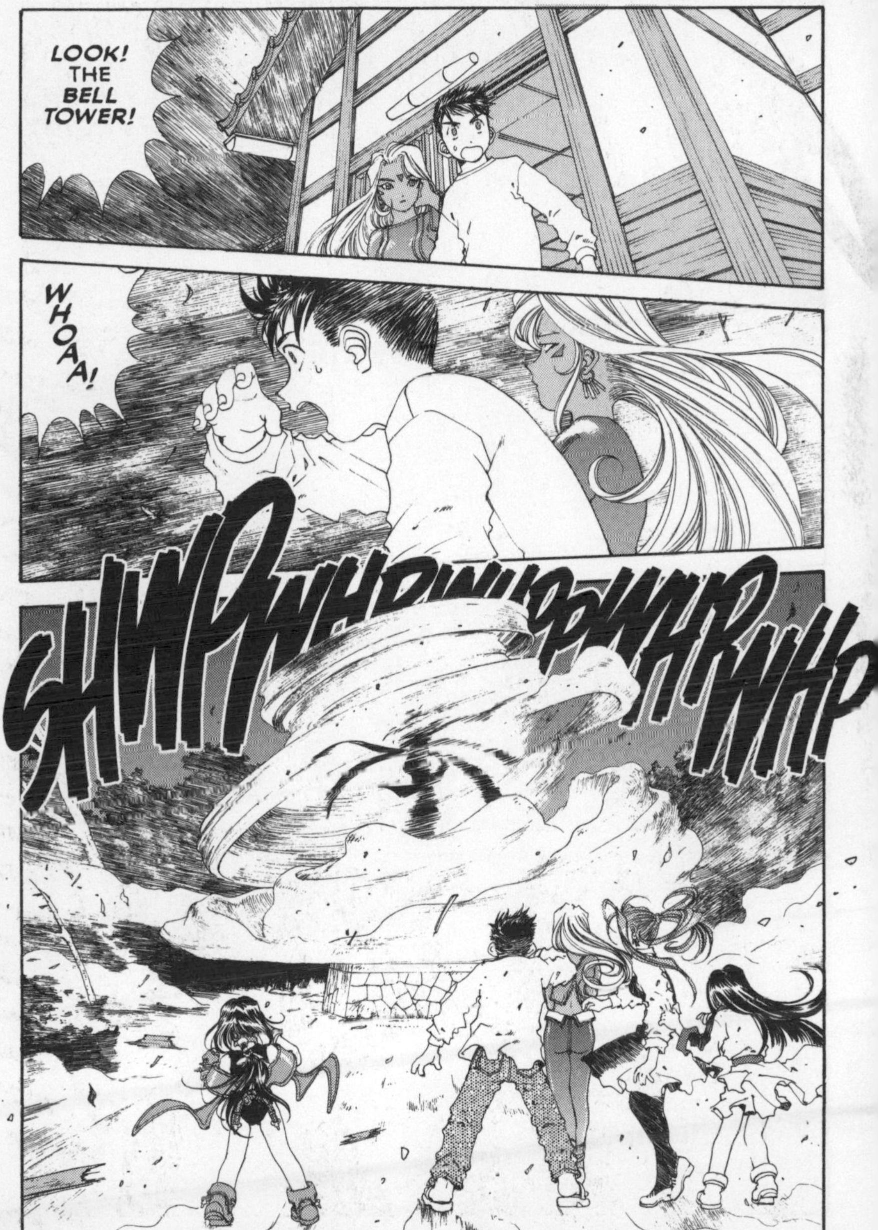
LOOK! THE BELL TOWER!
WHOAA!

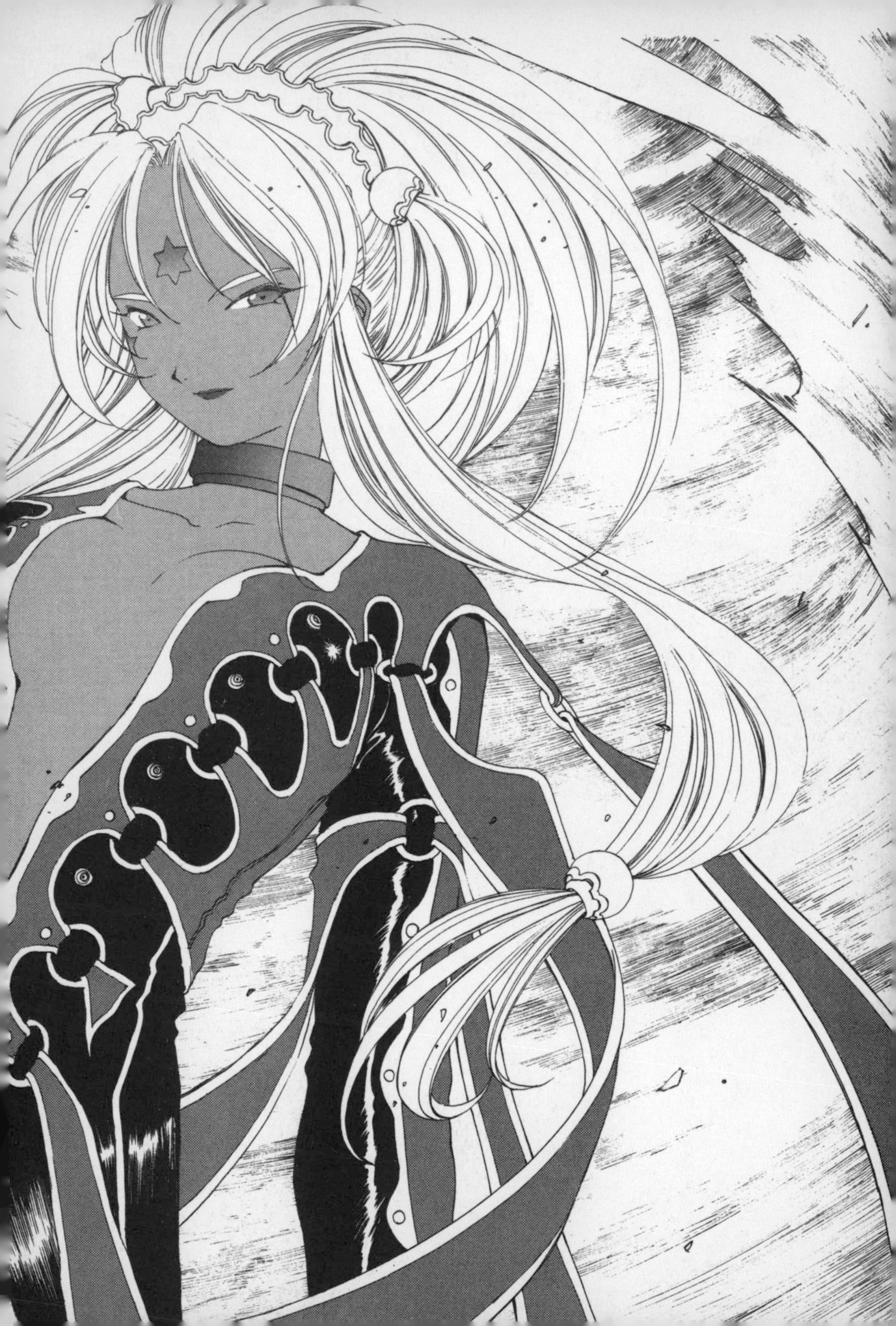

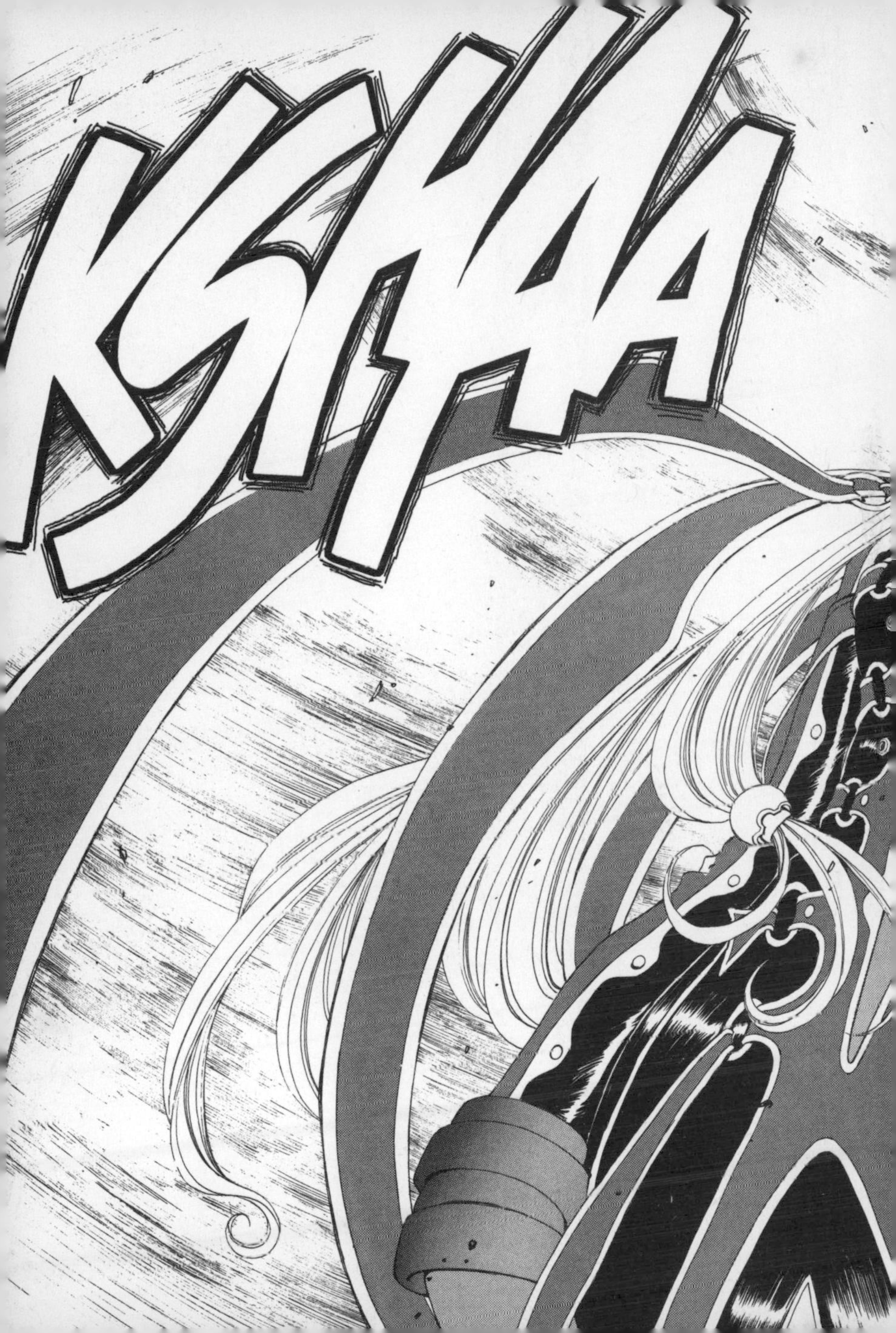
KSHAA

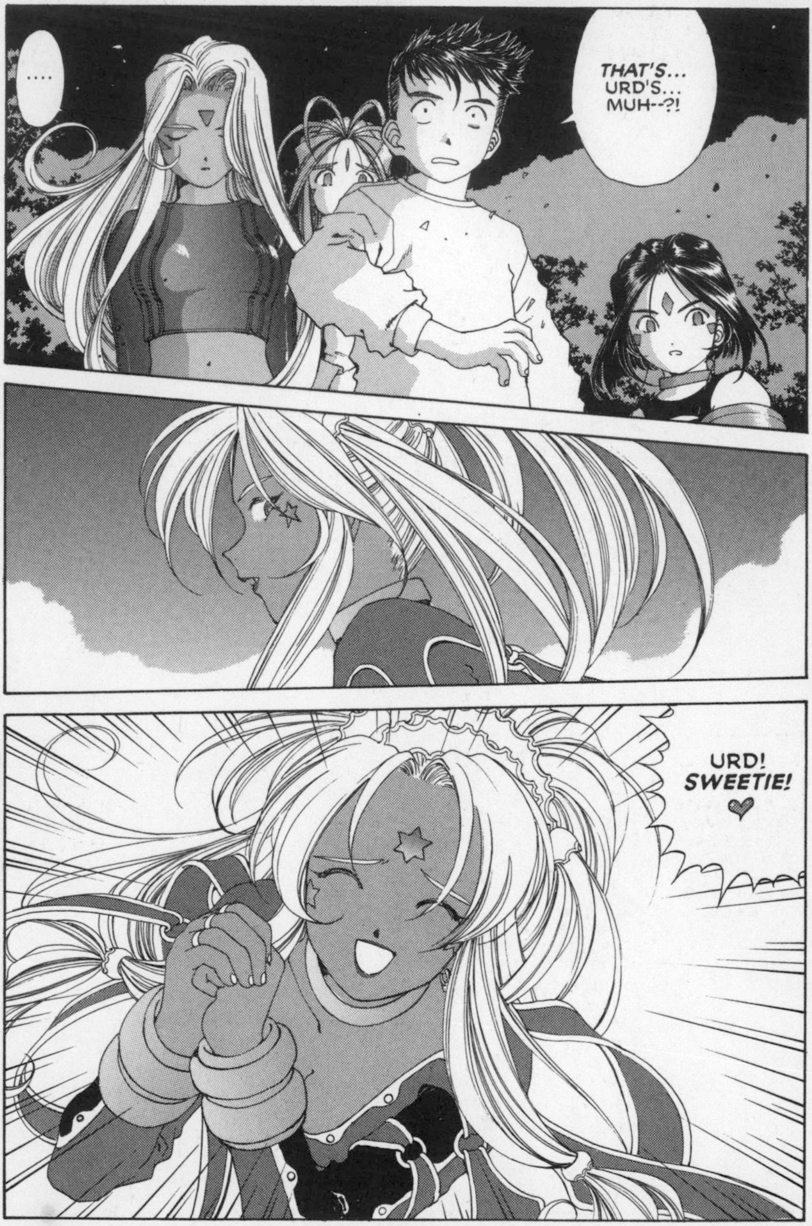
THAT'S... URD'S... MUH--?!
....
URD! SWEETIE!

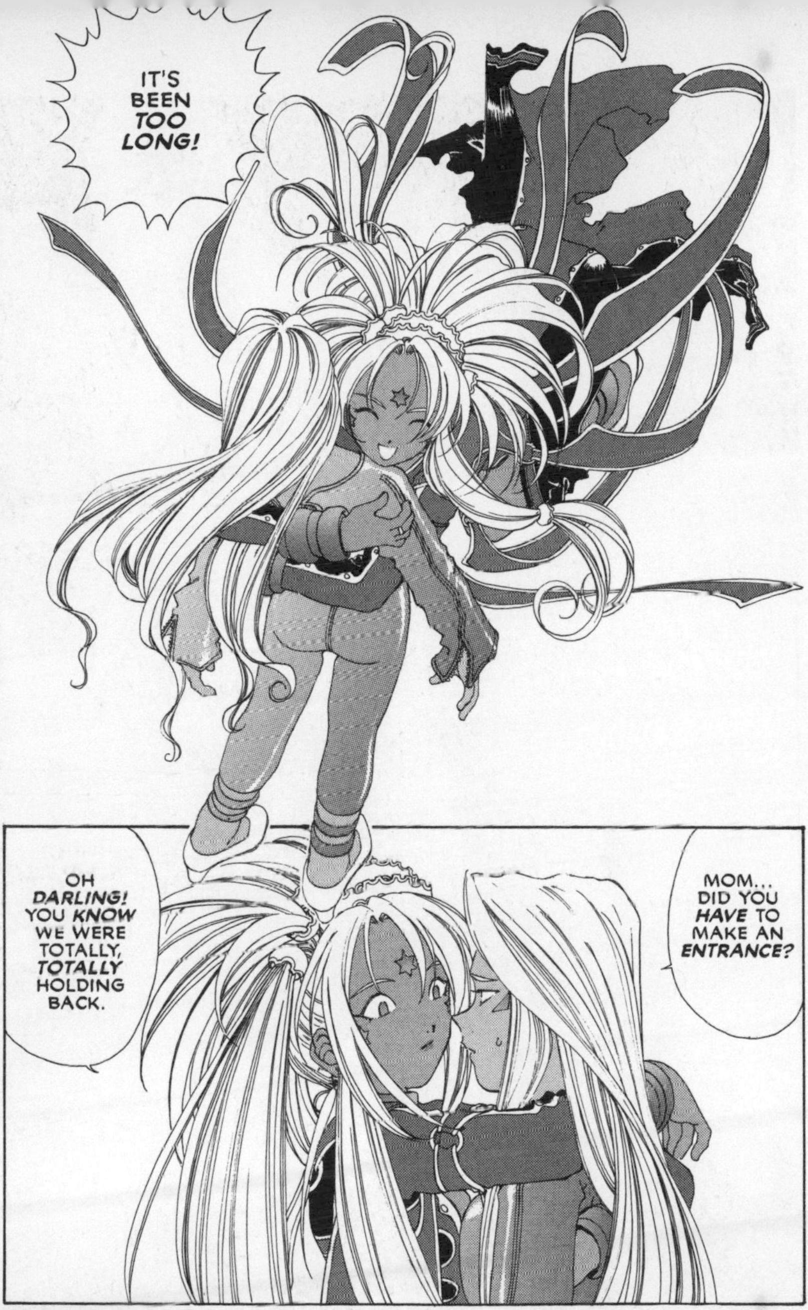
IT'S BEEN TOO LONG!
MOM... DID YOU HAVE TO MAKE AN ENTRANCE?
OH DARLING! YOU KNOW WE WERE TOTALLY, TOTALLY HOLDING BACK.

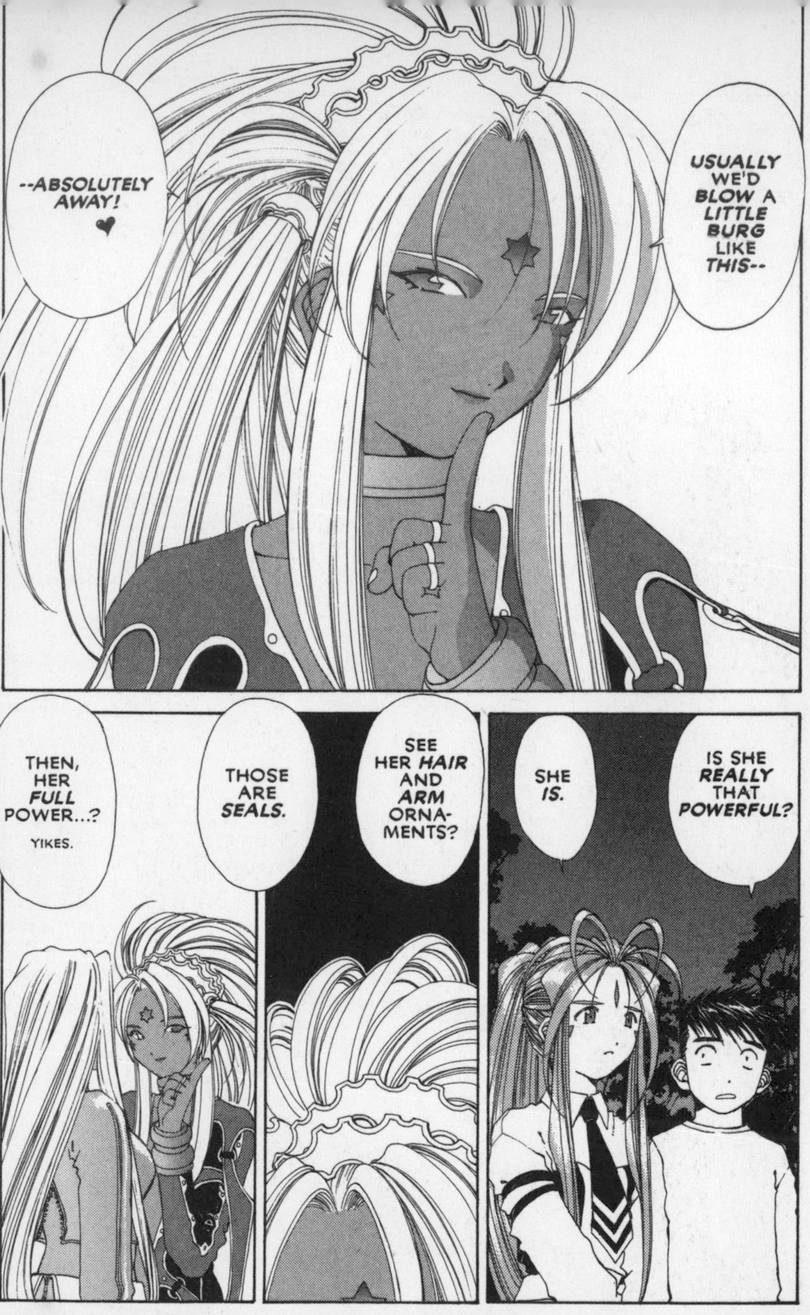
USUALLY WE'D BLOW A LITTLE BURG LIKE THIS--
--ABSOLUTELY AWAY! ♥
IS SHE REALLY THAT POWERFUL?
SHE IS.
SEE HER HAIR AND ARM ORNA-MENTS?
THOSE ARE SEALS.
THEN, HER FULL POWER...?
YIKES.

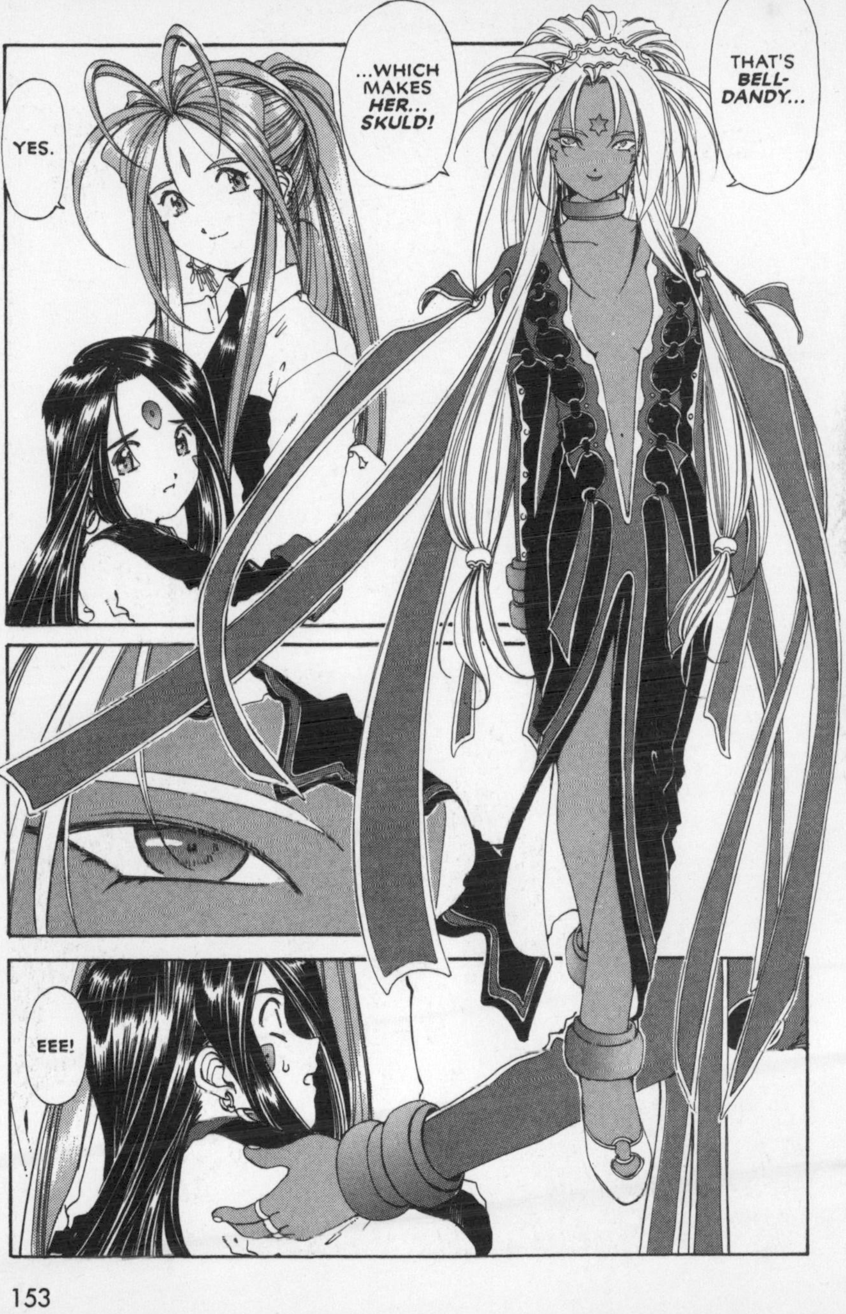
THAT'S BELL-DANDY...
...WHICH MAKES HER... SKULD!
YES.
EEE!

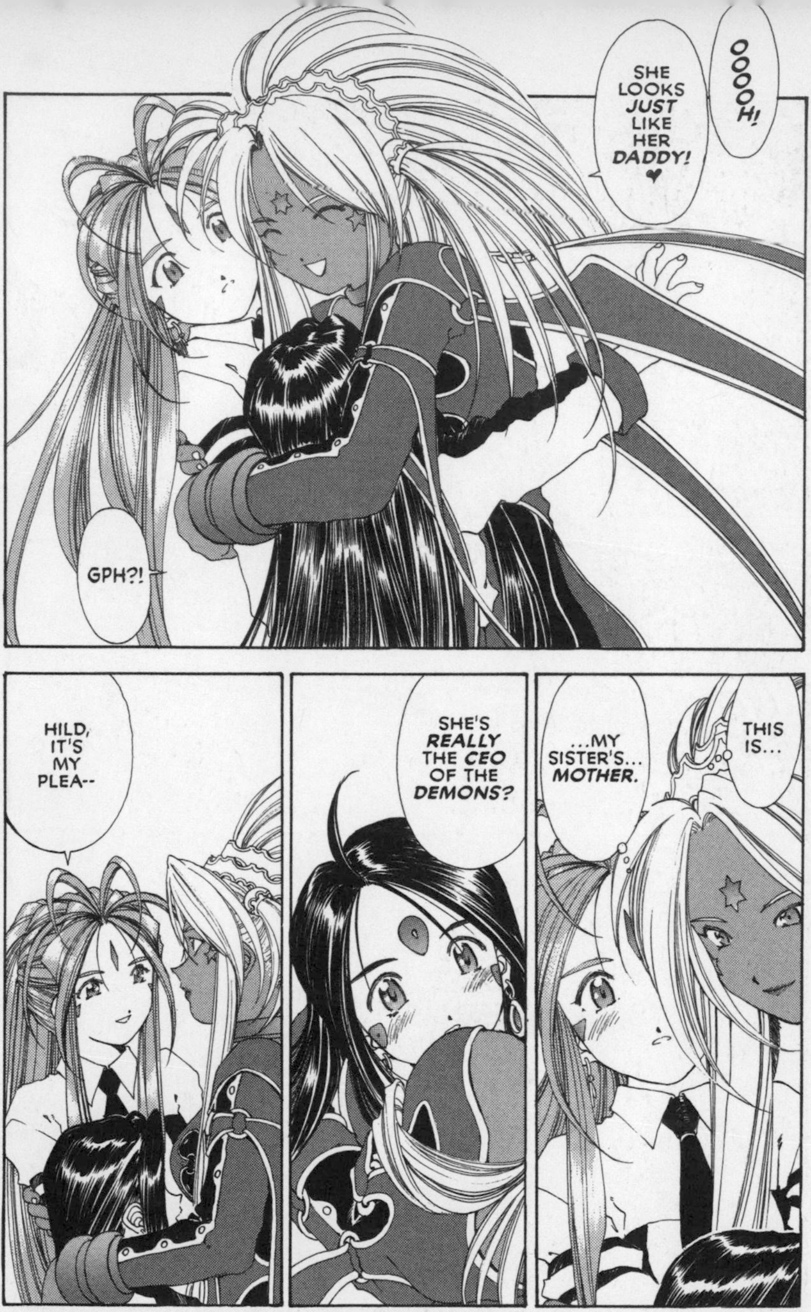
OOOOH!
SHE LOOKS *JUST* LIKE HER *DADDY!* ♥
GPH?!
THIS IS...
...MY SISTER'S... *MOTHER.*
SHE'S *REALLY* THE *CEO* OF THE *DEMONS?*
HILD, IT'S MY PLEA--

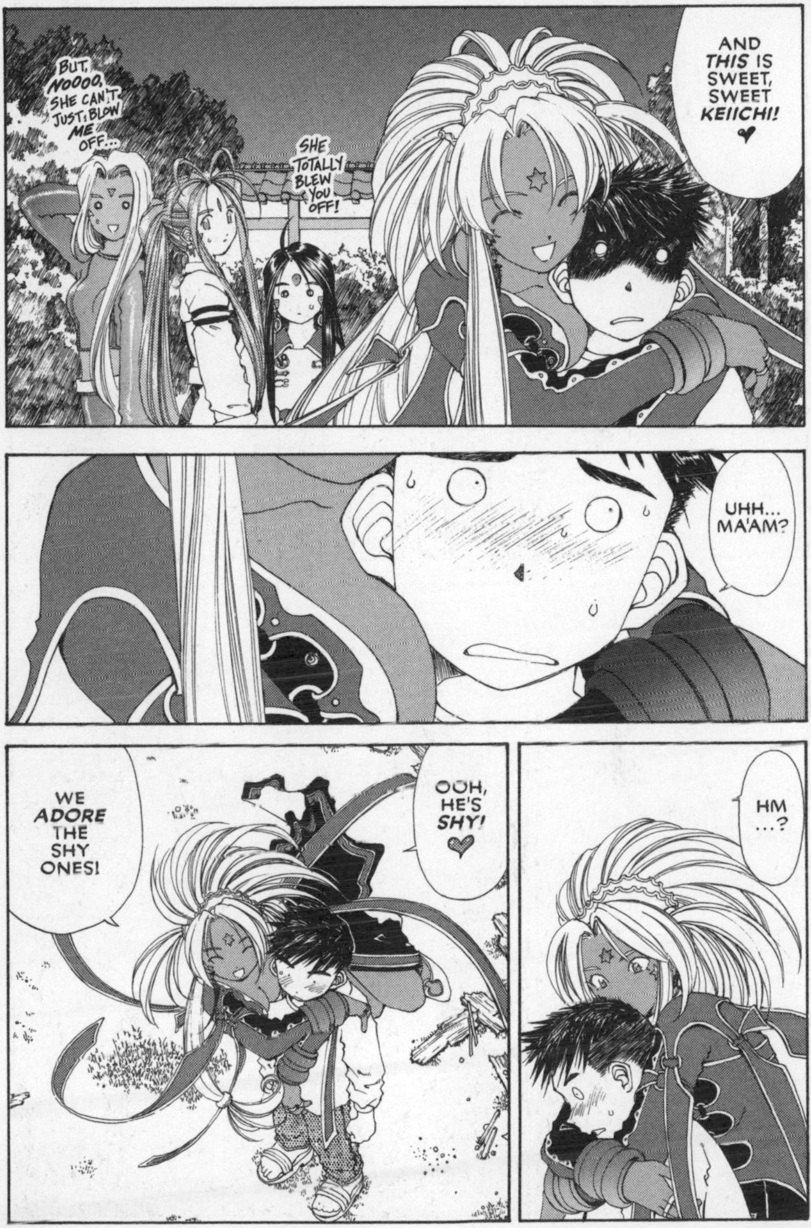
AND THIS IS SWEET, SWEET KEIICHI! ♥
BUT, NOOOO, SHE CAN'T JUST BLOW ME OFF...
SHE TOTALLY BLEW YOU OFF!
UHH... MA'AM?
HM ...?
OOH, HE'S SHY! ♥
WE ADORE THE SHY ONES!

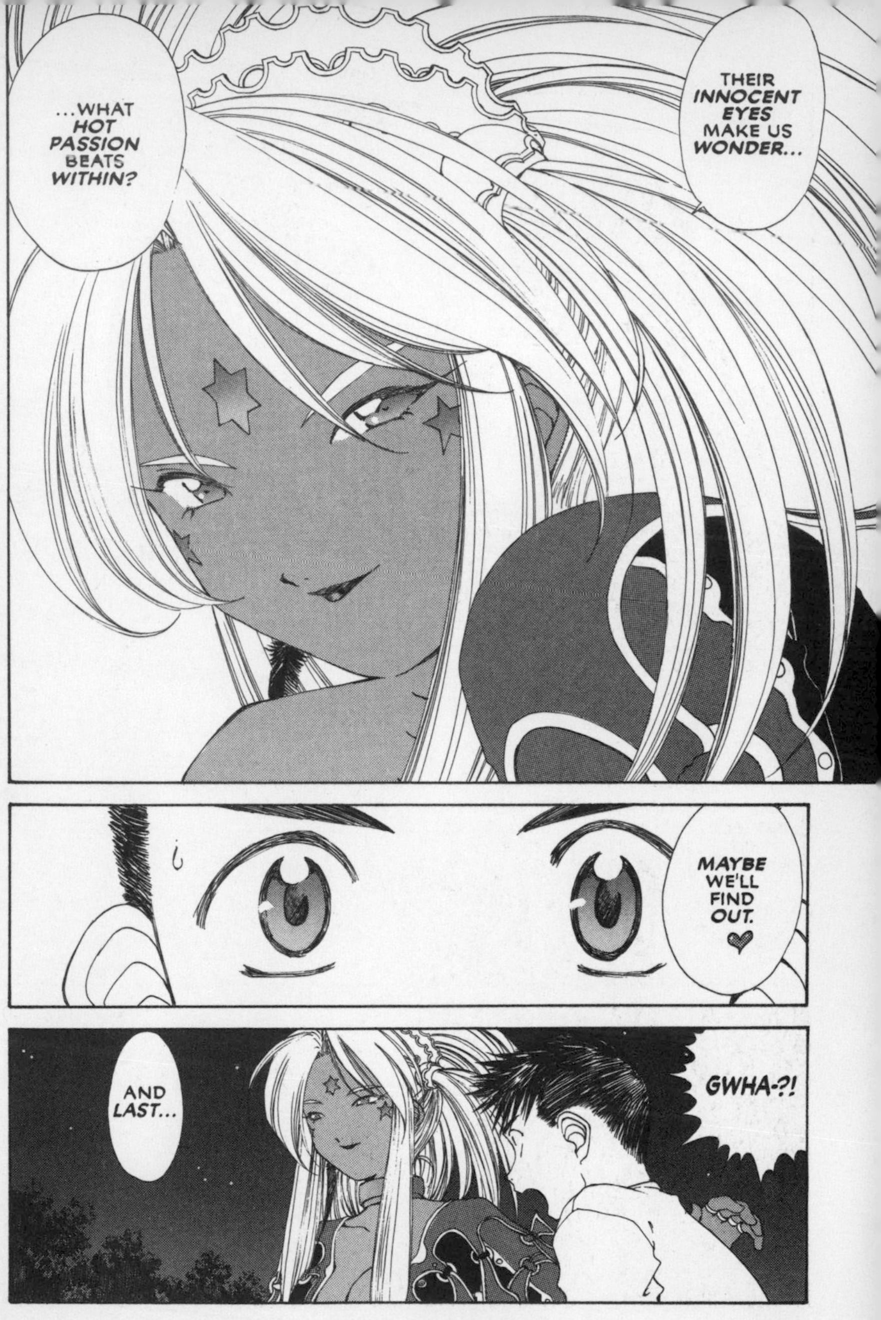
THEIR INNOCENT EYES MAKE US WONDER...
...WHAT HOT PASSION BEATS WITHIN?
MAYBE WE'LL FIND OUT. ♥
GWHA-?!
AND LAST...

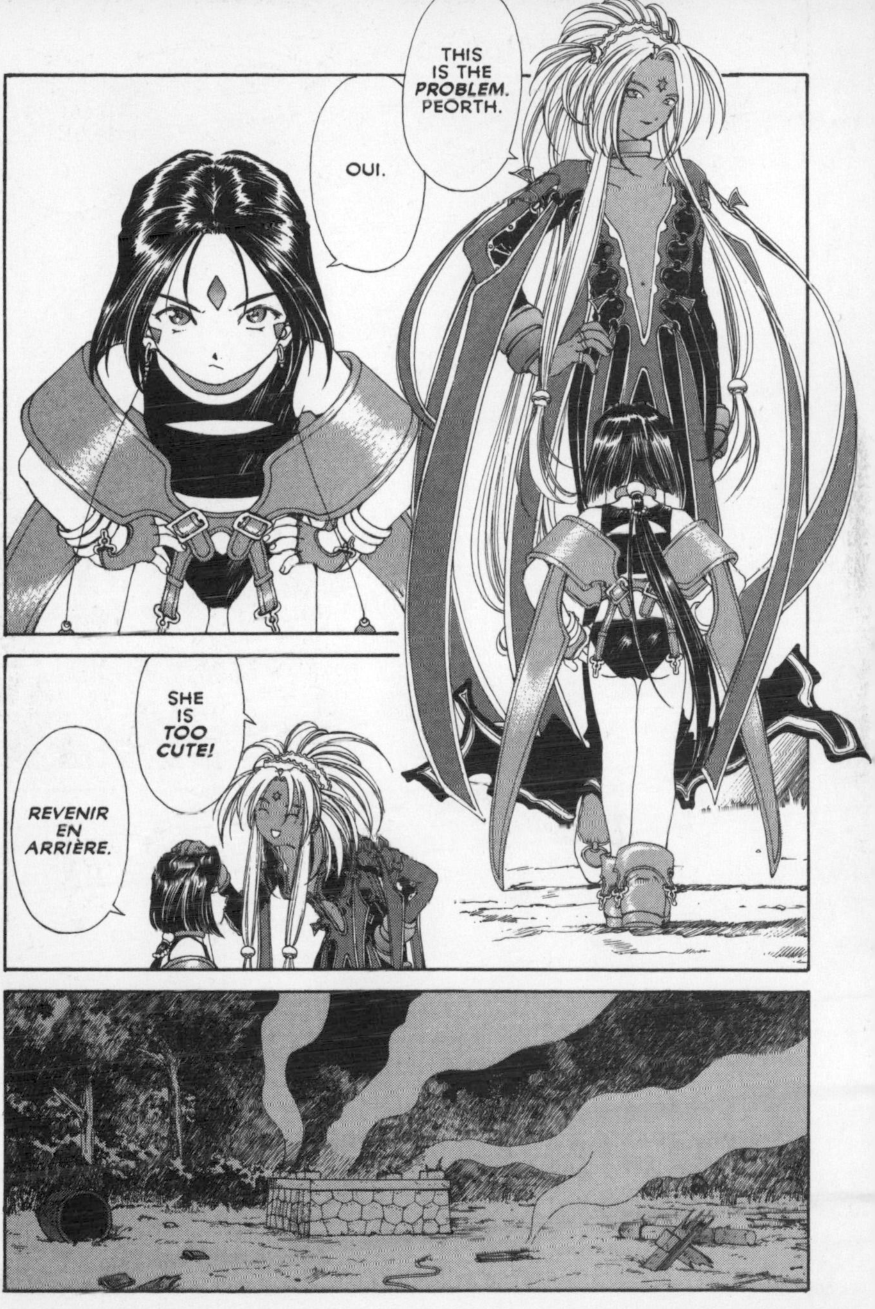
THIS IS THE PROBLEM. PEORTH.
OUI.
SHE IS TOO CUTE!
REVENIR EN ARRIÈRE.

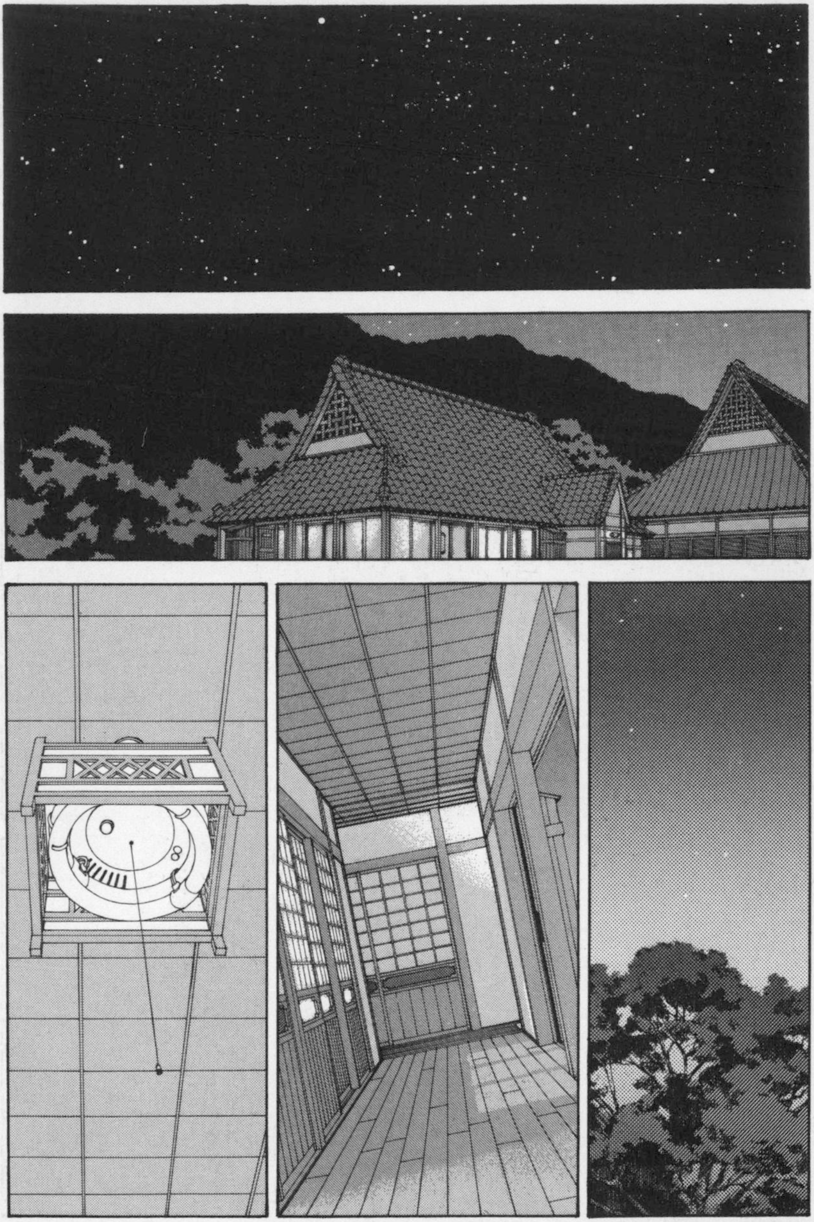

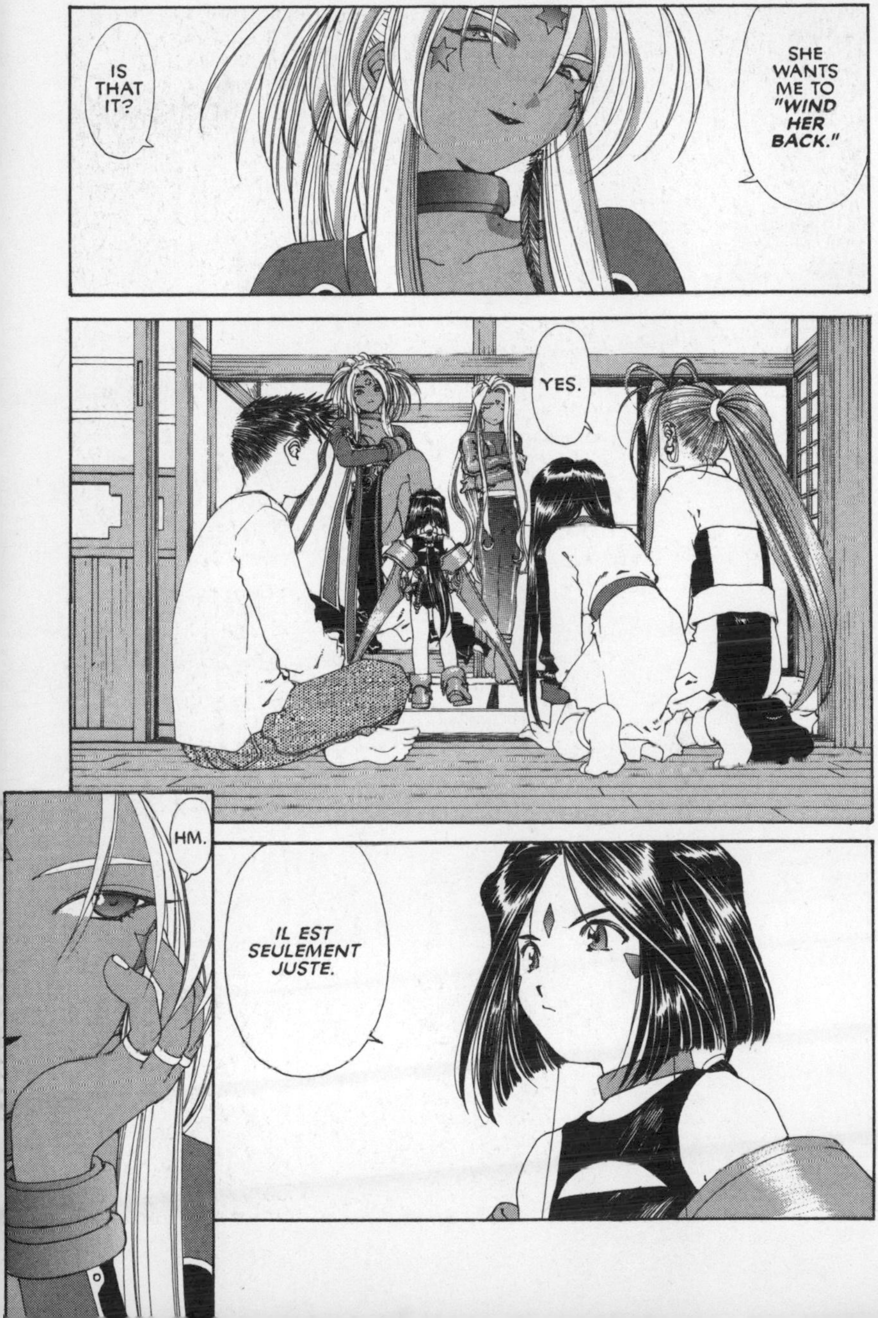
SHE WANTS ME TO "WIND HER BACK."
IS THAT IT?
YES.
IL EST SEULEMENT JUSTE.
HM.

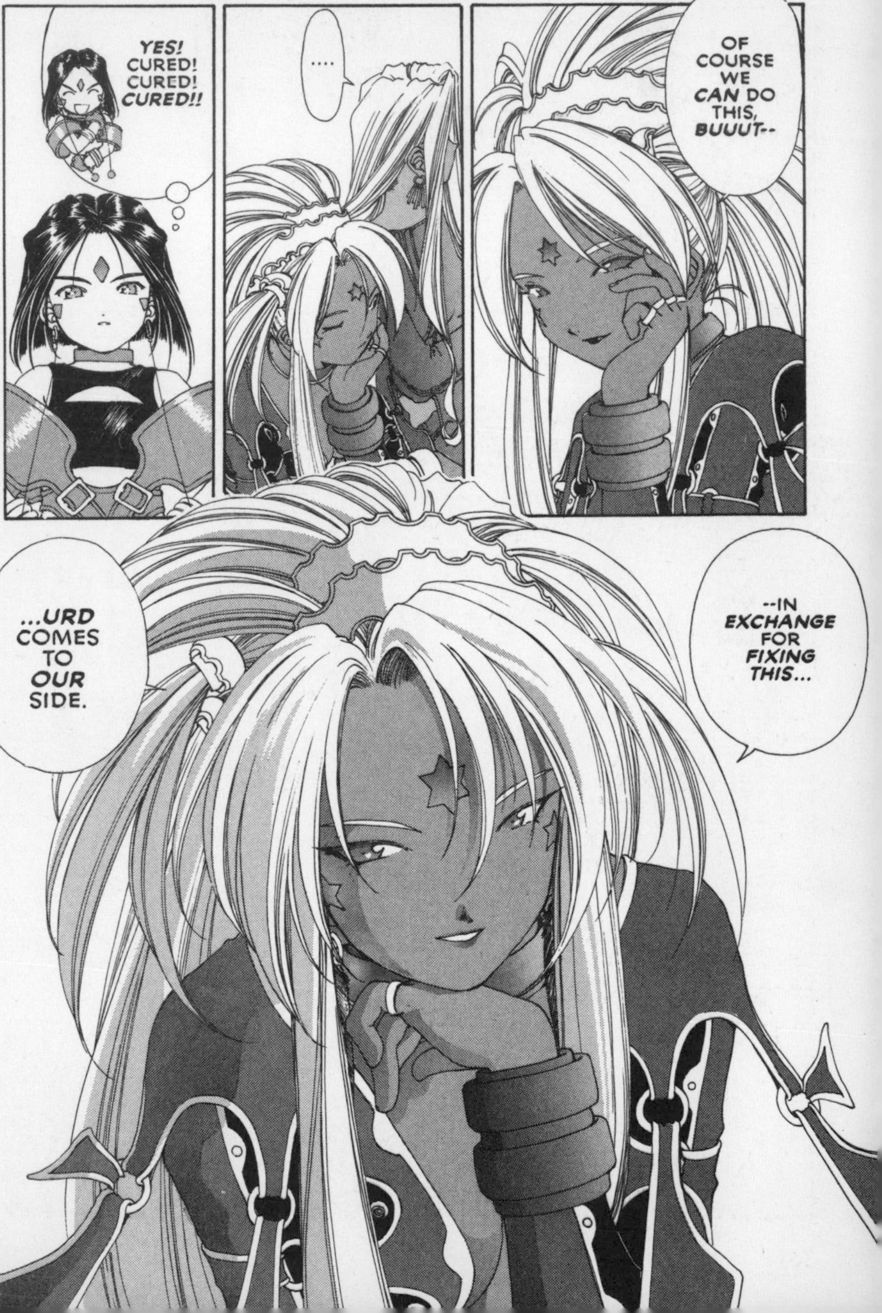
OF COURSE WE CAN DO THIS, BUUUT--
....
YES! CURED! CURED! CURED!!
--IN EXCHANGE FOR FIXING THIS...
...URD COMES TO OUR SIDE.

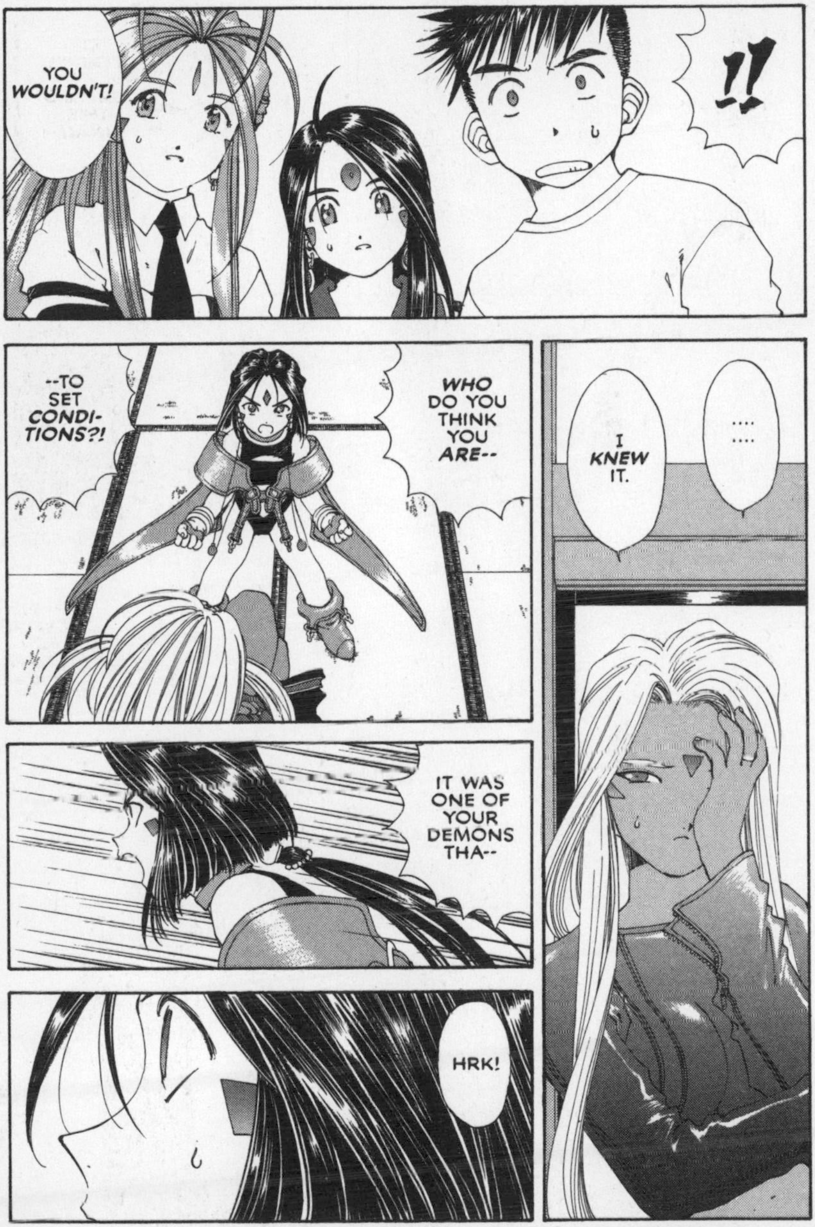
!!
YOU WOULDN'T!
....
....
I KNEW IT.
WHO DO YOU THINK YOU ARE--
--TO SET CONDITIONS?!
IT WAS ONE OF YOUR DEMONS THA--
HRK!

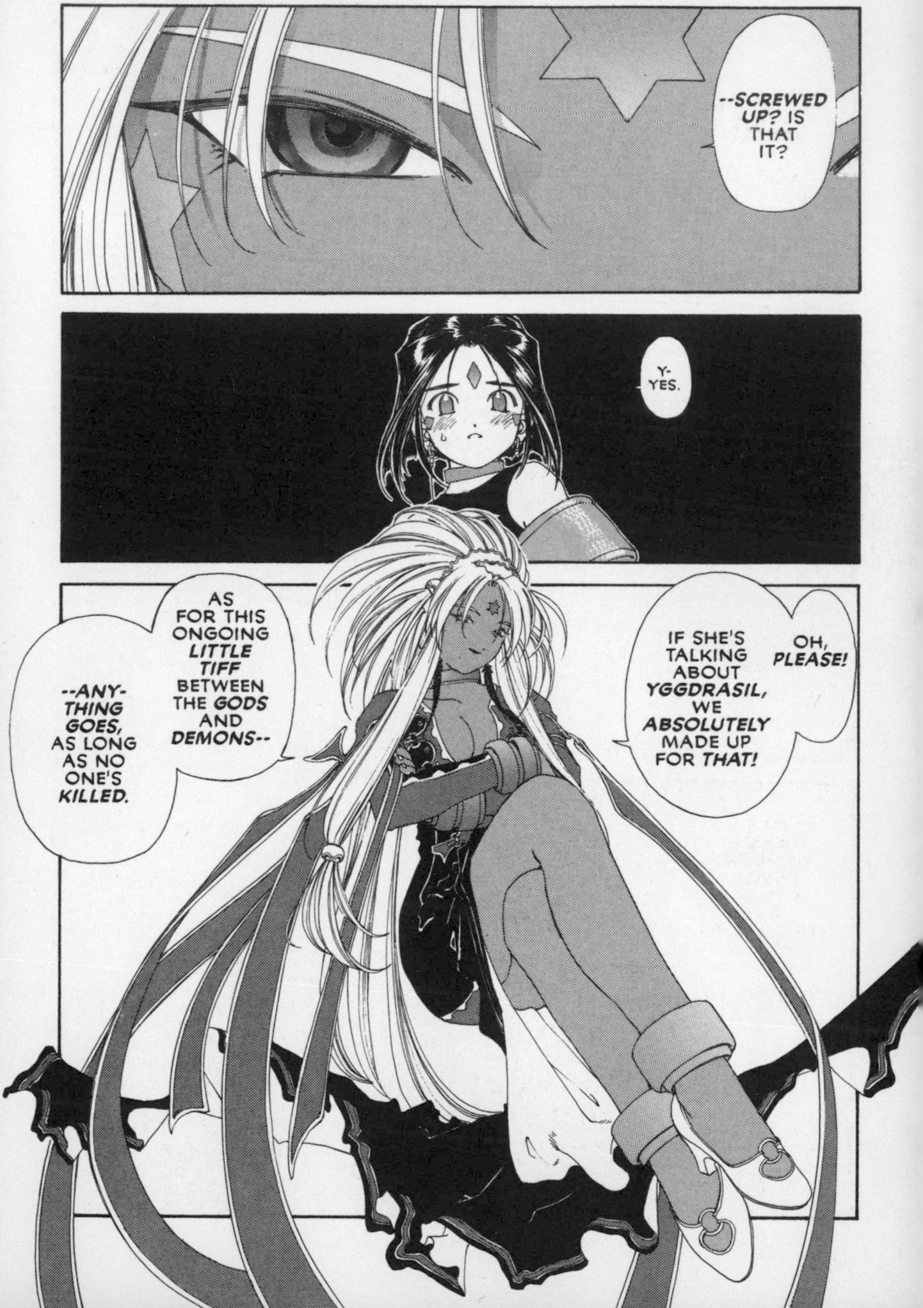
--SCREWED UP? IS THAT IT?
Y- YES.
OH, PLEASE!
IF SHE'S TALKING ABOUT YGGDRASIL, WE ABSOLUTELY MADE UP FOR THAT!
AS FOR THIS ONGOING LITTLE TIFF BETWEEN THE GODS AND DEMONS--
--ANY-THING GOES, AS LONG AS NO ONE'S KILLED.

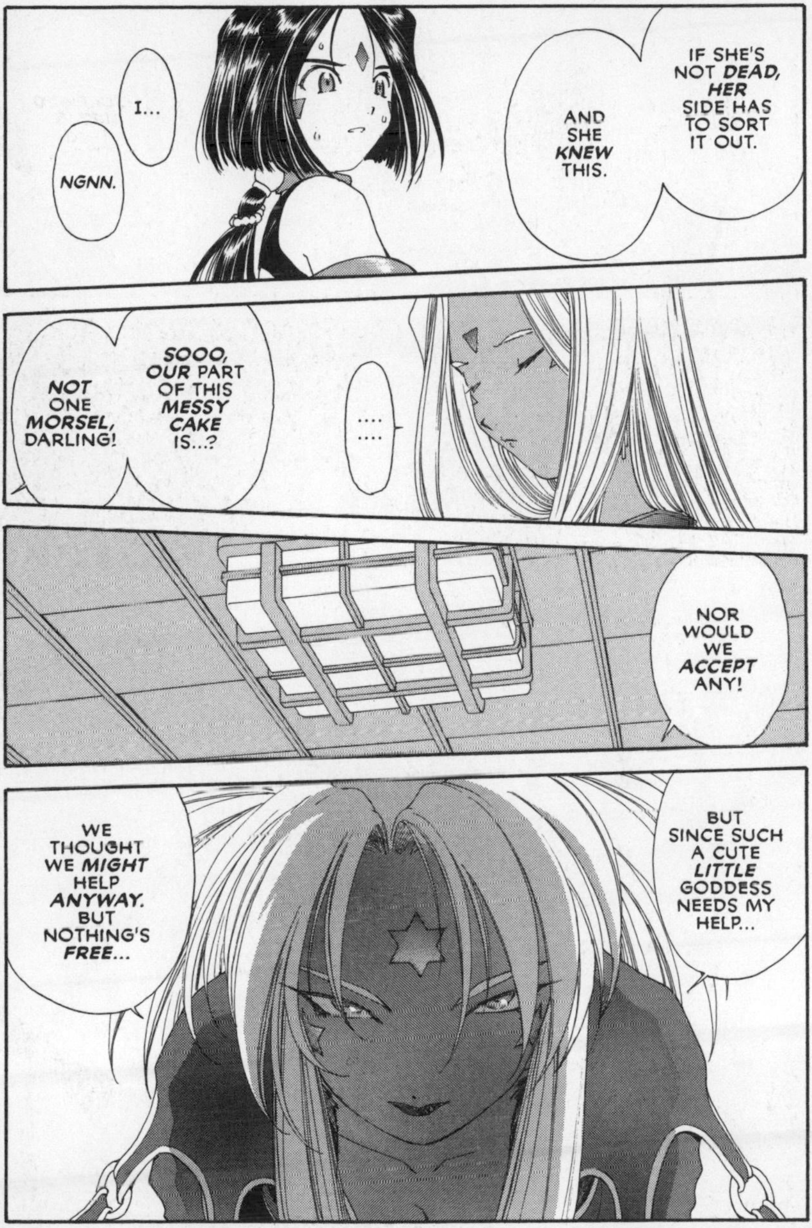
IF SHE'S NOT DEAD, HER SIDE HAS TO SORT IT OUT.
AND SHE KNEW THIS.
I...
NGNN.
....
....
SOOO, OUR PART OF THIS MESSY CAKE IS...?
NOT ONE MORSEL, DARLING!
NOR WOULD WE ACCEPT ANY!
BUT SINCE SUCH A CUTE LITTLE GODDESS NEEDS MY HELP...
WE THOUGHT WE MIGHT HELP ANYWAY. BUT NOTHING'S FREE...

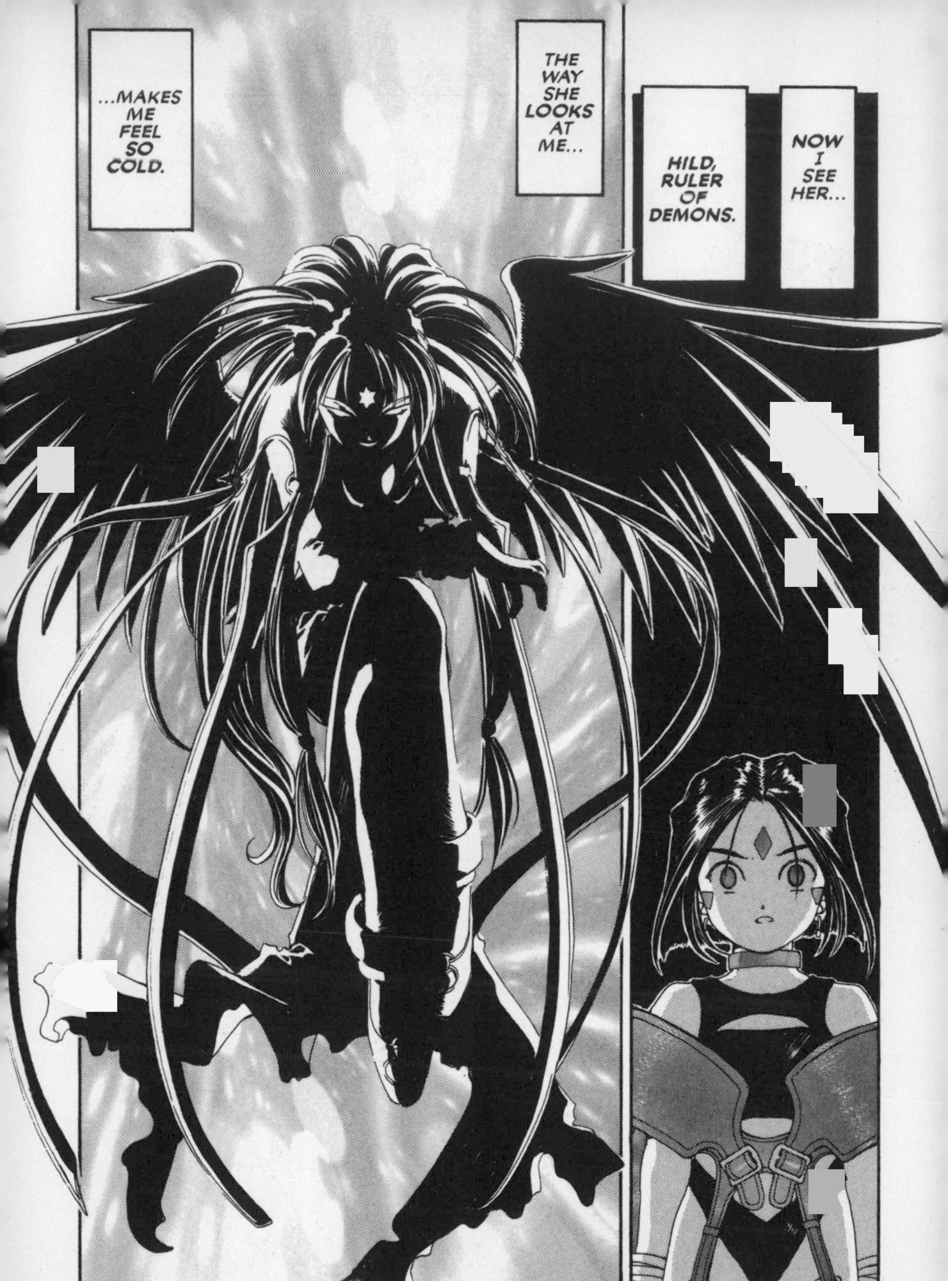
NOW I SEE HER...
HILD, RULER OF DEMONS.
THE WAY SHE LOOKS AT ME...
...MAKES ME FEEL SO COLD.

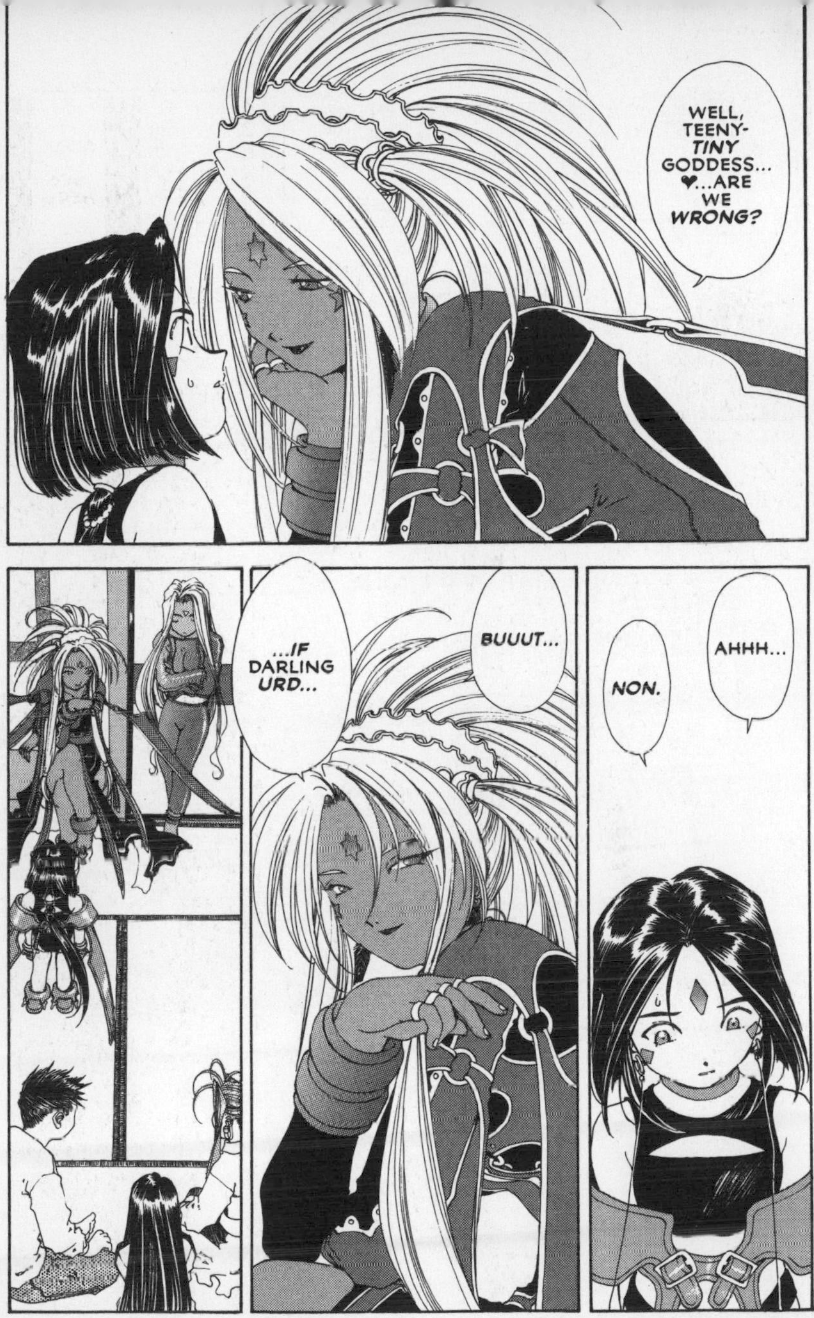
WELL, TEENY-TINY GODDESS... ❤...ARE WE WRONG?
AHHH...
NON.
BUUUT...
...IF DARLING URD...

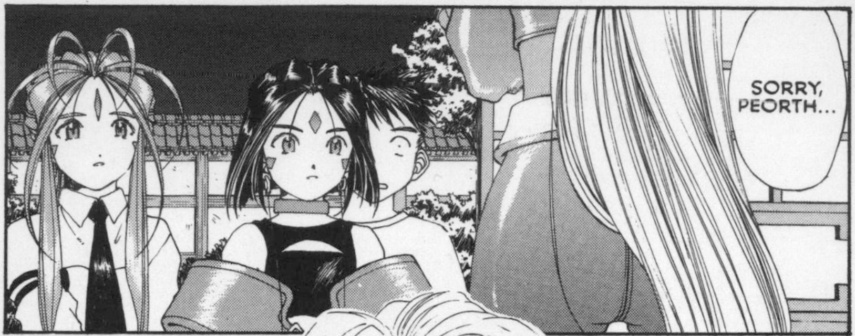
SORRY, PEORTH...

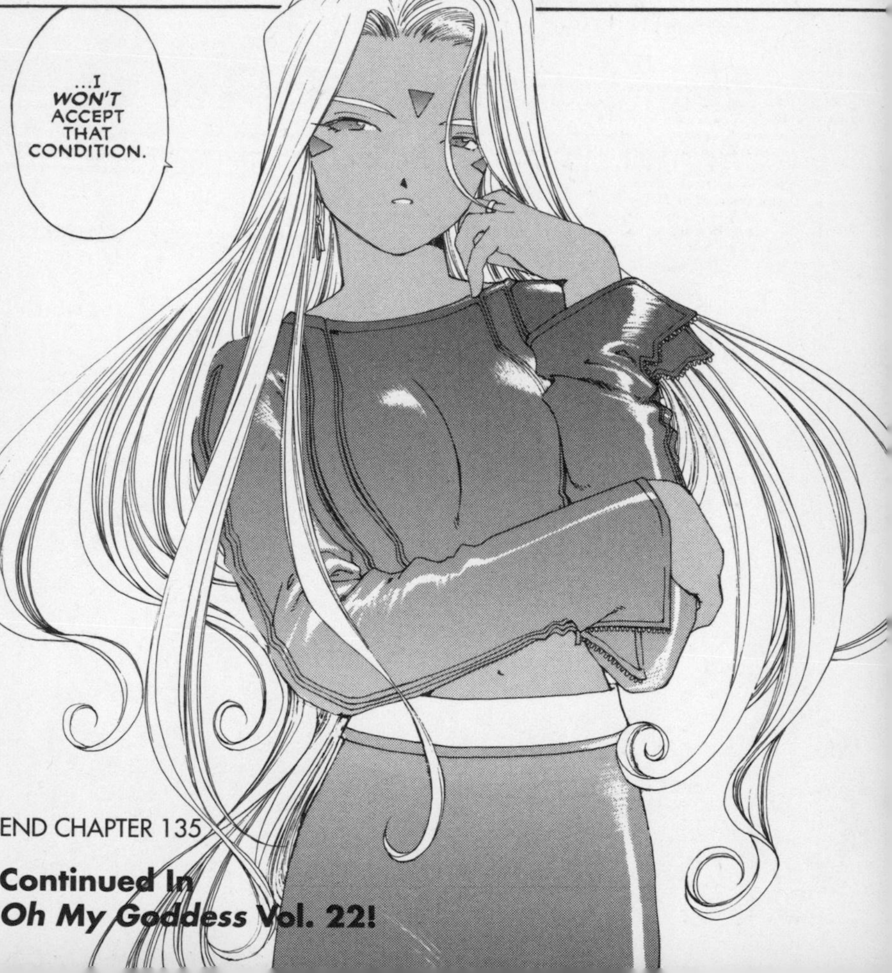
...I *WON'T* ACCEPT THAT CONDITION.

END CHAPTER 135

Continued In *Oh My Goddess* Vol. 22!

EDITOR
Carl Gustav Horn

DESIGNER
Debra Bailey

ART DIRECTOR
Lia Ribacchi

PUBLISHER
Mike Richardson

English-language version
produced by Dark Horse Comics

OH MY GODDESS! Vol. 21

©2005 by Kosuke Fujishima. All rights reserved. First published in Japan by Kodansha, Ltd., Tokyo. English translation rights arranged through Kodansha Ltd. This English-language edition ©2005 by Dark Horse Comics, Inc. All other material ©2005 by Dark Horse Comics, Inc. All rights reserved. No portion of this publication may be reproduced, in any form or by any means, without the express written permission of the copyright holders. Names, characters, places, and incidents featured in this publication are either the product of the author's imagination or are used fictitiously. Any resemblance to actual persons (living or dead), events, institutions, or locales, without satiric intent, is coincidental. Dark Horse Manga™ is a trademark of Dark Horse Comics, Inc. Dark Horse Comics® is a trademark of Dark Horse Comics, Inc., registered in various categories and countries. All rights reserved.

Published by Dark Horse Manga
A division of Dark Horse Comics, Inc.
10956 SE Main Street
Milwaukie, OR 97222
www.darkhorse.com

To find a comics shop in your area,
call the Comic Shop Locator Service
toll-free at 1-888-266 4226

First edition: July 2005
ISBN: 1-59307-334-8

1 3 5 7 9 10 8 6 4 2

Printed in Canada

letters to the ENCHANTRESS

10956 SE Main Street, Milwaukie, Oregon 97222
omg@darkhorse.com • www.darkhorse.com

NOTE: Full addresses and e-mail addresses will not be printed, unless you ask! All fan artwork, letters, and e-mails submitted become the property of Dark Horse Comics.

Welcome back to the English-language edition of Kosuke Fujishima's *Oh My Goddess!* Before we get to readers' letters, a few words on the occasion of this, the big switch (if you're reading Vol. 21 from left-to-right out of force of habit, this section will explain matters ^_^) as to where *Oh My Goddess!* came from, and where it's going to.

OMG! first appeared in English from Dark Horse as a monthly comic book in August of 1994. Skipping a few months here and there, *OMG!* ran just over a decade in the comics format, up to issue #112, released in September 2004—a marathon matched by few manga in the U.S., in any format, before or since. Although the pace seems slow compared to today's rapidly released manga graphic novels, it's worth noting that one chapter a month is also the "natural" pace of release for *OMG!* in Japan, where it appears (alongside such other Dark Horse manga titles as *Exaxxion, Gunsmith Cats, Blade of the Immortal, Seraphic Feather,* and *Shadow Star*) in Kodansha's monthly magazine *Afternoon*.

Between 1996 and 2005, the stories from the monthly comics were collected by Dark Horse into 19 separate graphic novels (the last one having the number "19/20" on it— see below). In order, these were Vol. 1: *Wrong Number;* Vol. 2: *Leader of the Pack;* Vol. 3: *Final Exam;* Vol. 4: *Love Potion No. 9;* Vol. 5: *Sympathy For The Devil;* Vol. 6: *Terrible Master Urd;* Vol. 7: *The Queen of Vengeance;* Vol. 8: *Mara Strikes Back!;* Vol. 9: *Ninja Master;* Vol. 10: *Miss Keiichi;* Vol. 11: *The Devil in Miss Urd;* Vol. 12: *The Fourth Goddess;* Vol. 13: *Childhood's End;* Vol. 14: *Queen Sayoko;* Vol. 15: *Hand In Hand;* Vol. 16: *Mystery Child;* Vol. 17: *Traveler;* Vol. 18: *The Phantom Racer;* and Vol. 19/20: *Sora Unchained.*

All of those monthly issues and volumes mentioned above—indeed, everything in the story before Vol. 21—were done "flopped," that is, reading Western-style, left-to-right. Starting here, with Vol. 21, and from this point forward, the story will be done "unflopped," that is, reading as it was originally printed in Japan, right-to-left.

If you've been reading the Dark Horse edition of *OMG!* before, the most important thing to know is that this book, Vol. 21, is a direct continuation of the story from the last volume in the series published in Western (that is, "flopped") reading order, January 2005's *Oh My Goddess! Vol. 19/20: Sora Unchained.* You haven't missed a thing by going from 19/20 straight to 21.

Why "19/20"? While technically, as mentioned above, it was the 19th volume of *Oh My Goddess!* published by Dark Horse, *Sora Unchained* contained all the chapters of the story that ran in the 20th volume of *OMG!* as published in Japan. It's not that any Japanese volumes have been "skipped," story-wise, but that Dark Horse traditionally divvied up the *OMG!* chapters by story arc, unlike the Japanese original volumes, which often end in the middle of a story arc.

That means previous Dark Horse *OMG!* volumes have always contained a run of chapters that, in Japan, were spread out over two or even three volumes. For example, *Sora Unchained* may have been Dark Horse's 19th volume of *Oh My Goddess!*, but most of its material actually ran in the Japanese Vol. 20, with only the last two chapters of the Japanese Vol. 19 appearing in *Sora Unchained.*

The earlier chapters of the Japanese Vol. 19, by the way, appeared in Dark Horse's Vol. 18: *The Phantom Racer*—which also contained the last three chapters of the Japanese Vol. 18. So in reality, *The Phantom Racer,* like *Sora Unchained,* could have had a "split" number, too—in this case, *The Phantom Racer* would have been Vol.18/19. The same would have been true of almost every single volume of the previous edition of *OMG!*— Vol. 17: *Traveler* contained Japanese Vol. 17/18, Vol. 16: *Mystery Child,* contained Japanese Vol. 16/17...and so on, going back to the very beginning.

Of course, the fact that one Dark Horse volume of *Oh My Goddess!* almost always contained parts of two Japanese volumes (the single exception was the very first Vol. 1: *Wrong Number,* which only contained stories from the Japanese Vol. 1—but not the Japanese Vol. 1's last chapter, which became the starting point of Vol. 2: *Leader of the Pack,* and...you get the picture) was, practically speaking, irrelevant, as long as no stories were left out, and all the chapters were run in the correct order (the monthly issues *did* originally have some chapters out of order, but not the actual collected volumes).

AT LAST: THE POINT

The whole issue only becomes relevant at this time, because in addition to doing all future volumes of *Oh My Goddess!* right to-left, Dark Horse also is switching to be in sync with the content of the Japanese volumes. Therefore, what's in this book, *OMG!* Vol. 21, is exactly what's in the original Japanese Vol. 21. And *that's* why *Sora Unchained,* the 19th Dark Horse volume, had a "19/20" on it, as a reminder it also contains the Japanese Vol. 20. We felt that if we just called it "Vol. 19" and had the next one be "Vol. 21," people would naturally think they'd missed part of the story—which isn't true.

Well, that was simple. ^_^ The bottom line is that you're not missing any of the story by going from *Sora Unchained* to Vol. 21. The last chapter in *Sora Unchained,* "The Endless Battle, Part Two," is the 129th chapter in *Oh My Goddess!* The first chapter in Vol. 21, "The Devil Inside," is the 130th chapter. This, of course, brings up another difference you'll notice—in the original Japanese, the various story chapters of *OMG!* had not only titles, but were numbered in order. From now on, those numbers will be included with the chapter titles. Conversely, in the original Japanese editions, the volumes themselves only had numbers, but no titles. So Vol. 19/20: *Sora Unchained* was also the last Dark Horse volume with a title—Vol. 21 is just plain "Vol. 21."

Now that we're in sync with the Japanese arrangement of the series from Vol. 21 on, Dark Horse plans to also go back and re-release all the previous parts of *Oh My Goddess!*—that is, the stuff from Vol. 1: *Wrong Number* to Vol. 19/20: *Sora Unchained.* This time, however, the stories will be packaged in the same format as Vol. 21—right-to-left, broken up as the original Japanese volumes were, and with the same changes in titling and format mentioned above.

In October this program will begin with *Oh My Goddess* Vol. 1. At that point Dark Horse will switch off between "new" and "old" volumes every two months. So, in December will come *OMG!* Vol. 22; in February 2006, *OMG!* Vol. 2; in April *OMG!* Vol. 23, and so forth. The idea is to serve both those who are already established readers of *OMG!*, and those readers just discovering the story.

Hopefully I haven't made this explanation more complicated than it needs to be, and if you have any specific questions, please don't hesitate to contact *Letters to the Enchantress* by post or e-mail. That's what I'm here for. That, and making coffee that looks and tastes like the soil of the Mississippi Delta.

Having welcomed back the *Oh My Goddess!* readers, I would like to express special appreciation for the "Goddess Trio" that put the series together: translators Dana Lewis and Lea Hernandez (please note that *Sora Unchained*'s credit of Dana Lewis and Toren Smith was incorrect; rather, it should have said "Dana Lewis & Lea Hernandez," Lea having joined the staff with that volume) and lettering and touch-up ace Susie Lee, who works with Betty Dong and Tom2K.

The fact *OMG!* has been read in the West now for more than ten years is testimony also to their work and the fine adaptation it has produced. The truth is, despite all the changes in format described above, I really wished to change as little as possible about the *OMG!* English-language readers have come to love. That's why I'm grateful that Dana, Lea, and Susie were able to stay on and carry this work into *Oh My Goddess!*'s new era. There's a lot of stories, after all, still to be told!

Thanks also to those inside Dark Horse and out who since 1994 have brought *OMG!* to print: editors Philip Simon, Chris Warner, Lynn Adair, Mike Hansen, Tim Ervin-Gore, Rachel Penn, Dave Chipps, Peet Janes, Greg Vest, and Suzanne Taylor; collection designers Amy Arendts, Debra Bailey, and Lani Schreibstein; art directors Lia Ribacchi, Marx Cox, Julie Eggers, Brian Gogolin, and April Johnson; lettering and touch-up artists Tom Orzechowski, L. Lois Buhalis, Jason Hvam, and Digital Chameleon, and translator Alan Gleason.

This manga, like so many others, is here because of Studio Proteus's Toren Smith, whom I thank for past, present, and future.

> Sincerely yours,
> Carl Gustav Horn
> Editor, *Oh My Goddess!*

P.S. In addition to the nineteen "old style" *OMG!* graphic novels, there's also a one-shot *Oh My Goddess!* graphic novel, *Adventures of the Mini-Goddesses,* which collects the four-panel gag strips that ran as bonus features in some of the early volumes of the Japanese *OMG!* These strips aren't part of the regular story continuity, and were not included in the "old style" collections. However, they will be included in the new editions, although Dark Horse will probably also keep *Adventures of the Mini-Goddesses* around for those who like all the gag strips in one collection.

P.P.S. By the way, the original Japanese volumes of *Oh My Goddess!* themselves show a fairly wide variation in page count. In the Japanese Vol. 21, the story pages ended at p. 166—just like they do here, of course—but the Japanese Vol. 20 was considerably thicker, with the story pages going all the way up to p. 241! So even though future Dark Horse volumes will in fact contain the same number of story pages as the respective Japanese volumes, they won't necessarily all be the same size, because the Japanese originals weren't.

P.P.P.S. I should let you know about a change from the original Japanese Vol. 21. On page 30, panel 5, Peorth in fact does sing the first two words in the Japanese version of *Dona, Dona* (Secunda/Schwartz/Kevess). This folk-style Yiddish song is still heard around the occasional campfire in America, but also became popular in Japan—in fact the Tachikoma (the anime version of the Fuchikoma)sing it to Batou in episode 16 of *Ghost In The Shell: Stand Alone Complex!* (It also shows up in *Revolutionary Girl Utena*). I admit it's a little silly, but we were unable to obtain timely clearance to have Peorth sing it in the English version. Therefore readers are encouraged to get interactive and sing it themselves when they reach this page. The editor will accompany on acoustic guitar.

Dear Enchantress,

I, as a huge fan of *Oh/Ah! My Goddess*, am thrilled to hear you've decided to keep the letters and fan art section from the single issues present in the new graphic novel releases from Dark Horse. It's always refreshing to hear from other fans that love these characters and this series as much as I do. I was wondering if Dark Horse will also consider putting in the little pictures of the creator, Kosuke Fujishima, and the little inserts he writes for the Japanese TPB releases? He's my favorite mangaka and I'd definitely like to know more about the genius that created my favorite series of all time. Besides that, keep up with what you're already doing, you guys are doing an amazing job with this series!

Wesley aka "Keiichi-chan"
(Please feel free to print my email address.)
MorKeiichi@aol.com

"Mangaka," sometimes written "manga-ka," means manga creator, if y'all didn't know. Certainly part of our plan is to include such things as Mr. Fujishima's pictures and notes when they occur in the original Japanese volumes. This was something he more commonly did in the earlier volumes of *Oh My Goddess!* than more recent ones—for example, he doesn't do it in Vol. 21, whereas you should see it in when the new edition of Vol. 1 comes out in October. Thank you for your compliments on *OMG!*; as you can see above, the job has taken a lot of people to do!

When you go to redo the old OMG! stories in the "new" right-left format, PLEASE PLEASE PLEASE change the name "Blessed Bell" for

Belldandy's angel back to Holy Bell! I can't remember if the other angels were changed, but this one was and it sticks out like a sore thumb, and I hate it. She is called Holy Bell in original Japanese (I have an expensive Belldandy statue imported from Japan and it is clearly named Holy Bell) and this should have been retained in the English release, IMO. If the other angels have been changed (Noble Scarlet, World of Elegance and Gorgeous Rose), please return them to their original names as well. Please. Pretty please. Pretty please with sugar on top.

The only other thing I'd like to request is a speedier release on "new" volumes. I'd like 4 new novels a year, with the redone books coming out less frequently … since I've already read those stories (though I plan on buying them again, of course) and I'd like to catch up to the Japanese release ASAP. ;-)

I'd like to also request the redone books retain the bleached white paper of the originals. It gives the books a really high quality feel, and helped me justify the price I was paying.

I will admit I never really liked the price point of the TPBs, however, you could have charged $100 a book and I probably would have still bought it (don't let management read that, please!).

Thanks for taking the time to read my letter, and I hope you seriously consider my requested change, as it's the only real complaint I have with the current TPB releases.

Stephen Lerch
via e-mail

Did we say this book was "$10.95"? We meant "$100.95." Just dropped a decimal point there.

Part of going to the lower-price, 5" x 7 1/2" format is using the kind of paper that other Dark Horse manga in this format use, as in the case of *Trigun*, *Hellsing*, or *Berserk*. We don't receive complaints about the format in those manga; but, of course, Dark Horse printed those particular titles in that format from the very beginning—people are used to it that way. I acknowledge the new format may take time to get used to, but I believe it provides relative value to the older, more expensive edition.

Actually, the paper in this volume should still be slightly brighter than that in the standard Japanese edition (that is, the *Afternoon KC* volumes) of *Oh My Goddess!*. This volume is also almost exactly the same page size as the standard Japanese edition, so, although it has gotten smaller, it's not smaller than the original.

The new format of *Oh My Goddess!* is also going to have two visual "enhancements" that weren't in the original Dark Horse editions.

First of all, manga pages that Mr. Fujishima painted in color will also be printed in color in the new *OMG!* editions. This is something he only did on occasion—so you won't see it in every volume—but there will be eight such story pages, for example, in the new Vol. 1 in October. Second, a re-release of the *OMG!* manga, called the "Complete" edition, is currently ongoing in Japan, too (on the occasion of the new TV anime series) and Fujishima has painted new covers for these. We're going to use these new covers for the Dark Horse re-release (and include the old cover on a color page, too, if possible).

I understand your request for the new *OMG!* to come out more often, but we really do want to balance the interests of new readers (the reason for starting over from Vol. 1) and those of established readers (the reason for doing Vol. 21 before the "re-do" of Vol. 1).

I agree on "Holy Bell," but, as you may have seen in the previous volume, *Sora Unchained*, Dark Horse has already returned to that usage (for example, in the scene where Holy Bell conjures a cushion of air to break Keiichi's fall). Likewise, we plan to have the various Goddesses' angels names be the same in English as they are in Japanese, in any case where they were not already previously so in the "old" edition.

Dear Mr. Fujishima,

You write good and interesting material. It is evident, from what you have written already, that Belldandy, Urd, and Skuld are all important among the goddesses.

May I take note of a contrast, perhaps an inconsistency?

On the one hand, when Belldandy forgot to renew her goddess license she lost the ability to use her power. It was she who had to call Goddess Central. Given her importance it is interesting that the Almighty (Daddy) didn't call her up to rebuke her for forgetting to renew her license. On the other hand, when Urd's license was suspended she immediately got a telephone call informing her, and she had to refrain from trying to use her power, lest her license be permanently revoked. Interesting that we have seen Urd use her powers since *Terrible Master Urd*, even though she is still under suspension and Skuld and Keiichi have commented that she is still under suspension. Amazing that we haven't seen Urd, or Belldandy, punished for their infractions during *Terrible Master Urd*.

A query, or a story suggestion: What would Keiichi and Skuld do if they were left alone for a period of time? Imagine that Urd and Belldandy get called up to Goddess Central for a few days. Of course Belldandy and Goddess Central would ask Keiichi to permit Belldandy to go, and it would be important for Keiichi's maturity for him to grant that permission.

Imagine that Skuld is not required to go with Urd and Belldandy, or that Skuld is tasked to stay at the temple. Imagine also that Keiichi and Belldandy had been scheduled to do something. Perhaps they are entered in a race. Now Keiichi must find someone to take Belldandy's place, choosing among Skuld, his sister Megumi, his boss Chihiro, and his co-worker Sora. During all this Keiichi and Skuld are by themselves in the temple and must learn how to act towards each other when no one else is around, while respecting their ties to Belldandy and Urd.

Regards,
David Olson
Arlington, TX

"Almighty" seems to be used in a more respectful than literal sense in the *OMG!* cosmology, considering the rather large staff he possesses—not to mention the apparent strength of the competition; perhaps Hild's title of "CEO" would actually better fit the mark.

In a strange way, Skuld is the most like Keiichi of the Goddess sisters—her being the weakest and youngest of the trio makes her closer to K1's "normality," and, of course, she is the engineer among the three, whereas Urd specializes in alchemy and Bell-chan in incantations. It's odd that the way Keiichi has his hair cut now makes him look more like Sentaro, Skuld's first crush from the story "Crazy Little Thing Called Love" in Vol. 13: *Childhood's End.*

Skuld's earlier relationship towards Keiichi seemed a mix of resentment towards him for "trying to take Belldandy away," mixed with a jealousy towards Bell-chan for being involved in something more grown-up. Both, of course, are very normal feelings in a family with sisters of different ages. But Skuld indeed seems to have matured somewhat and adjusted to the situation, defining herself now more against Urd—perhaps, because when it comes to trying to find technical solutions to the strange problems always popping up in the *OMG!* world, Skuld and Urd can compete more as equals; social maturity doesn't enter into it so much—although maybe "maturity" isn't quite the right word to fit Urd. But you know what I mean.

As you say, though, take Urd and Belldandy away from the equation and it might

be interesting to see what happens. My first thought is that Skuld, more than anything else, would feel very lonely with both her sisters gone—having been around one or the other of them all her life—and it would probably be difficult for her to get over this. But it's an open question.

That's all for now! Next time, I'll leave out the long-winded explanations (maybe), which means we'll have more room for your letters and fan art. Look out for *Oh My Goddess* Vol. 1 in October and Vol. 22 in December! But wait, there's still more to the Goddesses' return! In November Dark Horse mmmmmdrops a special *OMG!* book never before published in English: the 192-page *Oh My Goddess! Colors.*

What's inside *Colors*? Original *OMG!* publisher Kodansha, working with Kosuke Fujishima, produced color versions of four of the best-loved stories from the whole series, each one centering around a particular Goddess, including "The Number You Have Dialed Is Incorrect," when Belldandy first comes into Keiichi's life; "Urd's Fantastic Adventure," when the eldest of the sisters shrinks to young-girl size; the above-mentioned "Crazy Little Thing Called Love," and finally Peorth's arrival in "Are You Being Served?"

In addition to the four stories, *OMG! Colors* also contains a bonus original *Oh My Goddess!* eight-page fan manga by, of all people, Yoshitou Asari (he's the guy who designed the Angels Sachiel, Shamshel, and Zeruel in *Neon Genesis Evangelion!*), plus special articles: Fujishima's eight-page personal profile of the Goddesses, an 18-page "Encyclopedia of Goddess Terminology," cross-referencing the people, places, and events of the manga series, four pages on the cars, bikes, and planes of the story, two pages on the "Rules of the Goddess' World"; and a six-page thumbnail guide to the OMG! story chapters. I think *Oh My Goddess! Colors* is something you will want to check out.

—CGH

DON'T MISS THESE OTHER FANTASTIC TITLES FROM DARK HORSE MANGA AND STUDIO PROTEUS!

STOP! This is the back of the book!

This manga collection is translated into English, but arranged in right-to-left reading format to maintain the artwork's visual orientation as originally drawn and published in Japan. If you've never read comics this way before, take a look at the diagram below to give yourself an idea of how to go about it. Basically, you'll be starting in the upper right-hand corner, and will read each word balloon and panel moving right-to-left. It may take a little getting used to, but you should get the hang of it very quickly. Have fun! If this is the millionth manga you've read this way, never mind.

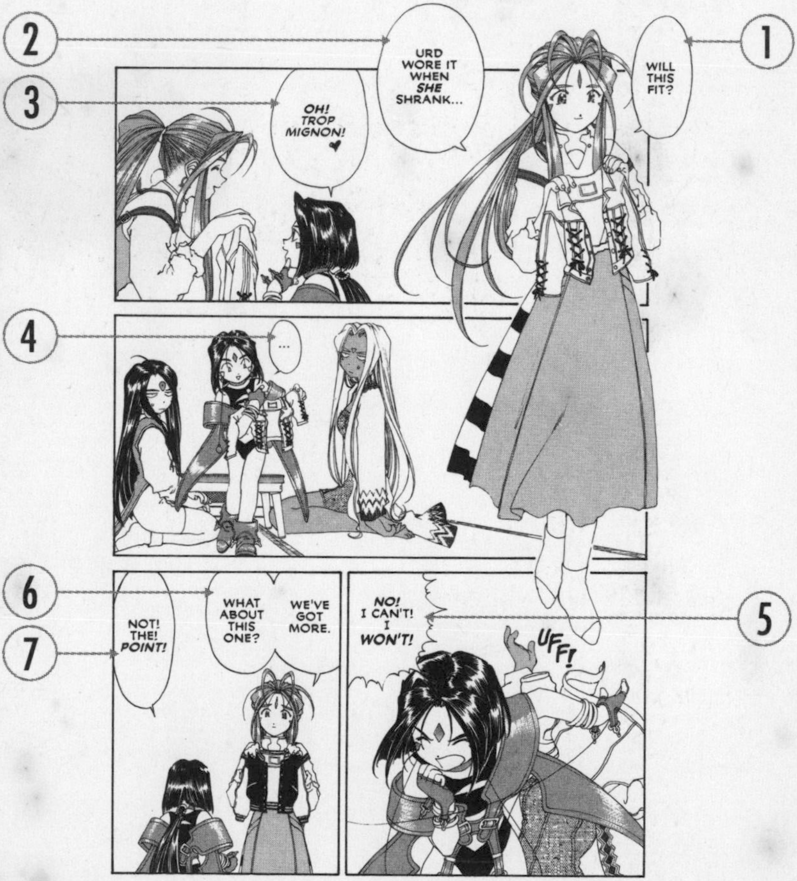
1
WILL THIS FIT?
2
URD WORE IT WHEN *SHE* SHRANK...
3
OH! TROP MIGNON!
4
...
5
NO! I CAN'T! I *WON'T!*
UFF!
6
WHAT ABOUT THIS ONE?
WE'VE GOT MORE.
7
NOT! THE! *POINT!*